Lords of Creation

Lords of Creation: The Origins

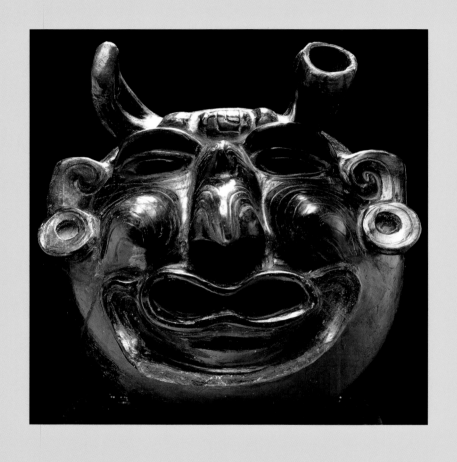

Virginia M. Fields and

Dorie Reents-Budet

# of Sacred Maya Kingship

with contributions by

Ricardo Agurcia Fasquelle

Jeremy R. Bauer

Ellen E. Bell

M. Kathryn Brown

Ramón Carrasco Vargas

Allen J. Christenson

Constance Cortez

Federico Fahsen

Enrique Florescano

David A. Freidel

James F. Garber

Nikolai Grube

Stanley P. Guenter

Julia Guernsey

Richard D. Hansen

Michael Love

Simon Martin

F. Kent Reilly III

Robert J. Sharer

Juan Antonio Valdés

Los Angeles County Museum of Art

in association with

Scala Publishers Ltd.

This catalogue was published in conjunction with *Lords of Creation: The Origins of Sacred Maya Kingship*, an exhibition organized by the Los Angeles County Museum of Art. It is proudly sponsored by Televisa, the largest media group in the Spanish-speaking world, as part of its commitment to promote and share its Mexican heritage. It was also made possible by a generous grant from the National Endowment for the Humanities, where great ideas are brought to life. Additional support was provided by the National Endowment for the Arts, which believes that a great nation deserves great art, the Arvey Foundation, and the Ethnic Arts Council of Los Angeles.

In-kind media support for the Los Angeles presentation was provided by Univision 34 Los Angeles.

Any views, findings, conclusions, or recommendations expressed in this publication do not necessarily represent those of the National Endowment for the Humanities.

Exhibition itinerary

Los Angeles County Museum of Art
September 10, 2005–January 2, 2006

Dallas Museum of Art
February 12–May 7, 2006

The Metropolitan Museum of Art
June 11–September 10, 2006

Note that credit lines and other specific information about objects in the exhibition are accurate as of March 15, 2005.

Thanks to the Consejo Nacional para la Cultura y las Artes and the Instituto Nacional de Antropología e Historia for their support.

CONACULTA · INAH

First published in 2005 by Scala Publishers Limited
Northburgh House
10 Northburgh Street
London EC1V 0AT
United Kingdom
and
Los Angeles County Museum of Art
5905 Wilshire Boulevard
Los Angeles, CA 90036

Distributed outside the Los Angeles County Museum of Art in the book trade by
Antique Collectors' Club Limited
Eastworks
116 Pleasant Street, suite 60B
Easthampton, MA 01027

ISBNs 1-85759-386-3 (cloth); 1-85759-405-3 (pbk)

British Library Cataloguing in Publication Data.
A catalogue record for this book is available from the British Library.

Director of publications, LACMA
Stephanie Emerson

Editors
Jennifer Boynton, Matt Stevens, and Nola Butler

Designer
Katy Homans

Supervising photographers
Peter Brenner and Steve Oliver

Rights and reproductions assistant
Giselle Arteaga-Johnson

Rights and reproductions coordinator
Cheryle T. Robertson

Produced by Scala Publishers Limited
Printed and bound in China

10 9 8 7 6 5 4 3 2 1

Front cover and p. 3: Mosaic Funerary Mask (cat. 135); p. 2, left: Lidded Bowl Depicting Mam (cat. 46); p. 2, right: Facade Mask (cat. 62); p. 6: Censer Stand Depicting Principal Bird Deity, Guatemala, Southern Highlands or Piedmont, AD 250–450, ceramic, 6¼ x 7¼ in. (15.9 x 18.4 cm), Los Angeles County Museum of Art, purchased with American Art Deaccession Funds (see also p. 150); p. 8: Tripod Vessel with Human Figure (cat. 115); p. 12: Cache Urn (cat. 36); back cover: Lidded Tripod Vessel (cat. 144)

To Linda Schele, whose passion and inspired teaching shaped our formative period

Contents

Director's Foreword

Divine kingship, whether used to describe the governance of societies from ancient Egypt or southeast Asia to feudal Europe, is an enduring worldwide phenomenon. The exhibition *Lords of Creation: The Origins of Sacred Maya Kingship* reveals for the first time how divine kings appeared in Mesoamerica, demonstrating that the origins of the institution preceded the earliest Maya expressions of royal authority. It addresses the reasons for the development of sacred kingship and the manner in which Maya kings elaborated the concept, professing their status through monumental art and architecture as well as precious objects of jadeite, shell, and ceramic. This exhibition provides an opportunity to present objects that have never been seen in the United States in an innovative context that is bound to stimulate further exploration of the subject.

A major undertaking for the museum, *Lords of Creation* constitutes an important component of the programming of the Center for the Art of the Americas at LACMA. The center represents LACMA's commitment to the collection, conservation, exhibition, and interpretation of art from the continents of North and South America from pre-Columbian times to the present, and to the translation of these objects into a meaningful viewing experience for our audiences.

The germination of the idea for *Lords of Creation* dates to the 1980s, when the exhibition curators, Virginia Fields and Dorie Reents-Budet, studied with the preeminent Mayanist Linda Schele. The extraordinary amount of new data about early Maya society led the curators to reinvestigate Maya kingship, and the exhibition is the culmination of five years of intensive research and planning. Their collaboration with a dedicated team of archaeologists, epigraphers, art historians, and linguists has resulted in this engaging and informative exhibition, which reflects and elaborates on the complexities of early Maya civilization.

The magnanimous support of the exhibition's national sponsor, Grupo Televisa, made the vision of the curatorial team a reality. The exhibition and catalogue were funded in part by grants from the National Endowment for the Humanities and the National Endowment for the Arts, recognition of the significant scholarly and aesthetic merits of the project. The Arvey Foundation and the Ethnic Arts Council of Los Angeles also provided key support for the exhibition's education programming.

Lords of Creation will reach a broad audience in the United States thanks to John R. Lane, director of the Dallas Museum of Art, and Philippe de Montebello, director of the Metropolitan Museum of Art, whose enthusiasm for the project led them to bring this large and complex show to their respective institutions. Finally, we are grateful to the many institutions and individuals who so generously lent the works of art and artifacts that made this exhibition possible.

Andrea L. Rich
President and Wallis Annenberg Director
Los Angeles County Museum of Art

Forewords

Maya culture has often been considered an anomaly in the Mesoamerican world: a peaceful community of artists and scientists, particularly astronomers, surrounded by bellicose societies that worshiped bloodthirsty gods. But in fact, archaeological, epigraphic, and ethnohistoric studies have established a deep connection among the different Mesoamerican cultures—including the Maya—so that now we can speak of a genuine civilization, the shared matrix from which a diversity of symbolic and artistic expression arose. This is one of the perspectives that, through approximately 150 works of art, the exhibition *Lords of Creation: The Origins of Sacred Maya Kingship* masterfully exemplifies.

The exhibition establishes a chronological line that runs from the Olmec, the "mother culture" that originated the idea of cosmos that would prevail for centuries in Mesoamerica, through the Maya Early Classic period. Curators Virginia Fields and Dorie Reents-Budet have assembled works that enable the viewer, for the first time in the United States, to appreciate the historic and religious profile of the sacred Maya lords and their fundamental role as the depositories of earthly power as well as the element of equilibrium between the realm of human life and the worlds above and below.

Lords of Creation presents a successful equilibrium: knowing the history of pre-Hispanic peoples gives us a deeper appreciation of the beauty and symbolism of their works of art. The fertile dialogue between art and science offers a new way of looking at one of the complex and beautiful systems through which human beings gave meaning to their brief passage on earth: Maya culture.

Sari Bermúdez

President

Consejo Nacional para la Cultura y las Artes/National Council for Culture and the Arts (CONACULTA), Mexico

Various civilizations throughout history have regarded thaumaturgic kings, priests, saints, monks, magicians, and demigods as the depositories of cosmic forces—men whose formidable task it was to transcend the immediacy of politics and maintain the equilibrium of the universe. The ancient Maya rulers are a historic model of this divine authority placed in mere human hands. The emergence of sacred lineages in this society of farmers demanded the acceptance of a political, military, and religious elite devoted to ruling and celebrating, to extending their domains over neighboring lands and expanding mathematic and astrological knowledge as part of the machinery of the cosmos. This concentration of power was manifest, in real life as in the art intended to perpetuate it, through an exuberant plastic language, a detailed ritual symbolism with tremendous narrative impact relating the origin of things and affirming the supreme authority of this absolute condition.

Lords of Creation: The Origins of Sacred Maya Kingship explores the role of kings and sacred dynasties from the middle of the Preclassic, when the first traces of this phenomenon appear in monumental Olmec art, through the Early Classic, when the dynasties achieved a grandeur eternalized in what today are recognized as masterworks of world art. There could be no better setting for this magnificent exhibition than the Los Angeles County Museum of Art, at the heart of a city that is home to the greatest number of Mexicans living outside of Mexico—a group that constitutes one of the largest minorities in the United States but often lacks access to the sources that illuminate its own past.

The wonderful curatorship of Virginia Fields, of LACMA, and Dorie Reents-Budet has produced a rich exhibition, the fruit of extensive archaeological research largely stimulated by shared efforts in Mexico such as the Palenque Round Tables, led by the National Council for Culture and the Arts through the National Institute of Anthropology and History. By presenting together the images and current interpretations of the symbolic and real, ritual and political worlds of the Maya, this exhibition brings the visitor face to face with ancient Maya civilization.

Luciano Cedillo

General Director

Instituto Nacional de Antropología e Historia/National Institute of Anthropology and History (INAH), Mexico

---

As we stand before these works of Maya culture, our senses, spirit, and creative imagination cross a threshold into the worldview of a prodigious people whose civilization flourished in a land located at the heart of the Americas, rich in biodiversity and ecological balance. Its history, thirty-five centuries long, displays a heritage that is profound in its values and knowledge, prolific in its languages and arts, and monumental in its architecture and spirituality.

Maya culture, like other world cultures, is at once ancestral and current, local and universal. One can be contemplating the majesty of the Temple of the Grand Jaguar at Tikal and at the same time greet a Maya woman from the Guatemalan altiplano dressed in a beautiful *po't* or *huipil* (an embroidered garment), whose filigree reproduces the hieroglyphs of the Cholq'ij, or lunar calendar, weaving the firmament with colors of the Mesoamerican landscape.

Janila yoj kikot roma ri samaj nib'an paruwi maya k'aslem: Great is our joy in the work that is being done to spread this culture and support the life of the Maya people. Guatemala's Ministry of Culture and Sports applauds the organization and mounting of the exhibition *Lords of Creation: The Origins of Sacred Maya Kingship* in Los Angeles, which presents to the world one of the oldest cultures of America, whose descendants are now part of the multilingual and pluricultural country of Guatemala. *Ruk'ux Kaj, Ruk'ux Ulew Ruk'ux Cho', Ruk'ux Palouj ti uk'uan rub'eyal ri samaj xti tikir wakamin:* May the heart of heaven and earth, the heart of freshwater and saltwater, bestow energy and illuminate the path for the exhibition that opens to the public on this day, that it may realize its fullest potential.

Manuel de Jesús Salazar Tetzagüic

Minister

Ministry of Culture and Sports, Guatemala

Sponsor's Statement

Televisa proudly sponsors the groundbreaking exhibition *Lords of Creation: The Origins of Sacred Maya Kingship* as part of its commitment to promote and share its Mexican heritage. *Lords of Creation* explores the development of sacred kings in the Americas and elucidates their roles in the emergence of urban society two thousand years ago in the Maya region.

Through its foundation, Televisa seeks to provide development opportunities for as many people as possible. To accomplish this, Fundación Televisa focuses on enhancing the nutrition, health, and education of children as well as encouraging values such as respect, honesty, generosity, and responsibility. Fundación Televisa is also committed to preserving and promoting Mexico's artistic heritage as well as generating more exchanges between Mexico and other cultures around the globe.

It is in this vein that Grupo Televisa is pleased to support *Lords of Creation* during the exhibition's tour of the Los Angeles County Museum of Art, the Dallas Museum of Art, and the Metropolitan Museum of Art, New York. These museums will enable a broad audience to become more familiar with one of the most outstanding civilizations of Mexico and the world.

Emilio Azcárraga Jean
CEO
Grupo Televisa

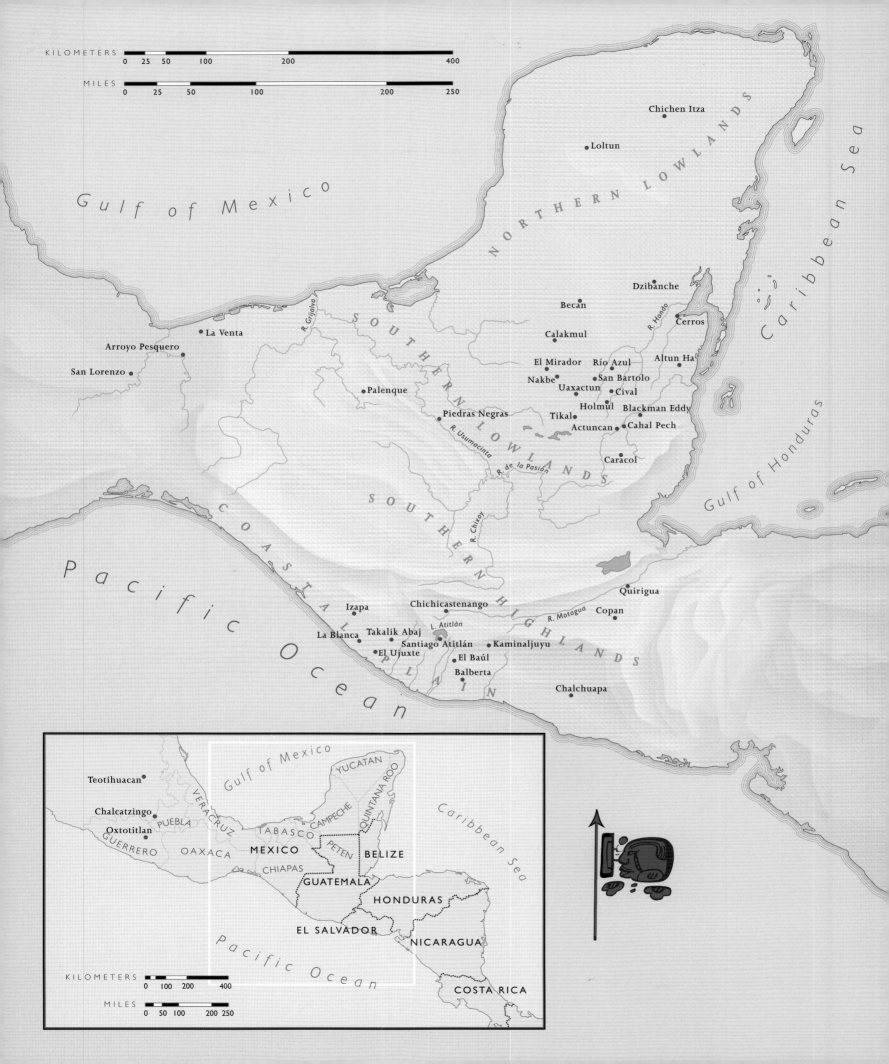

KILOMETERS
0 25 50 100   200   400

MILES
0 25 50   100   200   250

Gulf of Mexico

Caribbean Sea

NORTHERN LOWLANDS

Chichen Itza

Loltun

Dzibanche

Becan

Calakmul

Cerros

El Mirador   Río Azul
                           Altun Ha
Nakbe   San Bartolo
R. Grijalva   Uaxactun   Cival
SOUTHERN LOWLANDS
Arroyo Pesquero
La Venta
San Lorenzo
Palenque
Piedras Negras   Holmul   Blackman Eddy
                  Tikal
R. Usumacinta   Actuncan   Cahal Pech
                    Caracol
R. de la Pasión

R. Hondo

SOUTHERN HIGHLANDS

R. Chixoy

Gulf of Honduras

Pacific Ocean

COASTAL PLAIN

Quirigua

Izapa   Chichicastenango   Copan
                               R. Motagua
La Blanca   Takalik Abaj   L. Atitlán
          Santiago Atitlán   Kaminaljuyu
     El Ujuxte
              El Baúl
          Balberta
                    Chalchuapa

Gulf of Mexico

YUCATAN

Teotihuacan

Chalcatzingo   VERACRUZ   CAMPECHE   Quintana Roo
PUEBLA   Caribbean Sea
Oxtotitlan   TABASCO
GUERRERO   OAXACA   MEXICO   PETEN   BELIZE
              CHIAPAS
                    GUATEMALA
                       HONDURAS
          EL SALVADOR   NICARAGUA
Pacific Ocean
                          COSTA RICA

KILOMETERS
0   100   200   400

MILES
0   50 100   200 250

Notes to the Reader

Chronology

The traditional chronology of Mesoamerican civilizations assumes certain key characteristics to distinguish Preclassic, Classic, and Postclassic periods. To define the Classic period of Maya civilization (AD 292–909), archaeologists employed definitive criteria, such as the presence of Long Count dates on carved monuments. Dating the earlier periods of Maya history depended on archaeological excavations in which radiocarbon dating and stratigraphic relationships provided a sequence of culture history stretching back to the first millennium BC.

The Preclassic (or Formative) period of Mesoamerican civilizations traditionally comprises three periods (Early, Middle, and Late), lasting from approximately 2000 BC through AD 250, although the earliest Maya remains date to approximately 1000 BC. Over the past two decades, the increasing number of archaeological investigations in the Maya area, including the northern lowlands, the southern lowlands, the southern highlands, and the Pacific Coast, has provided locally specific chronologies that do not always fall within the standardized formula. Also, the cultural characteristics that previously defined the "Classic" period are appearing in earlier contexts. For the reader's ease, we follow the broadly defined parameters of dating the Middle (900–400 BC) and Late (400 BC–AD 100) Preclassic periods with the cautionary note that these dates are not fixed but rather serve as general guidelines subject to nuance and flexibility. Though the evidence is scanty, it now seems clear that the period known as the Early Classic, previously dated from AD 250 to 600, may have begun as early as the first century AD.

Orthography

The complexities of writing Mayan words in the present day are detailed in Freidel, Schele, and Parker (1993, 15–19). In this volume, we adhere to the system followed by those authors, which reflects the alphabet devised by Maya writing and language groups in highland Guatemala and published in 1989 by the Ministry of Culture and Sports (Margarita López Raquec's *Acerca de los alfabetos para escribir los idiomas maya de Guatemala*). In this volume, glottalized consonants are marked by an apostrophe, and plurals are marked by the suffix *-ob*.

Preface:
Images of the Ruler in Mesoamerica

Enrique Florescano, **CONACULTA**

The ruler is an omnipresent figure in the political imagery of Mesoamerica, surrounded by a scintillating yet diffuse mythological aura. Most of the studies devoted to the ruler have focused on the Postclassic Mexica *tlatoani* (one who speaks, great lord); few have looked into the origins of royalty and even fewer have considered the nature of political authority, the duties that the ruler fulfilled, and the symbols that represented him.

Despite the scant attention paid to this institution, it is universally recognized to have been the dominant form from at least 1500 BC to AD 1520. Thus, it left its mark on three millennia of Mesoamerican history. The ruler is the figure most represented in that history, as much in myths, annals, and chronicles as in art and symbols. The presence of the sovereign in these varied modes of expression has made of his image an eminently historical figure, one whose trajectory can be followed, in certain cultures of the Classic and Postclassic periods, from birth to death.

The founding of the kingdom and the birth of royalty were acts so significant in human history that the societies that witnessed the genesis of these institutions considered them the start of a new era, the watershed between chaos and civilization. In Mesopotamia, Egypt, China, Japan, or Mesoamerica, those events were linked with the ordering of the cosmos, the primal dawn, the birth of time and of civilization. The inauguration of the kingdom was tantamount to the rebirth of the world. In these ancient cultures this most important rite initiated the calendar year and celebrated the creation of the cosmos, the festival of sowing or harvest, the beginning of time and the foundation of the monarchy, the awakening of a new age in human development.

In Egypt the pharaoh was the founder of the monarchy and a divine being; he descended directly from the gods and incarnated their powers on earth, and his enthronement renewed the forces of nature (Frankfort 1948). In Japan the harvest festival, *Daijō-sai*, was celebrated by the emperor the day he ascended to the throne. In this ceremony, "the renewal of kingship united the renewal of nature, as in planting or harvest, with the renewal of society. The accession of the king, when celebrated as a great festival of renewal, bridged two ways in which man experienced time" (Ellwood 1973, 3). Two pioneering works, James Frazer's *Lectures on the Early History of the Kingship* (1905) and Arthur M. Hocart's *Kingship* (1927), strove to define for the first time the characteristics of royalty and promoted the study of royalty and its functions in different cultures and regions. Comparing the knowledge derived from those studies with what is known today of royalty in Mesoamerica, notable similarities are immediately evident in the nature, representations, and duties of the ruler.

The first studies on the forms of government among the Olmec show that a divine nature was attributed to the leader of men. He represented the ordering forces of the different regions of the cosmos and the territory of the kingdom. He summoned rain and fertility; he enjoyed the protection of the founding ancestors and held the power to make those forces work on behalf of the kingdom's people (Reilly 1994c; Reilly 1995b; Joralemon 1996a).

Figure 1

Drawing of figure on jade celt known as the Leiden Plaque. The king holds a double-headed serpent bar against his chest; two patron deities' heads emerge from the serpents' mouths. Other components of royal costume include the personified trefoil Jester God atop his headdress (see cats. 13–17) and the elaborate belt from which hang two belt heads with pendant plaques (see cats. 76, 77). Here, the king stands over a prisoner with bound hands.

In Mesoamerica, as in other cultures, public representations of the ruler focus on three critical moments of his life: his designation, his accession to the throne, and his death. When the acting ruler designated his successor from among his heirs, the official channels of communication would publicize the name and image of the favorite son, as can be seen on the tablet on the Temple of the Cross from Palenque, which was used to display the portrait of Kan B'alam II, the heir of K'inich Janaab' Pakal I.

In kingdoms of the Classic period the public square was a veritable forest of stelae, as Schele and Freidel (1990) have characterized it, which depicted rulers at the grandest moment of their lives, when they assumed their supreme office. The accession to the throne, the most significant ceremony among these portrayals of power, was represented in stelae, paintings, and monuments by the image of the sovereign holding the symbols of power in his hands—the scepter with a double-headed serpent, or the great ceremonial bar (fig. 1)—or seated on the throne, adorned in splendid finery and protected by the gods and the emblems of the kingdom.

One of the oldest duties of the *ajaw* was to intercede with the gods to assure a successful harvest. Communication with the ancestors—the primordial font of wisdom and legitimacy— was another of the sovereign's duties, also one of the oldest and best theatricalized, steeped in an aura of the frightful and the spectacular. In Mesoamerica ritual bloodletting was considered indispensable for realizing this communication, and its practice was one of the sovereign's cardinal tasks. According to Schele and Freidel, "The magical person of the king . . . was the conduit of the sacred, the path of communication to the Otherworld, the means of contacting the dead, and indeed of surviving death itself" (1990, 98).

The final chapter of the sovereign's life, his death, was immortalized by the royal tomb, from the Olmec monuments to the funerary crypt of Pakal in Palenque, perhaps the best Mesoamerican representation of the mortal body of the *ajaw* and his immortal effigy (fig. 2). In this mausoleum is the sarcophagus of the departed king; on the beautiful carved stone that covers the sarcophagus can be seen the resplendent figure of Pakal being reborn from the underworld, transfigured into an immortal, the ever youthful Maize God (Florescano 1995, 167–70). Thus, the designation, enthronement, and death of the sovereign were scenes through which the royal tomb theatricalized his presence in the public life of the kingdom. As Georges Balandier observed, "through the production of images, through the manipulation of symbols and their organization in a ceremonial framework," the prince was transformed into a "great political actor" (1980, 15, 16).

Translated by Rose Vekony

Introduction:
The First Sacred Kings of Mesoamerica

Virginia M. Fields, Los Angeles County Museum of Art, with
Dorie Reents-Budet, National Museum of Natural History

The primary focus of Maya cosmology and religious ceremony centers on the creation of the cosmos. The strength of this belief extends over the course of Maya history as revealed in religious practices among the Maya today (see Christenson 2001; this volume) and as documented in the sixteenth century, where a series of creations is recorded in the K'iche' epic, the *Popol Vuh*. Creation events are recorded in Late Classic period hieroglyphic inscriptions at such sites as Quirigua (Looper 2003) and on the Late Preclassic murals at San Bartolo (Saturno and Urquizú 2004), and apparently were first recorded in the Middle Formative monumental art of the Gulf Coast Olmec (Reilly 1994b). The essential nature of ancient Maya kingship rests in the concept that the most important rituals performed by the king involved reenacting the events of creation (Freidel et al. 1993).

Beginning with the Olmec, monumental art portrays human rulers in the guise of deities, especially the Maize God, proclaiming their sacred and secular authority to bring agricultural fertility and abundance to their communities. These rulers embody a system of governance known as divine kingship, a phenomenon found among ancient civilizations throughout the world (see, for example, Blier 1998; Chang 1984; Ellwood 1973; Feeley-Harnik 1985; O'Connor and Silverman 1995; Valeri 1985). The exhibition *Lords of Creation: The Origins of Sacred Maya Kingship* examines the factors that coalesced during the Middle and Late Preclassic periods in Mesoamerica to give rise to divine kingship, which was defined and sustained by the power and wealth of the rulers and sanctioned by their supernatural patrons and ancestors.

Over the course of the past several decades, archaeologists, epigraphers, and art historians have brought to light the complexity of the workings of the royal court among the Late Classic Maya, revealing nuances of palace life among the Maya elite at the pinnacle of their social, political, and artistic accomplishments (see Miller and Martin 2004). *Lords of Creation* addresses the question of how the Maya came to achieve such levels of wealth and sophistication.

Drawing on ethnohistoric evidence from the sixteenth century that the position of ruler entailed both secular and religious responsibilities and that these rulers claimed divine descent, J. Eric S. Thompson (1973) first posited that the same situation existed during the Classic period. David Freidel and Linda Schele (1988a, 1988b) later analyzed the extant body of Late Preclassic archaeological and iconographic developments and proposed how those developments were used to legitimize the power of rulers through supernatural sanction. Further investigations provided evidence that the source of the royal headband worn as a crown by Maya kings as well as the title of *ajaw* (lord, or ruler) could be traced back even further to Olmec antecedents in the Middle Formative period (Fields 1989).

Since the early 1980s, archaeological investigations into the Middle and Late Preclassic and Early Classic periods have proliferated at sites throughout the Yucatan Peninsula of Mexico and adjacent Belize, the northern Peten and Pacific slopes of Guatemala and nearby Chiapas, and the

Figure 1
Ceiba tree, Tikal, Guatemala

Figure 2
Rendering of Mural I, Oxtotitlan

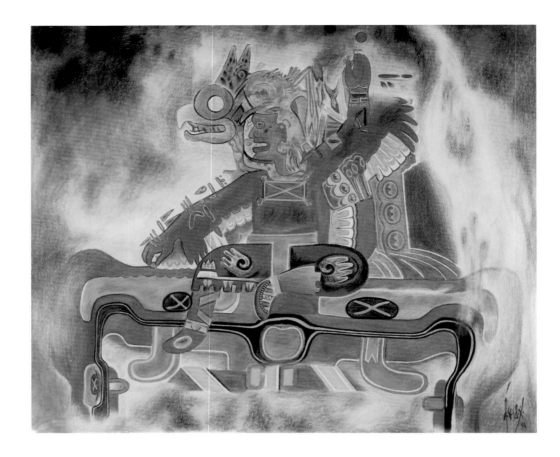

site of Copan in western Honduras, providing an abundant body of corroborating evidence for critical changes in Maya society during these periods. These data provide a substantial base from which to reexamine the concept of divine kingship and its origins among the Maya. The recent discovery of sophisticated murals, elegantly painted with the characteristic Maya line and palette, depicting hieroglyphic texts and accession ceremonies at the Late Preclassic site of San Bartolo in the northeastern Peten, also raises the question of how early such "Classic period" traits may have appeared. The murals portray a ruler dressed as the Maize God and reenacting rites linked to the deity's mythic actions at creation (Saturno and Urquizú 2004).

During the Middle Formative, Olmec populations in the Gulf Coast heartland responded to changing conditions in their society precipitated by a regular and abundant agricultural surplus by initiating increasingly more widespread exchange networks (Clark and Hansen 2001). The most precious commodities initially were jadeite and other greenstones, to be followed by spondylus shell in the Late Preclassic and cacao in the Classic period (Freidel et al. 2002; McAnany et al. 2002). The heartland Olmec, especially at La Venta, are credited with devising hierarchical forms of social and political life that were disseminated along the Pacific Coast, as revealed by the numerous Olmec-style monuments found from the Isthmus of Tehuantepec to El Salvador (Clark and Pye 2000b). Monumental art outside the heartland, however, especially in Guerrero and Central Mexico, implies comparable developments to those at La Venta. The mural at Oxtotitlan (fig. 2), for example, presages an enduring composition of a ruler dressed in the guise of a bird and seated on a personified throne (see cat. 6). Enthroned figures also appear in the Guatemalan highlands (fig. 3) by around 300 BC; these are substantial expressions of authority for this early date. Among the lowland Maya, the appearance of kingship reflected "stimulus diffusion of a high-status institution from one region to another" (Clark and Hansen 2001, 32), possibly via early centers in Chiapas, such as Chiapa de Corzo, into the Mirador Basin and spreading east into present-day Belize (see Brown and Garber, this volume).

Figure 3
Monument 65, Kaminaljuyu

Epigraphic and iconographic studies also elucidated the parameters of Maya kingship. Freidel and Schele (1988a, 1988b) documented the redefinition of political and economic power during the Late Preclassic that legitimated the social order governed by kings and described the appearance of attributes of kingship in the symbol systems at that time. The increasingly important trade in luxury commodities played a significant role in the evolution of complexity among the Maya, and highly valued ornaments of jade and shell were especially important because they were linked to the "cosmic power flowing through rulers" (Freidel et al. 2002, 43).

Such cosmic power constitutes a key criterion of divine kingship, which is characterized by the capacity of rulers to interact with supernatural powers, to intercede on behalf of the human populace. The role of supernatural beings in the expression of Maya royal authority is well documented in the Late Classic period (see Schele and Miller 1986). Stephen Houston and David Stuart (1996) closely examined the relationship between deities and kings in ancient Maya sources, identifying various strategies of divine kings, such as their impersonation of supernatural beings on certain occasions, and the participation by deities as ritual sponsors of such events as accession to office.

Increased wealth and political power of ritual specialists in ancient China, whose authority rested in their ability to gain access to divine and ancestral wisdom (Chang 1984, 2) parallels a similar responsibility for Maya kings, who reenacted the creation of the cosmos in the guise of the Maize God (Freidel et al. 1993, 55). Among the most important ritual actions performed by kings was that of raising a great world tree to separate the sky from the earth. The world tree is often identified as a ceiba (fig. 1), but when the tree was depicted as a fruitful maize plant, it symbolized the acts of creation; correspondingly, the *milpa*, or maize field, with its four corners and four sides, comprised the basic metaphor for the original order of the cosmos established at creation (Freidel et al. 1993, 55, 130). Raising the world tree was a primary royal responsibility dating back to the Middle Formative, as seen in San Martín Pajapan Monument 1 (fig. 4). The monument, found at the top of a volcano in Veracruz, portrays an early ruler performing this ritual action while wearing an Olmec-style Maize God headdress with a symbolic maize plant in the form of a trefoil atop the face of the deity (Reilly 1994b, 186–87).

A growing body of archaeological, epigraphic, and art historical evidence indicates three criteria that define the powers and legitimacy of the earliest lowland Maya kings. The first is the dedication of sacred space through the placement of a cruciform-shaped or quincunx-patterned cache, which appears in both Olmec and Maya archaeological contexts and signifies the king and his capacity to center the cosmos (Reilly 1995b, 38–39; Taube 2003b, 461–64). Quincunx-patterned dedicatory caches made up of precious greenstone celts, themselves symbolic representations of maize plants (Joralemon 1988, 38; 1996a, 57), appear at a number of sites during the Middle and Late Preclassic periods, including La Venta (Drucker et al. 1959, 128), San Ysidro (Lowe 1981), Seibal (Smith 1982; Willey 1978), and Cival (see Bauer, this volume). During the Late Preclassic period at Cerros and the Early Classic at Copan, quincunx-patterned offerings consist of royal jewels worn by the king (see cats. 19 and 20). This pattern and its association with the metaphor of maize agriculture and the acts of creation are apparent from its inception in the Middle Formative (Reilly 1994b). A seated figure from Arroyo Pesquero (cat. 16), for example, wears a headdress marked by a quincunx that is surmounted by a trefoil, which itself represents maize (Fields 1989, 1991).

The quincunx pattern as cosmic metaphor followed kings into death, as seen at Río Azul (Adams 1999; Freidel and Schele 1988a, 558). The walls of an Early Classic tomb were painted with the hieroglyphs expressing the cardinal directions, while the king's body would have been laid out as the central axis. Reiterating this belief in the present day, the *nab'eysil* of Santiago

Figure 4
Monument 1, 1100–900 BC, San Martín Pajapan

25

Atitlán in highland Guatemala dances with a sacred bundle, moving from the center to the four directions, in order to create the world as his ancestors did (see Christenson, this volume).

Receiving and wearing the trefoil crown is the second criterion defining early kings. The crown, a cloth headband with a central, typically trefoil, icon flanked by bifurcated ornaments (see cats. 13–17), is the precursor to the Jester God jewel of the Late Classic period (Fields 1991) and designates the king as the bringer of maize fertility to the community. The headband with its central maize motif flanked by four jewels marks the wearer as the central axis in a four-sided cosmos. The king may also be portrayed with a maize cob as his crown, with trefoil leaves sprouting and yellow maize silk hair (fig. 5).

Naming a ruler with the title of *ajaw* is the third primary designation of early Maya kings. The title is found on architectural facades and portable objects dating to the Late Preclassic as well as in brief hieroglyphic captions in the accession scenes on the San Bartolo murals (see cats. 22–26).

Lords of Creation traces the origins of Maya divine kingship and its expression in art through a series of ten themes, presenting well-known objects and recent discoveries in a revealing new context. The exhibition and the catalogue section of this volume begin with the first sacred rulers of the Middle Formative period and the earliest Maya kings followed by an examination of the nature of the cosmos and the supernatural beings who inhabit it. The first royal portraits and the paraphernalia of office are described, as are royal ritual responsibilities and the importance of feasting in the social and political arena. The origins of the calendar and hieroglyphic writing, which signaled new methods for legitimating the king's authority, are outlined. The widespread economic and political networks, which had a tremendous impact on the nature and expression of divine kingship in Maya society, especially in the fourth and fifth centuries, are also explored. The exhibition concludes with the king's ultimate journey through death and into the afterlife as a divine ancestor.

Our understanding of the nuances of early kingship is made possible by the research of scholars such as those who contributed to this volume. Recent excavations in the lowland Maya area and Pacific slopes, which reveal important new data for understanding the development of kingship, are detailed in the essays by Julia Guernsey and Michael Love, M. Kathryn Brown and James Garber, Juan Antonio Valdés, Ramón Carrasco Vargas, and Ellen Bell. Other significant components of understanding the emergence of the first Maya kings are provided in essays by Kent Reilly on Olmec antecedents, by Federico Fahsen and Nikolai Grube on the earliest Maya writing, and by Robert Sharer and Simon Martin, who consider the complexities of the interaction between Teotihuacan and the Maya area. Highlighting themes in the essays is a series of brief texts, by Jeremy Bauer, Constance Cortez, David Freidel, Richard Hansen and Stanley Guenter, and Ricardo Agurcia Fasquelle, that focus on key elements of the expression of early kingship. Allen Christenson concludes with his description of the enduring centrality of creation in contemporary Maya cosmology and religious practice.

This exhibition and catalogue mark a stage in ongoing research into the topic of Maya kingship, with many questions left to explore—for example, the role of women in formulating and legitimating royal authority or the nature and linguistic affiliation of the earliest hieroglyphic texts. In addition, the murals at San Bartolo raise a number of fascinating issues: What were the antecedents to this painting tradition, which is characterized by mastery of the elegant line and palette more typical of the Late Classic period? Why did painting apparently subside in importance during the Early Classic with its ceramic tradition of rich sculptural forms only to reemerge during the Late Classic as a primary form of artistic expression? Undoubtedly, ongoing research will continue to enhance our understanding of the origins of Maya kingship.

Figure 5

Plate Portraying Enthroned King (cat. 21), detail

Between Heaven and Earth: The Cival Cache and the Creation of the Mesoamerican Cosmos

Jeremy R. Bauer, Vanderbilt University

In Mesoamerica few concepts are as widespread as the notion of a four-part universe with a sacred central point from which emerged the structure of the universe, the forces of nature, and humankind. Manifested in Maya art as a quatrefoil or as a *k'an* cross, the origins of this concept can be traced back to the Olmec of the Early Formative period through the Classic period, and it survives today among modern Maya peoples (see Christenson, this volume). Mesoamerican elites utilized the *k'an* cross as the fundamental cosmic symbol to legitimate their claim to divine authority. By symbolically linking themselves to the center of cosmic creation within the context of public rituals, Maya kings asserted their role in the creation and maintenance of the world.

The act of re-creating and manipulating cosmic forces is clearly conveyed by a Preclassic period offering from the site of Cival, located in the northeastern Peten of Guatemala. Excavations in 2003 and 2004 at this large Preclassic center, which overlooks the Holmul River, revealed an elaborate expression of elite symbol manipulation in the form of a cache of artifacts placed in a specially constructed pit at the base of an E-Group architectural complex. Throughout the Maya lowlands, such architectural groups are associated with agricultural and celestial rituals commemorating sacred ancestors and creation events (Aveni and Hartung 1989; Aveni et al. 2003; Fialko 1988; Laporte 1995; and Ricketson 1928).

Figure 1 (below, at left)
Cache cut cleaned

Figure 2 (center)
Cache cut with fragmented water jars

Figure 3 (right)
Detail of central deposit, showing jade celts and fragments

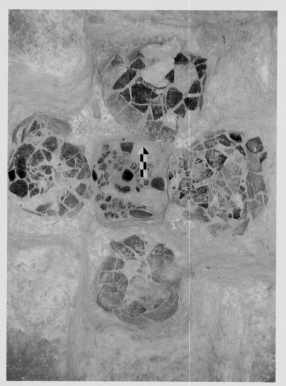

The Cival cache was placed on the structure's centerline at its base and was interred sometime before 350 BC, dedicating the earliest version of the structure. Oriented to the cardinal directions, the *k'an*-cross offering cut deeply into the dense limestone bedrock at the structure's base and framed the moment of creation, while its concentric stepped walls demarcated the conceptual levels of the Maya universe (fig. 1). The lowest level contained five upright jadeite celts that, throughout Mesoamerica, symbolize maize and especially sprouting maize plants (Taube 2000). A prized blue-green jadeite celt occupied the central place at the base of the cruciform cut as the conceptual center of the cosmos, while four additional celts stood upright along the cardinal sides of the cut. Ringing the base of the celts, a scatter of more than 110 small pieces of jadeite of various colors and degrees of finish surrounded the central axis (fig. 3). The blue and green colors of the jadeite refer to the precious color of the conceptual center of the Maya universe and evince links to the primordial sea of the pre-creation era as well as the watery underworld of the Maya (see Stross 1985). Underscoring the reference to water are five large *ollas*, or water-carrying jars, which were placed above each of the celts (fig. 2). The eastern arm of the *k'an* cross also contained a red-slipped ceramic disc made from the reused base of a broken vessel (not visible in the illustrations), which appears to represent the rising sun. A posthole was cut through the center of the thick plaster cap of the cache, indicating that a solitary post had been erected in its center. This wooden post creates a symbolic link between the buried jades as sprouting maize kernels and the wooden post that represents a mature maize plant as the cosmic world tree, or Na Te' K'an (Freidel et al. 1993, 53–57).

Collectively considered, the Cival cruciform cache represents one of the clearest manifestations of the Mesoamerican cosmic diagram and its related creation myth. According to recent discussions of the Maya creation myth based upon the sixteenth-century *Popol Vuh* and Classic period hieroglyphic texts, the origin of the cosmos involved the creation of a four-sided maize field or terrestrial realm that emerged from the watery darkness of the primordial sea (Freidel et al. 1993; Tedlock 1985). The jade pebbles scattered around the cache's base and the water jars refer to this body of water from which emerges land in the form of the cornfield. The four *ollas* and jadeite celts mark the four sides of this symbolic *milpa*, or maize field. The water vessels also relate to the four directional Chaaks, or rain gods, who nourish the agricultural cycle, as recorded in the Dresden Codex and later Colonial period texts. In the center of this four-sided cornfield, the Maize God separated the earth from the heavens and erected in its center the world tree (depicted as a ceiba tree or maize plant during the Classic period). In the context of the Cival cache, the central jade celt represents the seed from which the celestial-terrestrial axis (the wooden post) emanates. At a later point in creation, the Hero Twins set the sun in motion, represented by the red ceramic disc in the eastern arm of the cache.

Through its symbolic contents and placement on the central axis of the agricultural and celestial commemorative E-Group complex, the elite patron of the Cival cache placed himself directly within the context of mythic creation, cosmic order, and the forces of nature so necessary for agricultural and spiritual prosperity. This patron, who likely was a ruler of Cival, oversaw the creation of the cache, from its architectural beginnings to the amassing of the precious objects to the elaborate public ritual and symbolic placement of the cache. Through his actions, the ruler asserted his role in the re-creation and maintenance of the cosmic forces of the Maya world for his community, who congregated in the plaza to witness their ruler's performance and control of these universal forces.

Olmec Ideological, Ritual, and Symbolic Contributions to the Institution of Classic Maya Kingship

F. Kent Reilly III, Texas State University at San Marcos

Ancient kings lavished their artistic, monumental, and architectural legacies across all geographical regions in which pristine civilizations developed. Although veiled by time and tropical verdure, the lingering remnants of ancient Maya kings and their civilization adorn the central Peten lowlands of Guatemala and Mexico. The stunning works of art and architecture attest to the importance they bestowed on royal sacred kingship. Many public monuments of the Maya Classic period may be understood best as these Maya kings' impassioned striving to memorialize their reigns and secure their place within the recurring cycles of Maya time, myth, and history. The interpretation of Maya hieroglyphic inscriptions continues to progress greatly. Along with the general Maya term for king (*ajaw*, see cats. 22–26), recent discoveries now allow the knowledge of personal names of many kings, as well as the names and titles of their nobles (Coe and Van Stone 2001). While Maya epigraphic inscriptions record historic, mythical, and preternatural information, their execution and rendering serve as crucial components of Maya hieroglyphic writing, art, aesthetics, and metaphysics. The vocabulary of the inscriptions focuses on the identities and actions of the *ajawo'ob*, their temporal relationships with the supernatural, their dynastic names and titles, their participation in royal rituals, their success in war, and their relationships with other *ajawo'ob*.

The origin of Maya *ajawship* and its role in the development of state-level societies throughout the Americas comprise major study areas in both Classic and Preclassic, or Formative, period research. Many recent investigations clearly indicate that the office of *ajaw*, indeed the glyph itself, originated among non-Mayan speakers (Fields 1989) during the earlier Middle Formative period (900–400 BC). Many of the symbols and much of the elaborate ritual deployed to enhance and publicly validate the Maya *ajaw* during the Classic period originated specifically with the Olmec culture in its Gulf Coast heartland during the Formative period (Reilly 1991).

The relationships between the Classic Maya and Formative Olmec cultures have long been acknowledged and debated (Coe 1977; Clark and Blake 1994; Lowe 1977). The term *Olmec* can be used at least two different ways. In the Formative period, *Olmec* is best understood as: (1) an archaeologically definable culture that flourished in the Gulf Coast heartland between 1200 and 400 BC; and (2) an art style that spread throughout Mesoamerica during the same period (Reilly 1995b, 27). The people who constituted the Olmec archaeological culture likely spoke a language belonging to the Mixe-Zoque—rather than the Maya—linguistic family (Campbell and Kaufman 1976). Temporally, the archaeological framework of the Olmec heartland falls into two time periods, or horizons, deriving their names from two important archaeological sites: the San Lorenzo Horizon (1200–900 BC) and the La Venta Horizon (900–400 BC). During the La Venta Horizon, Olmec artistic and political interaction with the developing coeval Maya cities of

Figure 1
Drawing of Monument 1,
Chalcatzingo

the Peten probably was most intense. Unlike the later Classic period Maya, no unassailable archaeological or iconographic evidence exists to indicate the Mixe-Zoque inhabitants of the Olmec heartland had developed a writing system (but see Pohl et al. 2002).

Although Olmec archaeological culture was limited temporally and geographically to the Gulf Coast heartland, objects created in the Olmec style were distributed across Mesoamerica. Within the heartland area, Olmec sculpture could reach monumental proportions and was often rendered as fully rounded, three-dimensional carvings. Sculptural categories included tabletop altar/thrones wrapped in bas-reliefs and the hallmark colossal heads that popularly distinguish Olmec art. During the La Venta Horizon, Olmec artists also carved low-relief compositions on stelae at La Venta. Outside the heartland, members of other language groups also carved large-scale monuments. At the singular, upland site of Chalcatzingo, Morelos, artists carved bas-reliefs in a characteristically Olmec style onto the boulders strewn along the talus slopes of a cleft mountain (Grove 1987) (fig. 1). However, most often the symbolic elements so crucial to defining the Olmec style adorn small-scale objects in the media of stone, clay, and wood. Interestingly, the Olmec art style continued functioning long after the evident demise of the archaeological culture in the heartland. Indeed, a stunning Maya mural (ca. 100 BC)—which William Saturno discovered recently at the site of San Bartolo, Guatemala (Kaufman 2003)—dramatically incorporates elements of the Olmec style into renderings of the Maize God and other preternatural figures. A solid body of iconographic studies consistently recognizes that Olmec architecture, public monuments, and other works of art—within the heartland and beyond it—clearly function to validate elite political authority by linking it to the supernatural power of the cosmic order (Joralemon 1976; Fields 1991; Reilly 1989, 1994a, 1994b, 1995b; Taube 1995, 1996).

Although Olmec artists lacked writing, they did express narrative and meaning by grouping individual sculptures into programs of tableaux (Cyphers 1999; Reilly 2002). The heartland Olmec arranged their large-scale sculpture into groupings that conveyed meaning and narrative through their relative placement, much as a Christmas nativity scene communicates shared narrative through the grouping of specific figures. Similarly, Olmec small-scale figures were intended to be grouped in tableaux, such as the well-known Offering 4, excavated at La Venta

(Drucker et al. 1959), and the recently discovered ritual caches in the ball court at La Merced, Veracruz (Rodríguez and Ortiz 2000).

Shared Patterns in Cosmological Modeling

Like all Mesoamerican peoples, the Classic Maya conceived of their cosmos as a multileveled configuration, always at tension between natural and supernatural oppositions (Schele and Freidel 1990, 66–77). The levels of the cosmos were joined by a traversing axis mundi that could be represented iconographically as a god, as a sacred tree or mountain, or even as the image of the *ajaw* ceremonially garbed, enacting the world tree (90–91). Within these artistic depictions of the Maya cosmos, bicephalic monsters and serpents, as well as dragonlike creatures, play important roles (Schele and Miller 1986, 45–47; Schele and Freidel 1990, 67–73), such as the Celestial Monster, which carries the sky upon its serpentlike body. The Kawak Monster personifies stone, and the Witz Monster personifies mountains and cave openings. Another cousin, the Water Lily Monster, in its dragonlike form embodies still waters such as lakes. Finally, the powerful Vision Serpents in their several varieties personify the smoke rising from the blood offerings that conjured up the spirits of royal ancestors (see cat. 60).

The Olmec art style deploys a similar program to depict the multileveled cosmic model, its oppositions, and its supernatural inhabitants (Reilly 1995b). The Mize-Zoque people also shared the belief in a multileveled cosmic order corresponding to the sky, earth, and under- or otherworld realms, but in their art they do not seem to have interpreted the cosmic levels as separate and distinct constructions. Rather, they are conjoined realities in a living and completely interconnected universe, traversed by the axis mundi. Like their Classic Maya counterparts, the heartland Olmec also expressed the cosmic axis as the Maize God in his role as the God of the Center. Incised images on greenstone and jade celts recovered from the heartland site of Arroyo Pesquero (Reilly 1995b, 38–39; Taube 1995, 46, fig. 6e) dramatically express this concept. Olmec artists clearly used the convention of placing the Maize God (in his manifestation as world tree or God of the Center) within the middle of four sprouting maize seeds to symbolize the cardinal directions.

Also like their Maya counterparts, Olmec dragons serve as metaphors for cosmic realms, locations, portals, and ritual actions (Joralemon 1976). One spectacular example, La Venta Monument 6, is a large sandstone sarcophagus that assumes the form of the great dragon as the surface of the terrestrial realm, floating in the primordial waters of creation with vegetation growing from his back (fig. 2). Ceramics, created in the Olmec style, from such Central Mexican highland sites as Tlatilco and Tlapacoya, in the Valley of Mexico, and Las Bocas, Puebla, have produced numerous near-abstract dragon variants by their elegant and economical schematization, which explicitly identify the cosmic realm that they inhabit. For instance, when these images carry the hand-paw-wing motif on their bodies, with the fingers pointing down, they most likely represent terrestrial dragons; fingers that point up almost certainly indicate a celestial dragon (fig. 3; cat. 30).

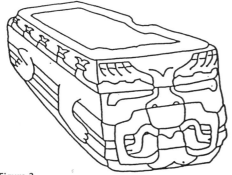

Figure 2
Drawing of Monument 6, La Venta

Figure 3
Rollout photograph of Carved Bowl (cat. 30)

The Jester God Royal Headband: Supernatural Sanction through Association with the Maize God

In most societies a crown or head regalia distinguishes the king from ordinary mortals. The crown royal for Classic Maya kings, the *sak hu'unal*, was a white bark headband adorned in the center with the Jester God carved from jade or greenstone (see cat. 90). By the Classic period, Maya kings wore the Jester God image, representing a variant of the Maize God, to link themselves to divinity. The crown announced the king's pivotal ideological and societal roles as the living incarnation of the Maize God. In Maya belief systems, this god had established the present creation, the latest in a series of creations. He also functioned in time and space as the pivot on which the cosmic oppositions balanced and renewed themselves. In wearing the Jester God headband, Classic Maya kings identified themselves with the Maize God; painted ceramics often depicted them in the god's full regalia in a ritual dancing pose, known as the Holmul Dancer (Reents-Budet 1991) (see Christenson, this volume, fig. 2). The backrack comprises another important part of this sacred ritual costume. Indeed, the Holmul Dancer carries on his back an elaborate model of the cosmic order that the Maize God established at the beginning of the present creation (Reents-Budet 1991, 219–21).

The so-called Jester God takes his name from his headdress, which resembles a medieval jester's cap (Schele and Miller 1986, 53). In fact, his unique trefoiled head represents uncurling maize vegetation (Fields 1982, 1991; Freidel 1990). The Jester God personifies the trefoil symbol in the center of the headbands, such as those on facade masks of divinities and in portraits of Late Preclassic period Maya rulers (Schele and Freidel 1990, 411). One of the earliest Maya manifestations of its use as an actual element of royal costume was recovered from excavations at Cerros, Belize, dating from around 50 BC (96–103). By the Classic period the Jester God also assumes the form of a long-snouted-zoomorphic variant for the *ajaw* glyph (411).

The Olmec were already using the Jester God as a royal symbol in elite costuming, where it was often expressed as a trefoil motif (Fields 1982, 1991; Reilly 1994a), which like its Classic period descendent stylizes growing maize leaves. One representation of an Olmec ruler appears to provide an antecedent for the Classic Maya Holmul Dancer. This small, carved jade figure from Arroyo Pesquero presents a seated male personage, not only wearing the Middle Formative trefoil forerunner of the Jester God headdress, but his elaborate backrack seems to depict the primordial waters of creation (Benson 1971; Reilly 1994a) (see cat. 16). However, the Holmul Dancer format was not the usual Maize God representation found in Olmec-style art. Karl Taube has identified many of the infant images (commonly known as "Olmec babies") in Olmec-style art as representations of the Formative period Maize God. This distinction between Classic period Maya and Olmec Maize God representations reflects an artistic emphasis on different periods of the life cycle of maize. The Olmec Maize God is almost certainly a metaphor for sprouting maize. The fact that Olmec rulers are frequently depicted cradling the Olmec Maize God illustrates that their relationship was a nurturing one. For the Maya, the Holmul Dancer complex is a personification of the Maya *ajaw* as mature maize and the source of life itself.

Olmec artists created both the trefoil and the preternatural long-snouted-zoomorphic variants of the Jester God. Significantly, several Olmec Jester God jewels have survived the centuries and have been displayed as heirlooms in Classic Maya contexts. The most striking example, from a Maya tomb in Yucatan, was worn as a pectoral by the high-status occupant (see cat. 90). The presence of an actual article of Olmec royal regalia in a Classic Maya tomb is further indication that many specific aspects of Maya *ajaw*ship had been borrowed from the Formative period Olmec.

The Ritual of Accession

In a dramatic episode depicted on the recently discovered San Bartolo murals, a Late Preclassic period Maya ruler sits enthroned on scaffolding, awaiting his crowning (Kaufman 2003, 76). This specific ritual moment undoubtedly prefigures similar Classic Maya coronation rituals and sacrificial episodes, such as the one carved on Piedras Negras Stela 11, dedicated 22 August 731 (Taube 1988) (fig. 4). Has an analogous ritual moment been captured in the art from the Olmec heartland?

A recently published celt from the Middle Formative period clearly illustrates that there were Olmec antecedents for this Maya scaffold enthronement ceremony. The incised imagery depicts a human figure with a *k'an* cross in his eye (fig. 5) seated on a scaffold that is dramatically similar to the scaffold depicted in the San Bartolo murals. At La Venta, on the east mound within the basalt-columned Enclosed Court, Robert Heizer excavated what may very well be the remains of an Olmec enthronement scaffolding (Drucker et al. 1959; Reilly 1999). He uncovered six postholes associated with a number of cached offering deposits, which the excavators labeled as burials (Drucker et al. 1959, 162–79). However, each posthole was so large that it surely must have supported a construction significantly heavier than the ubiquitous, ordinary thatched roofs found on *champa* structures of the Gulf Coast. The offerings positioned between the posts contained jade jewelry as well as other regalia and accoutrements. Offerings 5, 6, and 7 contained the remains of Olmec versions of the Classic Maya *sak hu'unal* along with jade earflare assemblages and belts. Undoubtedly, these offerings constituted the coronation regalia of La Venta's past rulers (Reilly 1999, 328–32). I suggest that the six large postholes indicate the placement and size of the scaffolding on which these rulers assumed the regalia of royal office. This evidence from La Venta—the offerings, the regalia vestiges, and these traces of a monumental raised structure—in addition to the incised celt, once again provides dramatic archaeological proof that a specific episode in Olmec ceremonies of royal accession was ancestral to the accession ceremonies of the Late Preclassic and Classic period Maya kings.

The Stela Genre

Stelae are generally oblong, standing stones, often incised or carved with information. They vary in size from portable examples that can be held in the crook of an arm (see cat. 56) to monumental ones that reach many feet in height and tons in weight. The Classic Maya preferred the stela as the public format to display royal images and texts. Besides recording royal accessions and victories, Maya stelae also were linked closely with ceremonies that marked the beginning and ending of sacred cycles of time. In addition to their public effectiveness, stelae played a sacred role in the ceremonial landscape; often they even were kept wrapped as sacred bundles (Stuart 1996). In that article, Stuart demonstrated that the act of ritually bundling or binding stelae with cloth or ropes was associated closely with the *ajaw's* tying on of the *sak hu'unal*.

In terms of the historical development of kingship, stelae gave Classic Maya rulers a means to record history publicly as linear time, while indelibly tying it in with the cycles of sacred time. Thus, a stela typically could record a historical ruler's ancestors, birth, accession, and even death, while simultaneously binding the linear progression of this individual human lifespan into the never-ending, recurring cycles of sacred time.

The earliest large-scale stelae have been found at the Olmec site of La Venta. La Venta's stelae fall into two categories: those that depict what appear to be historic human personages; and those that show images of clearly supernatural beings (Reilly 1995a, 1995b; Taube 1995). At La Venta, the origin of stelae has been linked securely to those greenstone celts that were ubiquitously cached as offerings throughout the site (Porter 1996). The excavated offerings of erect,

Figure 4
Drawing of Stela 11, Piedras Negras

Figure 5
Olmec-style incised celt

deliberately arranged celts are arguably the direct progenitors of the celtiform, full-scale stelae (Porter 1996; Taube 1996). Extending the argument, those celtiform stelae bearing the image of the Olmec Maize God surely must portray that deity in his role as the axis mundi, world tree, or God of the Center (Reilly 1994b; Taube 1996, 51).

Like their later Classic Maya counterparts, Olmec stelae and other monuments were active participants in the ritual landscape, and as such were often carved with rope or cloth bindings (Reilly 2001). At La Venta, the images of kings as well as the stelae were often carved so as to appear bundled (Guernsey Kappelman and Reilly 2001). La Venta Monument 77 in particular, in the frontal view, depicts a seated Olmec ruler wearing a cape and an elaborate Maize God head-dress (see cat. 4). When viewed from the rear, his cape appears as bundle wrapping, while the headdress assumes the aspect of a cleft-maize motif (Taube 1996).

The first Mesoamerican examples of large stelae appeared at La Venta, and the later Classic Maya used stelae to tie royal history into cyclical time. Thus, one can posit a specific accession or coronation site on the Northeast Mound in La Venta's enclosed court. All these factors strongly suggest that the rulers of La Venta themselves led the ideological transformation from paramount chief to king sometime between 900 and 500 BC. All the evidence points to La Venta being the site where Classic Maya kings' regalia was first visualized in the permanent medium of stone, both monumentally and in miniature.

What may we deduce about the nature of the interaction between Formative period Olmec and Maya royal ritual and regalia? I have long argued that the best explanation for borrowings of symbols and ideology among Mesoamerican Formative period cultures is the mechanism of long-distance exchange and interaction among elites (Reilly 1991, 1995b). Olmec art and symbols within the Gulf Coast heartland are unquestionably more ancient. However, recent explorations and the discoveries at San Bartolo clearly indicate that the Late Preclassic Maya also were a dynamic and expanding culture. The spread of ritual objects and ideological concepts—including the symbolic visualization of cosmology, the Jester God headband, scaffolding as the site of accession rituals, and the stela cult—are explained best through a geographically dis-persed, Middle Formative Ceremonial Complex. In this overlapping, competitive, dynamic ambience, a range of ideological and political concepts were sown and cross-pollinated through an evident, though incompletely understood, series of interactions among the emerging ethnic identities of the peoples who would form the elites of the polities of the Mesoamerican Classic period. Undoubtedly, the template for Classic period belief, politics, and ritual was first essayed and visually inscribed in the Middle Formative Olmec heartland.

Late Preclassic Expressions of Authority on the Pacific Slope

Julia Guernsey, University of Texas at Austin, and
Michael Love, California State University, Northridge

There is significant variation in expressions of authority within the Pacific coastal region of Guatemala and Chiapas, Mexico, during the Middle and Late Preclassic periods. While some fundamental aspects of kingship remained consistent, the institution was reinterpreted as social conditions changed through time.

The roots of rulership in this region can be traced to the Middle Preclassic period, during which time Early Preclassic chiefs appear to have been transformed into kings. By the Late Preclassic period, new sculptural modes focused on the office of rulership alongside traditions that emphasized site layout, axial alignments, or, quite literally, the mapping of authority onto the natural landscape. Archaeological and art historical evidence from several key sites within this region presents a more encompassing view of kingship that acknowledges patterns of continuity while also accommodating variation.

These transformations may have been, in part, a response to the unique nature of this region, which was situated at the nexus of two great cultural traditions in ancient Mesoamerica. To the west was the Mixe-Zoquean-speaking region, which stretched from the eastern boundary of Chiapas near the site of Izapa, through the Grijalva River basin, the highlands of Chiapas, the Isthmus of Tehuantepec, and into the Gulf Coast Olmec heartland. To the east was the Mayan-speaking region, which extended from the piedmont area near the site of Takalik Abaj, through the Guatemalan highlands, and north into the Maya lowlands. This location at the juncture of two linguistic traditions may have fostered a tendency to articulate messages of rulership in terms that were not always language dependent. In other words, the choice by rulers at specific sites to express messages of authority in monumental architectural or sculptural form—often without accompanying hieroglyphic inscriptions—should be seen as deliberate. Its success may have rested on its very lack of dependence on language and, instead, an emphasis on well-established pan-Mesoamerican concepts of sacred knowledge that were broadly understood to audiences of diverse cultural backgrounds.

The Middle Preclassic Period

The first chiefdoms, or societies dominated by hereditary leaders, emerged in Mesoamerica during the Early Preclassic period. By Middle Preclassic times, an ideology of rulership in which powerful individuals portrayed themselves as able to manipulate and control natural and supernatural forces had clearly developed, as evidenced at the Olmec site of La Venta (Reilly 1994b, 1995b, this volume) and Pacific Coast sites such as La Blanca (Love 1991, 1999) and Takalik Abaj (Graham et al. 1978; Orrego and Schieber 2001; Schieber 1994). Takalik Abaj Monument 16/17, for instance, depicts a figure—probably a ruler—with a "were jaguar" mouth, fleshy jowls, and a tall headdress that terminates in a mask capped with a trefoil motif; similar features characterize La Blanca Monument 1 (figs. 1 and 2). A figure from Middle Preclassic

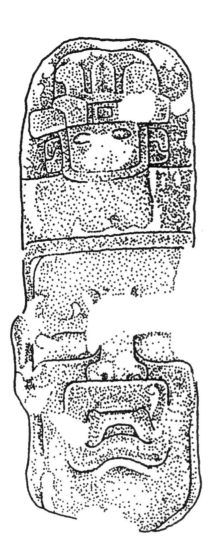

Arroyo Pesquero, in the Olmec heartland, depicts a ruler with a similar physiognomy who also wears the trefoil crown of kingship (Fields 1989, 1991; Reilly 1994b) (see cat. 16). Such consistencies demonstrate that rulers along the Pacific slope were participating in shared systems of elite insignia and stylistic conventions that extended from Chalchuapa, El Salvador, to Tiltepec and La Union, Chiapas, through the Isthmus of Tehuantepec, and into Guerrero, Morelos, and the Olmec heartland.

During this same period, monumental architecture—a hallmark of social complexity that attests to the control of economic surpluses and the deployment of large labor forces—also appeared along the Pacific slope. Large earthen mounds were constructed during the Conchas phase (900–600 BC)[1] at La Blanca, Guatemala, which appears to have become the major center within the region at this time (Love 1991, 1999, 2002). Mound 1 at La Blanca was a massive structure, 25 meters (82 feet) in height, built entirely of rammed earth capped by clay walls. It served as the center around which other public mounds were constructed in order to create a sacred space. At the site of Izapa, the earliest platform phases within Mound 30a also date to the Middle Preclassic (Ekholm 1969), although it was not until the latter part of that period—following the decline of La Blanca—that Izapa would rise to a position of relative importance within the region (Love 2002; Lowe et al. 1982, 12). Several public buildings at Takalik Abaj appear to have been constructed during this period as well, including Mound 5, a 20-meter- (65-foot-) tall pyramid.

The achievements in sculpture and monumental architecture that took place along the Pacific slope during the Middle Preclassic marked the emergence of rulers and an ideology that supported their claims to power. Sacred spaces created by the organization of these forms were undoubtedly the loci of ideologically charged rituals, performed before assembled audiences. Other forms of ritual took place in households without kingly supervision or intervention, as testified by the omnipresence of figurines in Middle Preclassic domestic contexts along the Pacific Coast at sites such as La Blanca. Did household rituals parallel, on a more intimate scale, the themes performed in the central plazas and conceptually buttress the claims of Middle Preclassic kings? Or did they represent a challenge to the rulers, whose claims to divinely sanctioned power may not have resonated with the masses?

The Late Preclassic Period

With the advent of the Late Preclassic period, two types of knowledge—calendrical and astronomical—emerged as central themes in expressions of rulership. They appear to have had a significant impact on how statements of authority were formally conveyed in sculptural and architectural terms. For instance, evidence for the Long Count first appears at this time. The Long Count, a linear calendrical system, tallied the days elapsed since the last creation of the universe on 4 Ajaw 8 K'umk'u, or 13 August 3114 BC. It was, however, far more than a calendar. It was an ideological tool, manipulated by Late Preclassic Mesoamerican elites to link themselves to an even more ancient creation mythology. Its novelty rested on its role as a means through which rulers highlighted their actions within greater cycles of time and defined themselves as responsible for the maintenance of cosmological order. This explicit association between rulership and a calendrically based creation cosmology is a Late Preclassic innovation that enabled rulers to transform from powerful ritual practitioners into supernatural forces in their own right.

The majority of Mesoamerican monuments with early Long Count dates come from the Pacific Coast region: two at Takalik Abaj (Stelae 2 and 50) and one at El Baúl (Stela 1). On Takalik

Figure 3
Stela 5, Takalik Abaj

Abaj Stela 5, which dates to around AD 126, the organization of the composition gives immediate priority to the centrally placed inscription, which is flanked by two individuals in elite garb that identifies them as rulers (fig. 3). While not deciphered, this text clearly indicates that, already by the Late Preclassic period, rulers in this region chose to anchor their deeds and actions to historical dates, creating a powerful statement of their control of sacred calendrical knowledge.

While astronomy had played a role in site orientations and organization from very early on, its overt use by Late Preclassic elites to couch political statements is another noteworthy innovation. The night sky, as has been well documented for the Classic Maya, served as a storyboard upon which the creation narrative unfolded each night (Freidel et al. 1993). This is illustrated by Classic period inscriptions that correlated a ruler's political actions with astronomically observable events. For ancient Mesoamericans, the sky provided empirical evidence of—or justification for—elite activities and claims. Late Preclassic Pacific slope rulers were already aware of the implications of this.

Sculpture

The ideology of rulership was communicated in dramatically contrasting ways during the Late Preclassic period along the Pacific slope. One example, Izapa (in present-day Chiapas, Mexico), reached its apex of growth during the Guillen phase (300–50 BC), which was characterized by extraordinary construction activity in which all of the central plaza groups reached their maximum proportions. The majority of monuments at the site also appear to have been carved during this period (Lowe et al. 1982, 133). The primary sculptural vehicle employed at Izapa was the stela, carved or plain, which was often paired with an altar at its base. These stela-altar pairs punctuated the site center with their imagery, working in tandem with architectural surroundings to create a unified program of sacred space. Oriented so that their highly narrative imagery could be viewed from the plaza center, they defined the space as one of performance, designed to accommodate and engage a large audience.

Although stelae first appeared in sculptural assemblages during the latter part of the Middle Preclassic period, they quickly became the primary sculptural mode along the Pacific slope for the dissemination of potent messages during the Late Preclassic period. With their more regular contours and smoothed stone surfaces, they provided an ideal—and permanent—means for recording rulers' performances and complex mythological narratives. The development of the stela format may also have been a response to external pressures and culturally diverse interaction spheres that were in place across Mesoamerica by at least 600 BC. Their appearance at Izapa—as well as Takalik Abaj, El Baúl, Kaminaljuyu, and elsewhere—was probably one symptom, manifested in sculptural form, of the amalgamation of power at selected Late Preclassic sites (Parsons 1986, 7).

While stelae functioned as one means through which the events of creation and the ruler's role within them were visualized to audiences, they did not stand merely in mute testimony to performances from the recent or distant past. Stelae played active roles in the ritual life of the community, as Stuart (1996) observed, and they were continually revitalized through ceremonies and processions performed within their midst. Their effectiveness may also be related to their human scale, which readily accommodated and engaged audiences gathered around them (Clancy 1999, 126; Newsome 1998).

But what were the themes recorded on the stela monuments in this region and how, specifically, did they articulate themes of rulership? One recurring image is that of rulers costumed as birds—replete with feathered wings, towering avian headdresses, and dramatically hooked beaks as on Izapa Stela 4 (fig. 4) and Kaminaljuyu Stela 11 (cat. 6). This imagery, which

Figure 4
Drawing of Stela 4, Izapa

was invoked throughout a broad geographic region during this period, was predicated on the myth of the Principal Bird Deity (Bardawil 1976; Cortez 1986; Guernsey Kappelman 1997). This avian deity, closely associated with the previous creation in the K'iche' Maya *Popol Vuh*, appears during the Early Classic period as the *way*, or alter ego, of Itzamnaaj, the primordial shaman or ruler (Bardawil 1976; Hellmuth 1986, 1987; Guernsey Kappelman 1997, 2004; Taube in Houston and Stuart 1989: n. 7) (see cat. 50). By wearing the costume of this bird deity, kings defined themselves as analogous to Itzamnaaj, who also transformed into the bird. They also wore the avian costume in death: the principal occupant in the Late Preclassic Tomb II, a royal burial in Kaminaljuyu Mound E-III-3, wore an elaborate greenstone mask that may represent a three-dimensional version of the bird mask worn by rulers at Izapa, Kaminaljuyu, and elsewhere (Shook and Kidder 1952, 115). On Takalik Abaj Altar 30, the relationship between this imagery and the office of rulership is explicit: a ruler costumed as the bird deity decorates the top of a Late Preclassic throne (Vinicio García 1997, 169; Orrego and Schieber 2001, 923). Clearly, wearing the avian costume was central to statements of rulership during the Late Preclassic period in this region and beyond, as evidenced by La Mojarra Stela 1, pulled from the Acula River in Veracruz, upon which another king appears in a remarkably similar bird costume (Winfield Capitaine 1988).

Rulers must have commissioned monuments that recorded their avian performances to demonstrate their abilities to communicate with the supernatural realm. This, in turn, buttressed their claims to political power. Moreover, the geographic spread of the imagery attests to a standardized vocabulary of forms and actions that signaled participation in an elite communication network spanning southeastern Mesoamerica during this period. This narrative directly inserted the ruler into a cosmological framework. This theme was also invoked in Group B at Izapa. There, three monumental stone pillars, each capped with a stone sphere, formed a triad at the base of Mound 30. This triad referenced the three-stone hearth—a symbol of the center of the universe—which was the locus of important creation events according to Classic Maya inscriptions and reflected in the sky in the triadic arrangement of stars in the constellation Orion (Freidel et al. 1993, 79–84; Looper 1995, 25; Taube 1998, 439; Tedlock 1985, 261). Rulership was cleverly inserted into the astronomical and mythological framework of Group B: Throne 1 sat at the central pillar's base, effectively placing the seat of rulership at the apex of the cosmic hearth.

Monuments at Izapa were not carved with the elaborate calendrical and hieroglyphic inscriptions that characterize monuments at sites such as Takalik Abaj and Kaminaljuyu. It should not be assumed, however, that a lack of inscriptions indicates unfamiliarity with nascent hieroglyphic traditions. Rather, it more likely reflects a deliberate choice by the elite at Izapa to commission public royal artworks that communicated to audiences of diverse cultural and linguistic backgrounds on a purely visual level.

Caches and Cosmograms

At El Ujuxte, located nearly equidistant between Izapa and Takalik Abaj, major occupation began immediately after the decline of La Blanca, around 600–400 BC, and continued into the Late Preclassic period. Despite its proximity to these two sites with substantial sculptural corpuses, only three large monuments are known from El Ujuxte. All three were uncarved altars (Monuments 1–3), like similarly plain altars from Izapa and elsewhere during this period (Love and Balcárcel 2000, 65). Their placement at the base of Mound 2 along one of the main axes of El Ujuxte indicates a ritualistic significance that was underscored by the offerings associated with Monument 1, which consisted of two vessels and a ceramic cross. Another offering consisting of ceramic crosses, bowls, and small plates was encountered farther to the west, very near the intersection of the two central axes of the site (fig. 5).

Figure 5
Feature 27 offerings, El Ujuxte

The significance of these crosses is revealed in the rigid, almost gridlike organization of El Ujuxte, which was constructed as a cosmogram with two axes forming a cruciform plan. The principal axis of the site aligned with the point on the horizon where the bright star Capella rose, while other alignments marked important astronomical phenomena, such as the zenith transit of the sun, winter solstice, and summer solstice (Poe 2000). The elite of El Ujuxte, through the astronomically significant formal planning of the central zone, created a powerful statement of their authority that reverberated on a cosmic level.

While the ceramic crosses echoed the architectural organization of the site, they also invoked the *k'an* cross, which, for the Maya, marked the location of the Maize God's rebirth. Yet

Figure 6
Drawing of Stela 27, Izapa

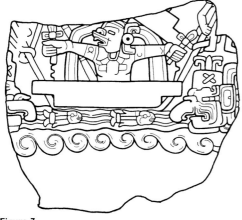

Figure 7
Drawing of Stela 67, Izapa. See also Christenson, this volume, fig. 7

this motif was incorporated by sites outside Mayan-speaking regions, such as at Izapa on Stela 27 (where it marked the trunk of a tree) (fig. 6) and Miscellaneous Monument 38 (where it occupied the center of a rectangular stone). On Izapa Stela 67, the lidded canoe bearing an Izapa ruler in the guise of the Maize God forms a *k'an* cross as well (Guernsey Kappelman 2002; Taube 1996) (fig. 7). At El Ujuxte, an alignment running from the outlying Chabela group through the northwest group pointed to where Gemini rises on the summer solstice, preceding the sunrise (Love 2004). Gemini appears in the night sky adjacent to Orion and its three hearthstones (Freidel et al. 1993, 81), suggesting that this alignment at El Ujuxte was linked to notions of centering and the creation narrative of the Maize God. On a broader scale, secondary centers surrounding El Ujuxte adopted the same cruciform central plan, indicating a regional standardization of site organization that may have echoed the themes of the primary center (Love et al. 1996, 11; Poe 2000).

These associations also characterized the elite residential sector at El Ujuxte, which formed a ring around the central zone to ensure elite control (Love and Balcárcel 2000, 65). In the only burial that included bones covered in cinnabar—a marker of royalty throughout the Maya region—three bowls were placed behind the individual.[2] The grouping of three vessels, repeated in many burials at El Ujuxte, recalls the triad of hearthstones that symbolized the place of the Maize God's rebirth, which could also be marked by the *k'an* cross. Through this reiteration of patterns associated with the Maize God narrative, the elite of El Ujuxte constructed a series of embedded cosmograms that ranged in scale from monumental to modest.

Substantiating the power of this new ideology was the near cessation of household rituals at El Ujuxte (Love et al. 1996, 8). Figurine use, so dominant at Middle Preclassic La Blanca, fell to nearly nothing at Late Preclassic El Ujuxte. Other household rituals associated with feasting similarly declined. This evidence suggests that the elite of El Ujuxte succeeded in deemphasizing ritual at the household level and moving it—figuratively and symbolically—into the sacred center of the site. In so doing, they successfully defined themselves as intermediaries between El Ujuxte residents and the divine.

Expressions of authority were varied during the Preclassic period along the Pacific slope. While extensive sculptural assemblages at some sites serve as sensitive indicators of centralized authority, other sites allude to equally sophisticated institutions through the organization of space and the remnants of ritual activity. How, then, can one go about characterizing the nature of rulership in this region during the Preclassic? Clearly, there were a number of different polities and cultural groups vying for power, each articulating their authority through varied means. Yet, despite this diversity, common themes emerge, such as an invocation of creation narratives and a manipulation of calendrical and astronomical knowledge that provided a supernatural charter for the ruling elite during the Late Preclassic period. In fact, the evolving, heterogeneous expressions of divine rulership found along the Pacific slope during the Preclassic attest to the range of possible themes of political and supernatural authority within the built environment.

Notes

1. Conchas phase La Blanca was marked by increased population size, density, and social complexity. A corresponding reduction of population in neighboring zones suggests that La Blanca elites exercised a higher degree of political dominance than in the previous, Early Preclassic period.

2. A fourth vessel, at the front of the burial, contained lime. A fifth bowl was placed on top of the *taxcal* column that encased the body.

The Principal Bird Deity in Preclassic and Early Classic Art

Constance Cortez, Texas Tech University

One of the most significant icons associated with early Mesoamerican rulership is the Principal Bird Deity. The creature first appears in Olmec art during the Middle Formative period (900–400 BC) (Guernsey Kappelman 1997). In a mural painted above an entrance to the Oxtotitlan cave, Guerrero, Mexico (see introduction, this volume, fig. 2), the seated ruler is shown either dressed in the guise of the bird or having actually assumed the bird's spiritual identity. The placement of this image above a cave entrance is significant—caves were understood to be portals to the underworld where powerful deities and ancestors resided. Guernsey believes that by taking on the guise and powers of the deity, the ruler was able to act on behalf of his people as a kind of intercessor between this world and the next.

To understand the Principal Bird Deity's mythological significance and the source of its power, it is necessary to turn to early representations found in narrative sculpture from the sites of Izapa and Kaminaljuyu. At Izapa, the bird appears in its hybrid form—having components derived from avian, human, jaguarian, and serpentine sources. On Stela 2 from that site, the creature is shown falling headlong into the branches of a tree (fig. 1). Inserted into inner cartouches of the outstretched wings are crossed bands, well-known symbols for the heavens. On either side of the

Figure 1
Drawing of Stela 2, Izapa

Figure 2
Drawing of Altar 10, Kaminaljuyu

tree, small figures represent one of the earliest manifestations of Junajpu and Xb'alanke', Hero Twins from the K'iche' Maya book of genesis known as the *Popol Vuh*. As the myth goes, Wuqub' Kakix, an avian deity, had usurped power and was wreaking havoc and harassing man and beast alike. One of the Hero Twins, Junajpu, waited at the side of the bird's favorite fruit tree and defeated him by shooting him down with a blowgun. Later Maya rulers often linked themselves genealogically or symbolically to these twins. By doing so, they, like the twins before them, held in check the powers of the bird, and those who, like the bird, would attempt usurpation of kingly powers.

The power of twins over the Principal Bird Deity is also borne out by artwork from Kaminaljuyu, an ancient site located in present-day Guatemala City. On cylindrical Altar 10, the avimorph is shown in a rampant attitude with one leg raised and extended in front of the other (fig. 2). Inside each of the wings, the hieroglyphs *k'in* (sun, day) and *ak'ab'* (darkness, night) replace the crossed bands found on Izapan monuments. Although the twins are not physically present, they are indirectly referenced by these symbols. The hieroglyphs allude to the "Paddlers," another set of twins, who seem to be related to the twins of the *Popol Vuh* and who are often associated with the underworld. Like Junajpu and Xb'alanke', the Paddlers hold the avian in check by their very presence through their hieroglyphs.

The manner in which rulers accessed the Principal Bird Deity's power was by means of a transformative, ecstatic dance (see cat. 53). Late Preclassic texts from La Mojarra Stela 1, discovered in the Olmec heartland, support the notion that such performances were the prerogative and obligation of rulership. The stone monument implies the transformation of the ruler into a bird by listing the implements used and costume worn by the ruler during the bird dance. Since a ruler's position was dependent upon his ability to access both natural and supernatural power, such proclamations of his spiritual prowess on public monuments would do much in validating his position to his people.

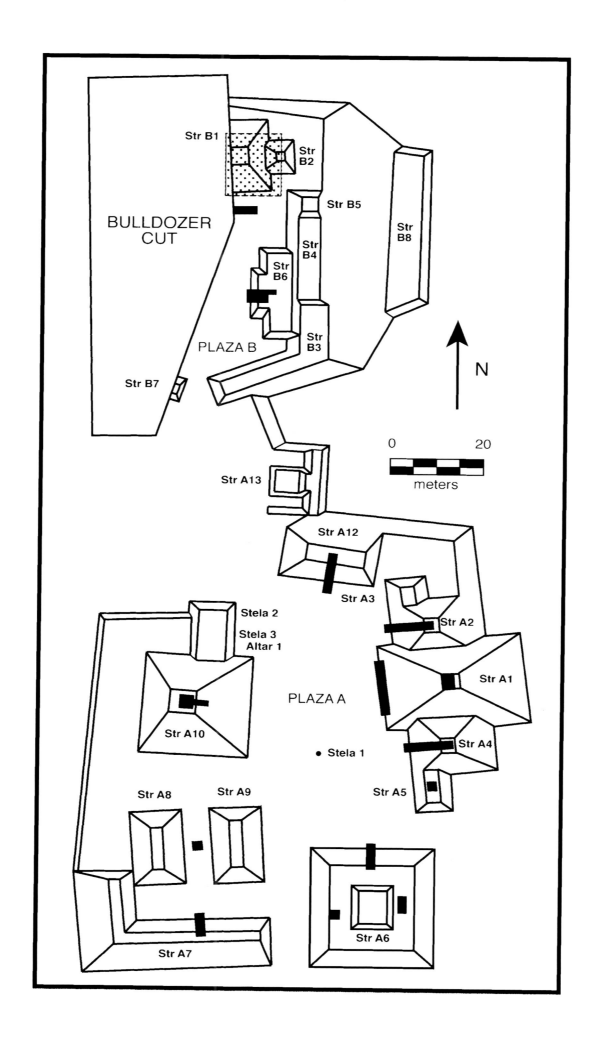

Preclassic Architecture, Ritual, and the Emergence of Cultural Complexity: A Diachronic Perspective from the Belize Valley

M. Kathryn Brown, University of Texas at Arlington, and
James F. Garber, Texas State University at San Marcos

The rise of Maya civilization has been a topic of great debate in Maya studies. New evidence from Belize has provided scholars with a better understanding of the processes behind the rise of complexity and the formation of the institution of kingship. Recent excavations at several sites in Belize, including Blackman Eddy, Cahal Pech, and Pacbitun, suggest that the Maya were present at least by the late Early Preclassic period (1000 BC) and that they continually inhabited the region for more than two thousand years. More than a decade of research at Blackman Eddy, one of the earliest settled communities within the Maya lowlands, has revealed much about the origins and development of Maya society through analysis of public architecture and ritual deposits.

The study of public architecture and sacred space is critical to understanding the development of complex societies and the emergence of kingship, because architecture played a role in perpetuating the ideology of social order legitimizing elite status. Investigations at Blackman Eddy revealed a developmental sequence of Middle Preclassic public architecture and associated ritual deposits. These data suggest consolidation of wealth, prestige, and power culminating in the use of public architecture and material culture as media to transmit ideologically related messages pertaining to social order, which in turn supported the institution of kingship (Brown 2003).

Ancient Maya ritual activities, such as sacrifice, bloodletting, and the consecration and termination of architecture have all been well documented for the Classic period. However, very little is known about the ritual behavior of the Preclassic Maya—more specifically the Middle Preclassic, when the institution of kingship was forming. This paucity of information can be attributed to the difficulty of uncovering Preclassic deposits due to the architectural overburden of later periods.

The data from Blackman Eddy suggest that the basis for Late Preclassic kingship and ritual activity developed out of an earlier communal feasting tradition associated with early public architecture. Feasting and communal ritual have been documented elsewhere in Formative Mesoamerica and played a significant role in the rise of complexity (Clark and Blake 1994). The role of ritual and public architecture changes through time and reflects the rise of sociopolitical complexity, and there is evidence that early public platforms functioned as integrative facilities for feasting, while later more elaborate pyramidal structures functioned as restricted performance space. Evidence from Blackman Eddy also suggests that public architecture became more elaborate as ritual deposits shifted toward a more restrictive form.

Blackman Eddy is a small ceremonial center, although it exhibits all the features of a major center, including monumental architecture, stelae, and a ball court (fig. 1). Unauthorized

Figure 1
Plan view of Blackman Eddy site core

Figure 2

Profile of Structure B1, Blackman Eddy

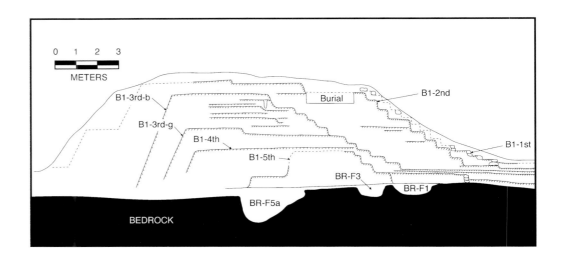

bulldozing activity partially destroyed Plaza B, cut Structure B1 in half, and presented a rare opportunity to investigate ritual remains associated with early Maya architecture through the use of extensive horizontal excavation (fig. 2). The construction phases document a history of architectural elaboration initiated at the end of the Early Preclassic that entailed increased costs for labor and materials over time. Ritual behavior may be inferred not only from the material remains but also from the attributes of architectural features. Early in the sequence (800–600 BC), ritual deposits represent the remains of feasting and communal ritual. Although they resemble domestic middens, they were deposited in single events and contain both whole and exotic artifacts mixed with ceramic serving vessels, riverine shell, and faunal remains, implying communal rituals associated with early public architecture. Communal wealth and labor were invested in the construction of platforms, which in turn reinforced group identity and solidarity, increasing the prestige of the sponsoring individual. Through time, certain individuals may have set themselves apart by acquiring exotic items and by gaining control over the organization of communal ritual, thus allowing them to limit access to public architecture and associated ritual.

By the end of the early Middle Preclassic (650 BC) the inhabitants of Blackman Eddy erected a new type of platform, which served a public nondomestic function. Structure B1-5th had a linear triadic arrangement composed of a central platform flanked by two lower platforms. It is a fairly large building for this time, indicating an increase in labor investment. The openness and unrestricted nature of B1-5th suggest it may have functioned as both a special ceremonial location and as an integrative feature. This is further supported by the presence of an elaborate deposit within the core of the central platform, which contained ceramic sherds, conch shell fragments, marine shell beads, jade, bone, obsidian blades, chert tools, riverine shells, a chloromelanite fragment, mano fragments, and carbon. The deposit was laid down after the construction of the building had started but before the building was finished. The variability of the remains suggests a communal event that coincided with the construction effort.

Structure B1-5th may be the earliest example of the triadic arrangement that was common during the Late Preclassic. This form appears to have been associated with kingship (Freidel et al. 1993), and it reflects the Maya worldview, symbolizing the three-stone place of creation. The basic themes of life, death, and rebirth are often symbolized through Maya ritual deposits and are evident within these Middle Preclassic deposits as well (Garber et al. 2004; Mathews and Garber 2004). Two deposits were encountered above B1-5th that have affinities to later Maya consecration and termination deposits. The first of these was in the "alley" between the B1-5th central and eastern platforms, where a polished deer-metapodial bloodletter, marine shell beads, and a bone bead were recovered. The deposit was capped with a lens of white marl—a practice common in termination deposits of the Late Preclassic and Classic (Garber 1983; Ambrosino et al. 2003; Pagliaro et al. 2003). Several types of animals, including dog, rabbit, white-tailed deer, brocket deer, peccary, armadillo, and fish were present (Norbert Stanchly personal communication 1997). Dog, deer, and fish are frequent components of elite ritual (Pohl 1983, 1985; Stanchly personal communication 1997).

A second offering was encountered above and to the east, and it appears to be a consecration or dedication feasting deposit/cache related to the subsequent construction phase, B1-4th. The deposit extended over several square meters and consisted of whole and partial ceramic vessels, a jade bead, deer mandible and scapula, a broken mano, and the inner core of a conch shell. This deposit (700–600 BC) was purposely placed above the marl lens capping the termination ritual and represented the rebirth or renewal of the structure. The elaborate character of this deposit—with numerous exotic items and several whole serving vessels—suggests increased wealth within the community, signaling emerging elitism.

Overlying B1-5th is B1-4th, a Middle Preclassic single-tiered rectangular platform decorated by a stucco mask facade that is the earliest documented architectural mask found within the Maya lowlands to date (Brown 2003; Brown and Garber 1998; Garber et al. 2004). Architectural sculpture dating to this time period can be found outside the Maya lowlands at Teopantecuanitlan and, slightly later, at Tzutzuculi (McDonald 1983). The summit surface of B1-4th was severely burned and the facade was desecrated in antiquity, possibly indicating warfare activity (Brown and Garber 2003). No iconographic information could be recovered; however, the ideological implications of a god mask flanking a Middle Preclassic platform include the use of public architecture to legitimize the elevated status of an emerging elite.

During the subsequent Late Preclassic period, mask facades were a common architectural decoration throughout the Maya lowlands. Although iconographic themes varied from site to site, these masks share certain elements that expressed ideas about Maya worldview and legitimize the role of kingship (Freidel and Schele 1988a; Garber et al. 2004; Hansen 1992a). Freidel and Schele argue that the institution of *ajaw* developed during the Late Preclassic and is evident in the material symbol systems. They suggest that kingship emerged at that time to accommodate "contradictions in Maya society between an ethos of egalitarianism and an actual condition of flourishing elitism brought on by successful trade and interaction between the lowland Maya and their hierarchically organized neighbors over the course of the Preclassic era" (1988a, 549). The iconographic themes of mask facades symbolize Maya worldview on a grand scale, and the role of the king would be legitimized through the ritual activities performed on these structures.

Until recently, evidence suggested that this style of architecture emerged abruptly in the Late Preclassic. It was also thought that prior to the Late Preclassic, there was little evidence for material implements of power. Freidel and Schele state, "An empirical difficulty with investigating the origins of the Late Preclassic institution of *ahaw* is the paucity of antecedent evidence pertaining to ideology because of the simplicity and ambiguity of the material symbol systems prior to the Late Preclassic transformation" (1988a, 549). The discovery of a Middle Preclassic mask indicates that Late Preclassic and Classic architectural decoration actually evolved from an earlier mask tradition; hence, the symbol system of kingship had antecedents in the Middle Preclassic. This is not to suggest that the institution of kingship was present at this early date, but rather that the ideological concepts that would have allowed the transition to, and acceptance of, the institution of kingship were in the early stages of development.

Structure B1-3rd was erected above B1-4th and marked a shift in architectural style involving an increase in labor and material investment. This occurred after what appeared to have been a hostile event and represented a dramatic increase in rebuilding activity. The basal platform was

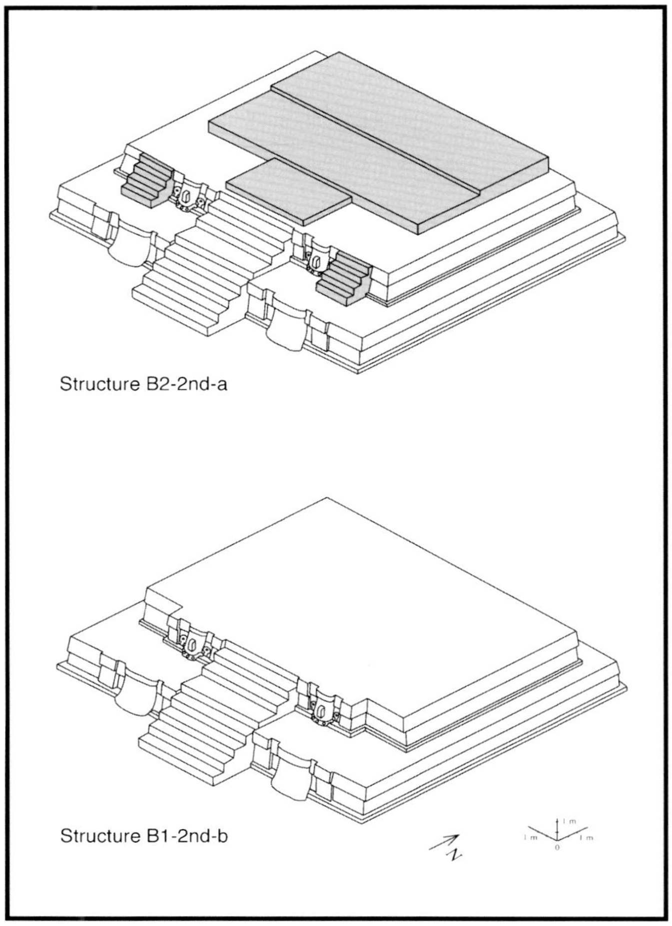

Figure 3
Structure B1-2nd, Blackman Eddy

Structure B2-2nd-a

Structure B1-2nd-b

constructed of monolithic cut limestone blocks and dates to the end of the late Middle Preclassic. Six additions to this platform were constructed, the final four dating to the Late Preclassic. B1-3rd-d signals a change in architectural style to a more pyramidal form. A Joventud Red bowl was placed in front of the building, intrusive into the associated plaza; this single-vessel dedication cache is important because it signals a change in ritual behavior from communal caching to a more restrictive form of caching that appears for the first time at the end of the late Middle Preclassic. Ritual activity is also transformed to restrict participation and reinforce the importance of special individuals. Caches placed within buildings and under associated plaza surfaces became the dominant form of caching during the Late Preclassic and Classic periods, as opposed to deposits placed on top of, between, and in front of platforms (Brown 2003).

The construction of B1-2nd during the Early Classic marks a change in the sequence, with the addition of large stucco mask facades flanking the central staircase (fig. 3). The presence of this form of architectural decoration, as discussed previously, signals a notable change in social order involving the creation of the formalized institution of kingship. The central section of the mask represents the severed head of the father of the Hero Twins (fig. 4). The head is emerging from a bloodletting bowl marked with three dots (Garber et al. 2004), and this emergence or symbolic birth reflects the transformation of the severed head into the Maize God. Bloodletting bowls are also perceived as an *ol*, or portal (Freidel et al. 1993). The three dots represent the hearthstones at the center of a Maya household and serve to center the cosmos for the creation events that follow (Freidel et al. 1993). Maize God insignia are intricately tied to the institution of kingship and are seen throughout the Classic on a variety of media (Brown 2003; Fields 1989, 1991). Such decoration clearly communicates the significance of sacrifice and bloodletting, which in turn helps maintain the social order. The ruler would perform sacred rituals

on this building, linking him to the supernatural and therefore legitimizing his role within the community.

A circular shaft, on the upper tier behind the mask facade, appears to be a large posthole that would have supported an enormous superstructure or scaffold. This shaft is remarkably similar to those encountered on 5C-2nd at Cerros, Belize. It is clear that by the Early Classic at Blackman Eddy, the institution of kingship was in place. Restricted access to rituals performed on the summit of pyramidal buildings disconnected the elite from the rest of the community, thus sanctifying their connection with the supernatural and legitimizing their elevated status.

The investigation of Structure B1 at Blackman Eddy has provided an unprecedented database of Preclassic architecture and ritual activity, and this evidence suggests that emerging elites initially used low platforms to host communal feasts, bolstering their prestige. As certain individuals gained support and power, new architectural forms and ritual caching behavior were introduced, which reflect a change in social order (Brown 2003) and reinforce the adoption of new ideological concepts to legitimize the new order and uneven wealth distribution, which in turn supported the institution of kingship.

The Creation Mountains:
Structure 5C-2nd and Late Preclassic Kingship

David A. Freidel, Southern Methodist University

Structure 5C-2nd at Cerros, Belize, is a remarkably well preserved early temple on an elaborately decorated small pyramid (fig. 1). When discovered in 1977, it was only the second known intact "sculptured pyramid" from the Preclassic period, and it remains a masterpiece of Maya art. The structure was a creation era place designed to enhance religious ritual performances by the king who commissioned it. Like modern churches, synagogues, and mosques, Maya temples were places of worship and prayer, where people remembered the sacred covenant with the divine established at the beginning of their particular revelation. Maya rulers were both religious and political leaders. Accompanied by shamans and priests, family members and courtiers, Maya kings led their people in the celebration of creation at sacred mountains like 5C-2nd.

Figure 1
Structure 5C-2nd, Cerros

Masterworks in religious architecture, like the Sistine Chapel at the Vatican, succeed in conveying the essence and totality of a revelation, but they do so in different ways. 5C-2nd is not like the Sistine Chapel, where Michelangelo depicted the entire creation from Genesis. The structure is more similar to the Sainte-Chapelle in Paris, commissioned by King Louis IX (St. Louis) in the mid-thirteenth century to house the Crown of Thorns, which he brought back during the Crusades. St. Louis's chapel, while a small Gothic church, is actually a monumental jewel box or reliquary for the most precious material evidence of the Passion of Christ. Sainte-Chapelle signals its function in its main rose window, which is uniquely designed to represent the Crown of Thorns. Thus the building makes the creation revelation real and tangible through allowing a key part to stand for the whole.

The challenge with 5C-2nd is determining which key parts of the Maya creation revelation it conveys. The four great stone and plaster deity masks on the terrace facades of 5C-2nd certainly embody central ideas about the sacrifice and resurrection of creator gods. We formerly thought that the masks represented the Hero Twin sons of the Maize God, who apotheosized as the Sun (lower two masks) and Venus (upper two masks) (Schele and Freidel 1990) (fig. 2). The twins rescued the bones of their sacrificed father Maize and his twin brother and managed, with the help of the shaman Itzamnaaj, to bring their father back to life. Just as dry maize kernels go into the ground like bones and reemerge as beautiful green plants, so too the Maize God resurrected and the Sun and Venus cycle through the underworld and heavens.

Today I think the lower masks represent funerary masks of the bundled bones of the Maize God and his twin brother. The upper masks represent Itzamnaaj and Chaak, the axe-wielding sacrificer god; these creator gods caused the death and resurrection of the Maize God. These were the gods impersonated by the king when he performed here as a lord of creation.

Precincts for Gods and Men: The Architecture of the Cities of the Peten, Guatemala

Juan Antonio Valdés, Universidad de San Carlos, Guatemala

The Maya built large and beautiful cities over an expanse of more than 350,000 square kilometers (approx. 135,000 square miles), which made it possible for regional styles to develop in the northern and southern Yucatan peninsula, in the Usumacinta River basin, in the central area of Peten, Guatemala, and in the extreme southeast of the Maya region.

The excavations carried out for more than a century in the Peten have shown that this central area was the heart of Maya civilization, in view of its great age, the high quality of its artistic expression, and the degree of cultural complexity attained by its early inhabitants. The first archaeological digs in the region, led by members of the Carnegie Institution of Washington in Uaxactun between 1926 and 1937, amazed the world with the discovery of the intact pyramid E-VII-sub, 8 meters (26 feet) high, with sixteen large stucco masks around its four sides (fig. 1). Dated to the Late Preclassic, approximately the first century BC, this edifice was long considered the oldest. But some eighty years later, now that excavations have been undertaken in other cities, it is known that the earliest constructions in the Peten go back as far as 700 to 600 BC, when the cities of Tikal, Uaxactun, and others were founded.

During the Preclassic period architects and builders experimented with limestone and stucco, achieving technological advances in the handling of volume and space that would come into systematic use over the centuries. The success in constructing elevated pyramids and palaces with stone corbeled-vault roofs set the standard for future monumental constructions and helped establish the character of each of the cities, and particularly the growing towns, as they moved toward a more complete urbanism.

Architectural and iconographic evidence indicates that during the first or second century BC, Tikal and Uaxactun had developed a strong system of centralized government, with a sovereign supported by a select group of nobles, learned men, and priests who together made up the royal court. These sovereigns proclaimed that they were direct descendents of the gods, and since this gave them the right to rule the destinies of their people, they never missed an opportunity to stress their divine nature before their subjects. No doubt the successful leadership of the sovereign and his court allowed them to gain in prestige and power over the centuries, their reputation enhanced by their proper handling of ideological and technological concepts. Great works and programs were undertaken by the leaders to display their authority and that of their gods. They commanded the construction of sumptuous pyramids that emulated the cosmos, and from them they transmitted messages to their faithful public.

The desire to have their cities achieve greater prestige on a regional level became a challenge for the rulers, so that by the second century BC the great cities found themselves caught up in rivalries to become the axis mundi, the heart of the cosmos and the favored place of the

Figure 1
Pyramid E-VII-sub, Uaxactun

Figure 2
North Acropolis, Tikal

gods. Tikal and Uaxactun were rivals in the central zone, while Nakbe, El Mirador, and Calakmul were all rivals a bit farther north.

Because rulers relied on architecture to perpetuate their cosmological ideas, their cities became a sort of map that copied and transmitted their beliefs. According to the Maya there existed five cardinal points: four to indicate north, south, east, and west, and one central point as the marrow of the entire system. To reproduce this scheme, they planned and built architectural groups with structures on the four sides, while in the center of the plaza was the fifth point, the space where communication between men and gods was possible, the link between the natural and the supernatural worlds.

The pyramids reached new heights with each passing century—from 8 meters (26 feet) for the oldest to 30 or 40 meters (100 to 130 feet) during the Early Classic. They were built for religious purposes, their elevation designed to bring human beings closer to the gods who lived in the heavens. However, once the religious precepts were fulfilled, the sovereigns' demands had to be satisfied, since they considered themselves demigods and thus required their own sacred space. The architects applied their talents to conceive a new space worthy of housing the king and his court. This led to the construction of limestone palaces with different numbers of rooms inside. The oldest known palaces with corbeled vaults were built during the Late Preclassic, and while their ruins have been found in Tikal, Uaxactun, El Mirador, Nakbe, and Calakmul, those at Uaxactun are the best preserved.

Each city was made up of clusters of buildings, all erected with an unerring sense of urban order. Careful study went into each structure's placement, chosen both for its suitability and for the play of light and shadow that would fall on the facades or the sides of the buildings, giving them greater movement and producing an almost magical effect at specific hours of the day. The Maya knew how to adapt their new constructions to the terrain, integrating nature into their cities and preserving most of the plant species. They thereby created exceptional and harmonious urban spaces that always combined perspective, aesthetics, and nature.

Nightly observation of the clear tropical skies gave Maya astronomers a detailed understanding of the movements of the planets, the moon, and the stars. From their observatories and other special buildings they studied sunrises and sunsets throughout the year as well, which led to knowledge of the seasons, the development of various calendrical systems, and a spectacularly advanced mathematics.

The acropolis was another distinctive architectural group (fig. 2). Located in the center of the city, it represented the seat of political and religious power. These structures consisted of grand, lofty platforms containing palaces and ritual precincts in the highest section, with a raised staircase in front. Three of the visual arts—architecture, sculpture, and painting—merged to infuse the walls and friezes with color and life. The front facades of the acropolis and its buildings also served as propaganda tools, offering a visual means of transmitting to the public the new ideological and social order that the sovereign had put in place and emphasizing images of gods and rulers to strengthen his charisma and power.

Clearly these complexes were planned and discussed before they were built. As proof we have a limestone model discovered in 1980 by Guatemalan archaeologists who were excavating the eastern part of the Great Pyramid, in the group known as the Mundo Perdido. This model has fourteen sculpted edifices, among them a ball court, various pyramidal bases, rectangular platforms, plazas at different levels, and stairways entering and exiting the groups. Whether the project was realized, the model provides reliable evidence that architects had to submit projects for the sovereign's approval before they could be built. Similarly, five stucco scale models of buildings were found at Yaxha during excavations in Structure 4 at the Mahler group (Morales 2001).

Figure 3
Hombre de Tikal

Figure 4
Marcador of Tikal, front. See also Sharer
and Martin, this volume, fig. 4

Over time, and as the number of nobles grew, larger palaces were built, beginning in the Early Classic; these were no longer situated exclusively in the center of the city but beyond the central zone as well. With greater interior space, more entrances, and more rooms, these palaces also served wider functions. For the first time two-story dwellings were built, but only for the elite. Also for the first time, nobles were authorized to erect monuments carved with their names, as seen in Group H at Tikal, where the sculpture known as the Hombre de Tikal was discovered (fig. 3). It bears an inscription announcing the arrival of a local noble named K'uk' Mo', with the title of *ajaw*, in AD 406, referring to events that featured the sovereign Yax Nuun Ayiin I. At almost the same time, in AD 416, a very fine stone known as the Marcador of Tikal, in Group 6C-16, was carved with reference to a historical warlike event that occurred between Tikal and Uaxactun (fig. 4).

By the Late Classic, during the seventh and eighth centuries, palaces had become intricate complexes with multiple rooms, vast chambers with private spaces, interior corridors, half-hidden doors, and internal and external stairways. They were three or more stories high, the Central Acropolis at Tikal being one of the best examples. But these complexes were not isolated; causeways both narrow and wide served as avenues to unify the most important sectors of the city. These were called *sakb'e*, meaning "white road," for the stucco pavement that covered their stone construction. Paintings on ceramic vessels and graffiti show royal processions on these roads, with men bearing the sovereign on their shoulders in a wooden litter covered with a canopy of fine linens or cotton cloth to shield him from the overpowering tropical sun.

Because most of the territory lacked rivers, another essential area in every city was the reservoir, known locally as the *aguada*, where water was collected during the rainy season to satisfy the needs of the city. In Tikal as in Uaxactun, these *aguadas* were used to breed fish and lizards, to raise herons, ducks, and other aquatic birds, and to grow water lilies and other flowers. One of the largest *aguadas* known was in the center of Tikal; when filled with water it must have seemed like a small lake, where one could swim, fish, or simply go for boat rides in the late afternoon.

Not everything in the rulers' lives was formal: there were moments of diversion, when the rulers enjoyed performances by professional magicians, actors, musicians, and dancers, as well as lessons by dance and voice teachers, all of whom gathered in the great urban centers to amuse and entertain the lords of the court. Even during the Spanish conquest, several Spanish chroniclers tell of seeing theatrical events when they arrived in the Yucatan, and they remark on the Maya's skill at illusionistic tricks. The clowns and musicians were engaged to entertain the nobles, who enjoyed these shows as much as the commoners did. Thus, the king would have been surrounded by other nobles and principal lords to share his delight in the spectacle.

Translated by Rose Vekony

Early Social Complexity and Kingship in the Mirador Basin

Richard D. Hansen, Idaho State University and the Foundation for Anthropological Research and Environmental Studies, and Stanley P. Guenter, Southern Methodist University

The Mirador Basin in the extreme north-central Peten of Guatemala and the extreme southern part of Campeche, Mexico, contains some of the earliest Maya cities, which arose during the Middle and Late Preclassic periods (Hansen 1990, 1992a, 1992b, 1998, 2001; Clark and Hansen 2001; Hansen et al. 2002). A limited occupation at Nakbe, for example, dates to around 1000 BC, and stone walls of structures and large platforms were built there by around 800 to 600 BC. Similar Middle Preclassic occupation has been found at La Florida, Xulnal, and Tintal. During this period, exotic commodities such as shell, jade, coral, granite, and obsidian document the existence of long-distance trade networks; other indicators of cultural complexity include the presence of figurines with trefoil Jester God or Maize God images, human incisors inlaid with hematite, and ceramics with incised woven mat elements, suggesting that the imagery that characterized organized governmental structures was present in the Mirador Basin by about 800 BC.

The most significant architectural innovation at this time—the E-Group complex, consisting of an elongated north-south platform on the east side of a plaza with a dominant pyramidal structure on the west—is represented at Nakbe, Tikal, and Uaxactun. Furthermore, early Maya cities appear to have been built on an east-west orientation (as opposed to the north-south orientation of other Middle Preclassic Mesoamerican cities). Nakbe Stela 1, intentionally smashed in antiquity, was found in forty-five fragments and associated with other very early carved monuments around a small mound in the site's eastern group of architecture. While the exact chronological placement of carved monuments in the Mirador Basin is generally difficult to determine because of monument veneration during the Late Classic period, early stelae such as Stela 1 portray paired standing human figures adorned with the regalia of divine rulers (fig. 2). The figure on the right wears the crown jewel of early kingship, the mask of the Maize God, as also depicted on the north wall of the murals at San Bartolo (ca. 100 BC) (see p. 138).

During the Late Preclassic period, the cities of the Mirador Basin were linked politically, socially, and economically, and paved causeways connected peripheral sites like Nakbe and Tintal with the giant capital city of El Mirador, located at the center of the region. Slightly northwest of Nakbe, El Mirador was the largest ancient Maya city, and its Danta Pyramid is the tallest and most massive structure ever constructed by the Maya. The scale of architecture found there and at other cities in the basin leaves little doubt that the apogee of political and economic power was highly centralized, as reflected in the estimated 10 to 12 million man-days needed to construct the Danta Pyramid (Hansen 1990, 1998). The Mirador state flourished until around AD 150 (Matheny 1987; Hansen 1990, 2001), when nearly the entire basin suffered a large-scale depopulation, although sites like Naachtun appear to have maintained an enduring population into the Early Classic period (Kathryn Reese-Taylor personal communication 2003). Five hundred years later, during the Late Classic period, the basin was reoccupied with a much more modest demographic density (Hansen 1996). Although it never reached the high population levels or the extent of the architectural

Figure 1
Late Classic vessel with early dynastic list

Figure 2
Drawing of Stela 1, Nakbe

construction programs of the Preclassic period, Late Classic El Mirador supported some of the era's best pottery painters, who created the distinctive codex style.

More than a dozen codex-style vases made at various sites in the Mirador Basin record a list of nineteen accessions to office by lords bearing the Snake Head emblem glyph (Martin 1997; Reents-Budet and Bishop 1987; Reents-Budet et al. 1998). While Calakmul in Campeche was the capital of the Late Classic period kingdom known as Kaan (snake) (Martin 1996), in earlier centuries the Snake Kingdom seems to have been centered elsewhere, including Dzibanche in Quintana Roo, Mexico, during the Early Classic period. Based on recent archaeological excavations, we suggest that the Snake Kingdom emerged during the Preclassic in the Mirador Basin, where the earliest examples of the Kaan emblem glyph have been discovered, particularly on bedrock carvings.

Many of the royal names of the Dzibanche and Calakmul kings appear in the dynastic list painted on codex-style vases (fig. 1). Their accession dates and dynastic sequence, however, do not match the hieroglyphic records at the two cities, which prompted Simon Martin (1997) to conclude that the dynastic list on codex-style pottery is not that of the Classic period Snake Kingdom rulers but rather may record a retrospective history of the Preclassic kings of the Mirador Basin commemorated by royal artists nearly one thousand years later. Thus, Dzibanche and Calakmul not only appropriated the name and emblem glyph of the Preclassic Snake Kingdom, their rulers also apparently took many of the names of the ancient Snake kings as their own. Such veneration compares to that of many other Maya sites, as well as to European models, such as King Arthur by the monarchs of Medieval Europe; like Arthur, the early kings of the Mirador Basin were also enduring exemplars, legendary rulers of a glorious past.

The Sacred Mountain:
Preclassic Architecture in Calakmul

Ramón Carrasco Vargas, INAH Mexico

Archaeological studies of Maya and Mesoamerican civilization have traditionally considered the Late Preclassic as the time when the urban centers and great architectural constructions of the Classic period began to be developed. But as continued investigation and new exploration have fleshed out the chronology of Preclassic sites, the evolution of establishments in certain regions has been shown to originate during the Middle Preclassic. By the Late Preclassic these establishments had already developed into complex societies with great urban centers.

Archaeological information formerly described the Maya of the Middle Preclassic as an egalitarian agrarian society of simple *cacicazgos*, or chiefdoms, scattered in towns across the Maya region. The Late Preclassic was considered the period during which Preclassic society began its process of urbanization and reached its apogee at sites such as El Mirador, Nakbe, Tikal, and Uaxactun. The most recent work in Nakbe, for example, has revealed architecture of the Middle Preclassic (late Ox phase, 600–400 BC) characterized by structures as high as 18 meters (59 feet).

Figure 1

Structure II, Calakmul

According to Richard Hansen (1998, 81), platforms constructed at this time reached 5 to 8 meters (16 to 26 feet).

It may be inferred from recent investigations in the region of Calakmul in Campeche, Mexico, and in Guatemala's northern Peten that during the Preclassic period, Calakmul, El Mirador, Nakbe, and Uaxactun formed a regional sphere of shared geopolitical history. When viewed together, they afford a panorama that could offer a more adequate explanation not only for the origins of Maya architecture but also for the evolution of the symbolism to which Maya art gives form—both aspects can be considered intimately related to a system of regional organization (Carrasco Vargas 2000).

Among the architectural clusters composing the urban center of Calakmul, Structures I and II are notable for their built volume (fig. 1). The original establishment must have evolved from those two constructions, forming two nuclei or nodules represented spatially by the presence of the two great bases that dominated the urban landscape. The placement of its two most representative structures, with their different orientations, reflects two distinct aspects of the site's organization at diverse historical moments. This urban plan persisted throughout the course of the city's evolution, until the beginning of the city's decline as a leading center of a wide network of associated and subordinate states in the Late Classic (Carrasco Vargas 2000).

The process of urbanization unfolded from a nucleus that was dominated from the start by the placement of Structure II, south of the present central plaza (the Great Plaza). The architectural sequence found inside this complicated edifice is the most complete of any reported for central lowland sites, with a total of six substructures covering more than twelve hundred years of architectural development (fig. 2).

Figure 2
Rendering of Structure II, Calakmul

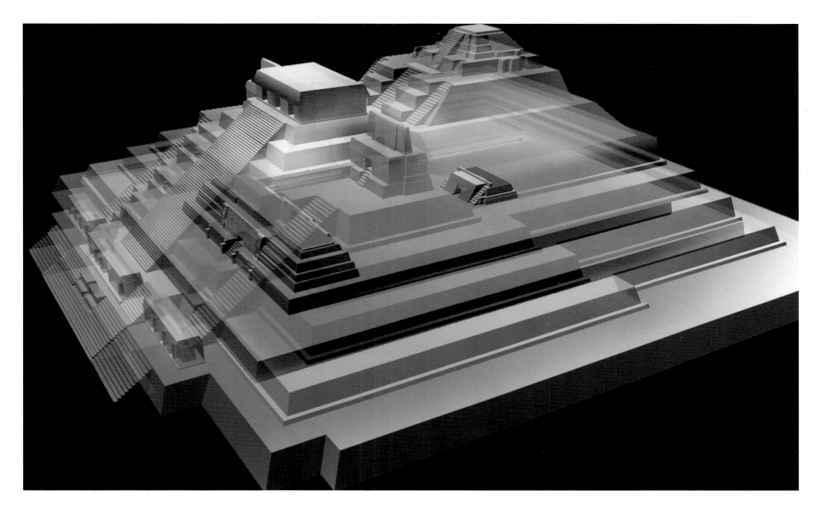

Substructure II-b, one of the so-called triadic complexes, was built during the Late Preclassic. A base with the attributes of a tall mountain, it was constructed at the height that would characterize Structure II throughout the urban history of the site, retaining its volumetrics and probably its architectural proportion as well. Sub II-b underwent modifications only on the north facade as a result of remodeling during the Early and Late Classic periods.

With the construction of Sub II-b, the buildings of the previous architectural complex, from the period that gave rise to the urbanization of Calakmul, were ritually buried. That earlier complex, beneath Sub II-b, is called Substructure II-c, and it is made up of some of the earliest structures reported for the site.

Sub II-c, dated to between 390 and 250 BC, consists of an 8-meter- (26-feet-) high platform over which edifices forming an acropolis-type group were built. On its northern facade, this acropolis presents a base called Substructure II-c1, one of the earliest edifices reported for Calakmul and one of the most completely preserved in the Maya region. Sub II-c1 suffered no significant mutilation when buried and covered by Sub II-b and thus retains both its structural and iconographic attributes.

To date, three edifices have been detected that make up Sub II-c: to the north, the aforementioned Sub II-c1; at the center, Sub II-c2, a small edifice that probably served as an altar; and at the far northeast, partly closing off this side, Sub II-c3, another edifice with a double corridor. Group H at Uaxactun, a complex with similar characteristics and probably based on the same model, was built at the end of the Late Preclassic; it primarily functioned as a site for ceremonies that legitimized power.

Viewed from the north facade, the base that constitutes Sub II-c1, more than 13 meters high and about 48 meters wide (approx. 43 by 125 feet), gives the Sub II-c complex the appearance of a mountain. A staircase flanked by large zoomorphic masks modeled in stucco leads into this mountain, through a corridor built with a barrel vault that is unique in the Maya regions of pre-Columbian America. Its design and construction demonstrate a building technique adopted by Maya architects at the end of the Middle Preclassic to re-create a natural space. This approximately 8-meter- (26½-feet-) long corridor re-creates the cave through which one enters the mountain's interior. Framed by a large 20-meter- (66-feet-) long frieze, this artificial cave leads into the ritual space formed by a large courtyard, whose three remaining sides are delimited by edifices that are still being explored.

Sub II-c1 represents the concept of the mountain-cave. The cave is the enclosure through which one passes to the regions dominated by rituals of death and rebirth; through it one enters the realm of the lords of the night. The walls of this corridor-cave were decorated with images outlined in black. A partial black outline shows a warrior holding a lance in his left hand and a shield in his right; a helmet protects his head, and Olmec characteristics may be discerned in his facial features. In the vault and on other sections of the walls are images of hands also imprinted in black (ek), the color that the Maya worldview associates with the west, the cardinal point from which the sun begins its passage to the dark regions. This association of ek with the corridor-cave reinforces the notion of Sub II-c1 as the threshold to the mountain's interior, the location of Xib'alb'a, the underworld.

The decoration on the frieze that frames the cave threshold further reinforces the mountain concept suggested by the form and structural design of Sub II-c1. In some of the earliest examples of public architecture the representation of the so-called Earth Monster and its association with the concept of witz, or mountain, seems directly linked to the ritual space in which the myths of origin are re-created. This association can be seen in Sub II-c at Calakmul, as well as in Group H at Uaxactun, where the four masks that decorated the base of Structure H-sub-3

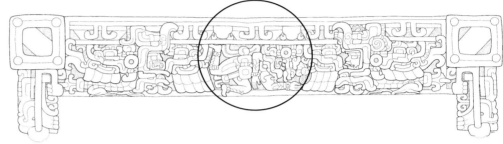

Figure 3
Detail of frieze from Substructure II-c1, Calakmul

Figure 4
Drawing of Calakmul frieze showing anthropomorphic figure

incorporated motifs representing both earth and sea. In Maya cosmology, hillside caves were considered entrances to Xib'alb'a. Associating the pyramid with the mountain and associating temple entrances with the mouths of caves ritually adapted the setting where communication rites with the supernatural realm were performed. That symbiosis between base and mountain, temple and cave—a symbiosis not found in the architecture of later periods—is more fully expressed in Sub II-c1. Sub II-c1 represents the mountain, and the vaulted corridor symbolizes the passage from profane level to sacred space, where participants in initiation ceremonies enter into contact with the ancestors and the supernatural powers.

The frieze decorating the facade of the base contains icons defining its character as a sacred mountain. Delimiting the upper portion of the frieze across its entire length is a band displaying symbols associated with the *witz*, which refers to the lower level of the Maya cosmos (fig. 3). The corners are defined by large earflares, from which rattlesnakes dangle like earrings, reinforcing the concept of the frieze as the representation of the personified *witz*. One symbol representing the mouth of the *witz* is a trilobed element that forms the logogram for "mountain." The same logogram appears in the iconography of the Classic period, such as that found along the edges of the stone lid of Pakal's sarcophagus at Palenque (see Florescano, this volume, fig. 2). The faces of the ruler's ancestors were carved within the trilobed elements, emphasizing that they are inside the mountain (Carrasco Vargas 2004).

Among the components that decorate the frieze, one in the central portion—an anthropomorphic figure with a zoomorphic head—stands out (fig. 4). In archaeological literature such figures are called "swimmers" because of the position they adopt, but actually this figure's posture is one of crawling, or sliding through the cave to the mountain's interior. This mythical figure represents the *ch'ulel*, the spirit entity of the Maya who dwells in Xib'alb'a as well as in human beings, plants, and animals (Carrasco Vargas 2004). Its centrality reinforces the cave identity and corroborates the interpretation of the upper band as symbolizing the mouth of the *witz*. Framing the spirit entity on each side are two birds, their wings spread and their open beaks emphasizing the mouth, the threshold to the mountain's interior. The birds' breasts and the edges of their wings present serpentine elements like those that identify the Principal Bird

Deity. Emerging from the beaks are anthropomorphic heads, each with its own features, which must be in direct relation to the myths of origin such as that recounted in the *Popol Vuh*.

At the spirit entity's wrists and ankles are knotted fillets followed by entwined bands symbolizing the mat (*pohp*) that signifies royalty and power in the iconography of the Classic period. Other knotted fillets, such as that supporting the spirit entity's belt, iconographically allude to the royal knot, which in writing is associated with the glyph of ascent to the throne for rulers of the Classic period. This affix is a logogram read as *hu'un*, one meaning of which is "headband," a direct reference to royal power. The presence of these elements—the *hu'un* and the *pohp*—at the spirit entity's extremities associates the frieze with acts relating to power, whether of ascent or of death. Considering the mountain-cave nature of Sub II-c1, the ceremonies performed would more likely relate to death and the entry to Xib'alb'a.

Given this connotation, the Sub II-c complex would have been dedicated to the cult of the ancestors, a feature that Structure II would retain until at least the middle of the Late Classic. The characteristics of the previous architectural complex indicate that from its earliest manifestation there existed restricted areas in which ceremonies were performed—rites and rituals of communication with mythical entities that were linked to supernatural forces or, more precisely, were their representatives in the earthly world. These primordial beings were always associated with caves, the context in which they were located; thus it may be inferred that the allegory expressed in this frieze refers to the entities that live in Xib'alb'a.

Although the Sub II-c complex has been only partly explored to date, elements such as its architectural characteristics, the frieze that decorates the facade of the building Sub II-c1, and the allegory that its iconography portrays, provide an idea of the function it served. This ideological message reveals that the presence of monumental architecture in the known societies of the Middle Preclassic reflects a social system with a degree of complexity that exceeds simple tribal organization. If we add to this architecture the presence of an elaborate iconographic complex and its associated rituals, we must accept these attributes as a form of state organization. This system of governance, expressed in the design and symbols on Sub II-c, clearly emphasize the character of the mountain-cave of this first great architectural work of Calakmul, the kingdom of Kaan.

Translated by Rose Vekony

Building a Dynasty:
Early Classic Kingship at Copan

Ellen E. Bell, Kenyon College

The tombs of Maya kings were often lavishly furnished with grave goods (Bell et al. 2004b), and from these rich tombs comes much of the evidence that informs the understanding of Maya kingship. John Lloyd Stephens (1969 [1841]) and other nineteenth-century explorers assumed that the ruined cities they encountered in Central America must have been ruled by powerful kings; however, scholars later questioned the scope of the rulers' authority (Webster and Freter 1990). Dramatic advances in the decipherment of hieroglyphic texts, iconographic analysis, and archaeological research have led to a broader understanding of the nature of Maya kingship, and the center of Copan, Honduras, provides ample evidence for an examination of divine kingship during the Early Classic period.

The fertile bottomlands of the valleys carved out by the Copan River in northwestern Honduras have attracted farmers for centuries. Ancient settlements can be found throughout the region, although they are concentrated around Copan, in the largest valley. Copan's Acropolis is an imposing accumulation of pyramids and buildings with origins dating to Preclassic times, and among its extraordinary structures are the Hieroglyphic Stairway, the ball court (fig. 1), the Popol Na, and Structure 16 and its underlying Rosalila building.

Elaborately carved altars depicting supernatural beings and tall stelae portraying Copan's sixteen divine kings, who governed from AD 426 to sometime after 822, are found in the Great Plaza at Copan. Their texts name the members of the royal dynasty, who traced their ancestry—and right to rule—to the first king and the founder of Copan's Classic period ruling dynasty, K'inich Yax K'uk' Mo' (see cat. 113). Recent research suggests that the Acropolis was built around a mortuary complex that held his remains as well as those of an elderly woman who was most likely his wife (Bell et al. 2004b). Portraits of the sixteen kings, who are seated on their name glyphs, are carved on the four sides of Altar Q, a small stone monument that provides the sequence of Copan's divine rulers. The inscription on the top surface commemorates the dedication of the monument and describes events around the installation of the founder of Copan's ruling dynasty (Stuart 2004). The royal figures are arranged around the sides of the stone in such a way that K'inich Yax K'uk' Mo' is shown handing a flaming torch to Yax Pasaj Chan Yoaat (r. 763–810) (fig. 2), the monument's patron and the last of the well-documented Classic period rulers. Altar Q was placed directly above the funerary complex in front of the last in a series of buildings within Structure 16 commemorating and celebrating the founding ruler (Sharer et al. 1999).

Maya kings relied upon a variety of means—in addition to wealth and military force—to establish and maintain authority: decorated buildings, sculpted monuments, and elaborate rituals created and increased their prestige and control. At Copan, K'inich Yax K'uk' Mo' exploited his political and social liaisons with rulers of powerful cities in the Maya area and in more distant regions. Recent research (see Sharer and Martin, this volume) suggests that K'inich Yax K'uk' Mo' enjoyed extremely close ties with the rulers of the Classic Maya center of Tikal and the Central Mexican center of Teotihuacan (Stuart 2004). His accession appears to have been part

Figure 1
Ball court, Copan

Figure 2
Altar Q, Copan

of a larger program of interaction between the elite of the Maya area and those of Central Mexico. K'inich Yax K'uk' Mo' became the ruler of Copan in AD 426, forty-seven years after Yax Nuun Ayiin I came to power at Tikal and five years before the accession of K'uk' B'alam I, the founder of the Classic period ruling dynasty at Palenque. All three rulers incorporated symbols with Central Mexican associations into their decorative strategies. While the nature of this inter-action (invasion and occupation; alliances formed to tip the balance of power in local factional struggles; a one-sided appropriation of foreign symbols to increase prestige; or a combination of these) remains unclear, evidence of some sort of relationship is intricately and inextricably woven into the architectural and material record of this period. This relationship is especially apparent in the mortuary complex, which contained the rulers' remains and which formed the core of the Copan Acropolis and the center—physical, ideological, and ritual—of the polity.

Excavations within the Copan Acropolis have uncovered buildings that date to the time of K'inich Yax K'uk' Mo' and his son and direct heir, Ruler 2 (Bell et al. 2004a; Fash et al. 2004; Sedat and López 2004; Sharer et al. 1999). These include the Hunal structure, most likely K'inich Yax K'uk' Mo's residence, which was subsequently altered for use as his tomb, and a series of later buildings constructed to encase his burial place and that of an important woman, probably his wife (see Agurcia Fasquelle, this volume, fig. 1). Both the buildings and their ritual deposits emphasize connections with Central Mexico and Maya centers, particularly Tikal.

The Hunal structure, one of the earliest buildings yet found in the Copan Acropolis, is below Structure 16; it was built in the *talud-tablero* style associated with Central Mexico and Kaminaljuyu (Sedat and López 2004). The tomb chamber held the remains of an adult male of advanced age (Buikstra et al. 2004) who had been buried with offerings of ceramic, jade, shell, and other materials. The origins of the twenty-one ceramic vessels in the tomb were determined through trace-element analysis; nine vessels had been made outside the Copan Valley (Reents-Budet et al. 2004a), providing further evidence that the ruler had close connections with for-eign powers. Of these nine, three were made in the Peten region of what is now Guatemala,

Figure 3
Drawing of left side of Stela 31, Tikal

near Tikal, and three were imported from highland Central Mexico. Other objects in the tomb echo Central Mexican iconography. Shell plates arranged around the head and over the mouth and jaw appear to be the remains of a shell helmet similar to that worn by Yax Nuun Ayiin I in his portrait on the side of Tikal Stela 31 (fig. 3). This helmet has been associated with the Central Mexican war serpent (Taube 2004a); as depicted on Tikal Stela 31, it forms part of a Central Mexican warrior costume.

Strong associations with the Peten, especially Tikal, are also seen in the offerings. Stable isotope ratio analysis of the bones suggests that the deceased was born and spent his early childhood in or near Tikal, before arriving in Copan as a young man (Buikstra et al. 2004).

Even though a ruler may have planned his burial during his lifetime, he was buried by his successor, and royal funerals provide a glimpse into the strategies of legitimation used by acceding kings. Ruler 2, who was responsible for the burials of both K'inich Yax K'uk' Mo' and his wife, appears to have emphasized local connections along with ties to powerful foreign centers.

Hunal and its tomb were encased within two new structures, known as Yehnal and Margarita, that shifted the focus from Central Mexican iconography to architectural styles and imagery linked even more closely to the Peten. A multi-chambered tomb was constructed inside Yehnal, although the whole structure was encased by another building, Margarita, before it could be used. The Margarita tomb held the remains of an adult woman and a variety of offerings. Like the Hunal tomb, the burial in Margarita included both foreign and locally made ceramic vessels. One of the vessels, the "Dazzler Vase," made in Central Mexico but decorated in Copan, depicts what may be the Hunal structure (see cat. 144). Additional objects, such as pyrite mirror backs decorated with Central Mexican iconography and Peten-style carved jade and shell jewelry, indicate foreign associations. Both tombs, however, also included a great deal of local material, and the prominence of the woman buried in the Margarita tomb suggests that K'inich Yax K'uk' Mo' may have solidified his position within Copan by marrying into a powerful local lineage.

This diversification of legitimation strategies is seen throughout the Maya world; the Early Classic rulers of Palenque and Piedras Negras, for example, also emphasized ties with Teotihuacan. Another way to legitimize rule was to emphasize descent selectively, as did Bird Jaguar IV of Yaxchilan in a sculptural program designed to highlight the royal ancestry of his mother and mask the lack of it on his father's side (Martin and Grube 2000, 127–33).

Throughout the Classic period, Maya rulers and their successors used a variety of strategies to underscore their right to rule. Elaborately decorated buildings, extravagant costumes, exotic pottery, weapons, and jewelry all emphasized the wealth, importance, and power of the ruler. Messages encoded in the decoration of the buildings that formed the backdrops for public rituals were reinforced through costume and regalia, presenting a unified idea that increased the power and prestige of the ruler himself.

Rosalila: Temple of the Sun King at Copan

Ricardo Agurcia Fasquelle, Asociación Copan

Rosalila was the principal religious temple at Copan in the late sixth century AD. Like the elaborate Gothic cathedrals of Western Europe, the facades of Rosalila were profusely decorated with complex religious messages. At the center of these was the Sun God, K'inich Ajaw, the divine patron of Copan rulers, and spiritual co-essence of the dynastic founder, K'inich Yax K'uk' Mo'. This extraordinary example of religious architecture from the Early Classic period placed the Sun King of Copan at the center of the cosmos and of Maya society. The physical presence of Rosalila, a sacred mountain, marked the heart of the city and ordered the social, political, and ideological world around it.

I discovered Rosalila on 23 June 1989, while directing tunnel excavations under Temple 16, at the center of the Copan Acropolis. Unlike most of the buildings found in our excavations at the acropolis, which were destroyed by the ancient Maya to stabilize the structures built above them, Rosalila was not systematically demolished. Instead, it was interred with great care and ceremony. Its rooms, moldings, and niches were cautiously filled with clay and rocks, while its enormous modeled stucco panels, painted in deep red and accented with yellow, white, and green, were covered with a thick layer of white stucco before the whole building was buried.

Figure 1
Rosalila temple within Structure 16, Copan. Below Rosalila are the Hunal and Margarita tombs (at lower left)

Figure 2
Detail of facade, Margarita temple, Copan

Rosalila is three stories tall, rising 12.9 meters (42 feet) above its main courtyard, and has a base measuring 18.5 by 12.5 meters (61 by 41 feet). Its principal facade faces west, the direction associated by the Maya with the entrance to the underworld, the world of the dead and the place where the sun sets every evening. On its main stairway, we uncovered a carved hieroglyphic text with a Long Count date reconstructed as 9.6.17.3.2 3 Ik' 0 K'umk'u (AD 21 February 571). This date is near the end of the reign of the tenth ruler of Copan, Moon Jaguar, who ruled from AD 553 to 578.

Twelve radiocarbon dates from our excavations agree with this early date for its construction and set its interment at about AD 690. Consequently, the temple had a long history: it was built by the tenth ruler, used by the eleventh, and buried by the twelfth. Rosalila occupies the middle section of a longer sequence of nested temples in the central axis of the acropolis. These were built by Copan's ancient rulers to venerate the founder of the dynasty, whose tomb was found deep in the bowels of the acropolis, directly underneath Rosalila.

The interior walls of the temple are covered with soot from the burning of incense and torches. Many of the objects I found inside further reflect the ceremonial practices carried out in this sacred building. Among these were seven ceramic incense burners with carbon still inside (two still placed on delicately carved stone jaguar pedestals), sacrificial stone knives, nine ceremonial scepters known as "eccentric flints," jade jewelry, precious seashells, stingray spines (perforators used in auto-sacrifice), shark vertebrae, jaguar claws, and vestiges of flowers. In its heyday, this marvelous building was an elaborate religious center from which rich colors, sounds, and aromas emanated. As in modern churches of highland Guatemala, copal incense burned continuously inside Rosalila, flowers and pine needles carpeted the floor, and ritual chants reverberated from its walls.

The Origins of Maya Writing

**Federico Fahsen, Universidad Francisco Marroquín, and
Nikolai Grube, University of Bonn**

Ancient Maya civilization is celebrated for the development of the most sophisticated writing system in the New World. Maya hieroglyphic writing can be regarded as a true writing system, where writing is defined as a visible record of speech rather than the representation of ideas. In true writing, a limited and clearly defined set of signs is arranged according to a canon of representational conventions in order to refer to another code of communication, that of language. In Mesoamerica there were also other systems of true writing, such as Zapotec and the little-understood Isthmian script, but Maya writing was by far the system with the largest written record.[1] The narrow definition of writing employed here excludes other recording systems such as the Peruvian khipus, whose connection to language has not been demonstrated.

The decipherment of Maya hieroglyphic writing has been greatly advanced in the last two decades. The nature of the script, which combines logographic (word) signs with syllabic signs, has been safely established. Dynastic legitimation, politics, and self-aggrandizement of rulers have been identified as the major topics of the written texts. Yet the origins of Maya writing have remained somewhat opaque. Our knowledge of Maya hieroglyphic writing is based almost exclusively on the texts that have survived from the Classic period, most of them carved or painted on stone monuments, architectural elements, and ceramic objects. At the beginning of the Early Classic period, Maya writing had already appeared in a fully developed stage. It seems that by about AD 300 all features of the script were already present. Very little is known about the evolution of the system or the early stages of phonetic writing. The earliest Maya texts are datable only by style and accompanying iconography. Most of the early texts lack dates, and almost all of the early texts are written on portable objects that lack archaeological provenance. A firm grasp of the development of Maya writing is further hindered by a dependence on evidence strictly from the Classic period. Scholars assume that the signs from the Classic period had the same reading in the Preclassic, when Maya writing began to emerge. A large number of Preclassic hieroglyphs—perhaps the majority—cannot be read because they have not survived into the fully functioning writing system of the Classic. What we know about early Maya writing is what later inscriptions allow us to project into the past.

Hieroglyphic Traditions from the Highlands and Pacific Piedmont of Guatemala

Yet another problem for the understanding of the development of Maya writing is the existence of different regional writing traditions in the Late Preclassic. Although the overwhelming majority of monumental inscriptions from the Classic period come from the lowland areas, Preclassic writing is also known from the piedmont area of the Pacific Coast of Guatemala and El Salvador. By the Late Preclassic a writing system was in place with sculpted monuments in such sites as El Baúl, Takalik Abaj, and Chalchuapa (Coe 1957; Fahsen 1995, 2001a; Chinchilla Mazariegos 1999). Some of the monuments at these sites carry Long Count dates that range from 36 BC to AD 126. Another set of undated monuments is from El Portón and Kaminaljuyu in the central highlands of Guatemala. The chronological frame embraces the six hundred years between 400 BC

Figure 1

Drawing of text on Stela 10, Kaminaljuyu

and AD 200, and all or almost all of these monuments deal primarily with rulership. The early Long Count dates on monuments from the coastal area and the highlands of Guatemala have been taken as evidence that Maya hieroglyphic writing developed in this region before it was exported into the lowlands. However, there is still considerable debate about whether the writing in the coastal piedmont and the highlands can indeed be regarded as a direct precursor to Classic Maya writing. Furthermore, although the earliest dates from inscribed monuments in the lowlands are AD 199 (see cat. 56, the reading of the date is debated) and AD 292 (Tikal Stela 29), some inscribed objects and monuments have been found in archaeological contexts that suggest their production in the first century AD (Hansen 1991).[2] It is possible that lowland Maya writing was at some time inspired by the developments on the coast and the highlands, but a direct genetic relationship cannot be proven.

Whatever the precise connection between the two traditions may have been, Preclassic lowland writing and coastal/highland writing are approximately contemporary and share various features. Hieroglyphs tend to fill an entire glyph block (see cats. 87, 89, 90, 91). There is no or very little evidence for suffixation, suggesting that grammatical morphemes were not represented. Most, if not all, signs were logographic and had an iconic origin, depicting real things or actions building on a conventionalized and preexisting iconography.[3] A good case for such an iconic logograph is the sign for "seating," which depicts the lower part of a body and bent legs in a highly conventionalized manner (see cat. 90:A5). This iconic sign was so common in Mesoamerica that it can also be found in early writing systems outside the Maya area, such as at Monte Alban or in the Isthmian script. Another word sign of wide distribution and iconic origin was the sign for "king." The sign is probably derived from a highly conventionalized illustration of a flower headband (Fields 1991). Some of the early word signs may even have been borrowed from late Olmec icons, such as the signs for "cloud" and "hill" (see cat. 85). These logographic signs usually appear in clusters and sequences, which seem to indicate a syntactic order reflecting spoken syntax. Where these sign clusters show up together with iconography, they are usually set apart and placed in cartouches or some otherwise clearly defined text areas. This suggests that Preclassic artists already were aware of the difference between the two representational codes—that of art and that of writing.

Hieroglyphic writing at the coastal sites of El Baúl, Takalik Abaj, Chalchuapa, and others did not progress very much beyond this stage of development. Only in a few later texts, such as on Stela 5 from Takalik Abaj dating to AD 126, signs for pronouns or grammatical suffixes can be identified. Otherwise, most of the texts from the highlands and the coast consisted of clusters of word signs arranged in a sequence that probably corresponded to spoken syntax, where the trained reader provided the lacking grammatical information. Around AD 200 the coastal piedmont writing tradition disappeared. The most plausible reason for this disruption is a major social and political transformation that must have occurred in this region in connection with the migration of speakers of K'ichean languages.

The Development of Syllabic Signs

The vast majority of early texts in the lowlands are found on portable objects, especially on greenstone and jadeite celts. There are also a few stone inscriptions on stelae, but they seem to be confined to names (and perhaps titles) of the individuals displayed (fig. 2). In contrast, many portable objects carry texts only and show that by that stage writing had become independent of art (see cat. 87). Images were not needed anymore to complement the written text, or to make a message less ambiguous. Stephen Houston has observed that some of the early lowland texts on portable objects are replete with head glyphs, which may stand for the names

Figure 2
Drawing of Stela from the Bajo de la Juventud, near Uaxactun

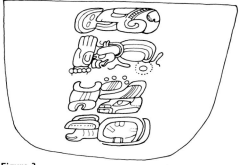

Figure 3
Drawing of Plaque with Maya Hieroglyphic Text (cat. 86), back

of supernaturals, perhaps the names of patron deities of places or the individuals who owned these texts (Houston 2000, 145–47) (fig. 3, cat. 86). Such lists could also consist of sequences of day names from the 260-day calendar, as on a Late Preclassic tripod vase from Mundo Perdido in Tikal (see cat. 95). Unfortunately, we do not know enough about the function of some of these objects in Preclassic ritual and whether they were used in divination or in order to be cached or displayed in sacred spaces.

Except for lists of supernaturals, most of the texts were self-referential, focusing on the dedication and presentation of the objects that carried the inscriptions (Mora Marín 1997, 2001). The fact that many texts stood alone without accompanying images may have led to a greater emphasis on syntactical relations in order to reduce ambiguity and strengthen the clarity of texts. We suspect that this situation and the need to express the relationship between possessed object and its possessor has led to the development of signs that were able to convey grammatical morphemes. The earliest ergative (possessive) pronouns are found on portable objects, such as jade celts, pectorals, and ceremonial axes (see cats. 86, 91–94). The need to write ergative pronouns probably also provided the incentive for the development of the first purely phonetic signs, which had no logographic value. This was particularly necessary when the word for the object that was possessed began with a vowel (Grube 1990a; Grube and Martin 2001, 37–41). In those contexts, the scribes had to represent the pronoun *y*-, which, as an isolated semivowel not only was difficult to pronounce, but which Maya scribes conceptually seem to have understood as a syntactical unit that was inseparably attached to the word for the object. The word for "darkness" was *ak'ab'*, and the phrase "her/his darkness" would have been *y-ak'ab'*. Apparently Maya scribes never made the step to write single sounds, as in an alphabetic system. Nonetheless, they invented syllabic signs consisting of a consonant and vowel that would allow them to write the prevocalic ergative pronouns. In the case of the word for "darkness," a Maya scribe would use the sign for the syllable *ya* in front of the word sign for "night," *ak'ab'*, where the vowel of the prefixed syllable matches the vowel of the possessed word (see cat. 90:C6). The vowel of the sign had to correspond to the initial vowel of the following word, thus the first syllabic signs we encounter in the Maya script are those for the syllables *ya, ye, yi, yo*, and *yu*. The expression "her necklace" was written *yu-ja* and analyzed as the possessive pronoun *y*- and the noun *u'j* (necklace) (in Maya writing, the last vowel in a syllabic spelling usually was not pronounced). The spelling of the prevocalic ergative pronouns seems to have motivated the development of further syllabic signs because once the initial syllable of a word was written with phonetic signs, the first step toward phonetic spellings was made and further consonant-vowel signs were added to complete the spellings. Approximately by the end of the third century AD, consonant-vowel (CV) syllables other than the *yV* syllables, which were needed to write the pronouns, came into existence, and by the beginning of the Early Classic period we find the first fully phonetic spellings, which do not incorporate any logographic signs. Examples for such spellings are *yu-ne* for *y-unen* (child of) from Copan Stela 63, *u-ka-ya-wa-ka* for *u kaywak* (his/her jade celt), and *tz'a-pa-ja* for *tz'a[h]p-aj* (it was erected). Houston suggests that the invention of a syllabary most likely was the work of a single individual or a small script community (2000, 146–47). Once syllabic signs were conceived as an option, they logically expanded to record all of their CV possibilities, leaving no possible combination empty.

The Language of the Earliest Texts

One of the paramount questions in the study of any ancient writing system is the linguistic identity of the people who invented it. The great majority, if not all syllabic signs in Maya hieroglyphic writing, are explicable in Cholan and Greater Tzeltalan words. Most syllabic signs are derived from logographic signs of the type CVC that had lost their final consonant. This was possible because the consonants in final position were weak. The sign for the syllable *ka*, for example, is based on the image of a fish fin. The word for "fish" in all Mayan languages is *kay*, where the final *-y* was considered weak. The syllabic sign for *cho* was derived from the image of a mandible, pronounced *choh*, and the syllable *hu* was based on the image of an iguana, *huj*. There is no evidence for a foreign origin of syllabic signs, although it is possible that the general idea of signs that had only a phonetic value was inspired by similar trends in other contemporary writing systems, such as the Isthmian script.

With the development of syllabic signs came the first fully spelled verbs. In earlier texts it is impossible to identify verbs due to the absence not only of pronouns but also of grammatical suffixes. However, the existence first of *yV* signs, and later of a whole CV syllabary, allowed the scribes to add all grammatical information and thus to represent the language of the aristocracy with considerable attention to detail.

An interesting feature of Late Preclassic and Early Classic Maya writing is the near absence of phonetic complements (Grube 1990a). Phonetic complements are syllabic signs attached to a logographic sign that provide pronunciation aids by highlighting initial or final sounds of the word. The few examples for phonetic complements in these early texts are *-na* suffixes under the logographic signs for "sky" (*chan*) and "cave" (*ch'e'n*). This suggests that for some reason the pronunciation of these signs may have been ambiguous. A possible explanation may be that the final consonant had undergone a sound shift. Proto-Mayan had an **ng* where the languages of the western branch of Mayan languages (among them the languages of the hieroglyphs) developed an *n* and the languages of the eastern branch have *j*. Perhaps the sound shift had not yet come to completion when the logographic signs for "sky" and "cave" were invented. There are occasional *-ji* suffixes under the sign for "sun" (see cat. 92:A7), which in the Classic period was pronounced *k'in*; they point to the relevance of the sound shift as the underlying motivation for the development of the first phonetic complements.

The use of ergative pronouns to express possession is a clear sign that the most ancient texts were written in a Mayan language. The Cholan or Greater Tzeltalan origins of syllabic signs suggest that the earliest script community in the lowlands was based on a very specific linguistic group. Recent research concerning the script traditions of the central highlands and the Pacific piedmont of Guatemala, especially at Takalik Abaj, Miraflores-Kaminaljuyu, the Salamá Valley, and sites at the Pacific Coast, not only points to a similarity of the signs and formats of the writing system to those of the lowland Maya area but also suggests that the scribes of these texts shared a Mayan language, probably even the same Cholan language of the lowland inscriptions (Fahsen 2001a). One of the most important centers of writing in the Late Preclassic central highlands was the important city of Kaminaljuyu. Numerous inscriptions have been found as the result of various archaeological excavations. Unfortunately, with the exception of Stela 10, most of the inscriptions are badly weathered and can no longer be deciphered. Stela 10 carries a long, incised hieroglyphic text that contains many signs known from lowland Maya inscriptions (fig. 1). Some of the logographic signs seem to be combined with syllabic signs, which could be phonetic complements, such as the syllable *na*, which is attached to the logographic sign for *hu'un* (paper, book). These complements point to Cholan, or at least a western Mayan language, as the language used by the scribes of Kaminaljuyu. At the same time, the inscription of Stela 10 also contains various signs, which do not occur in other Maya texts, and it remains to be proven whether the highly sophisticated writing system of Kaminaljuyu was a close relative of lowland Maya writing or whether it represents an independent development sharing only common roots with the lowland Maya system.

Writing as an Instrument of Dynastic Legitimation

The available data suggest that writing in the Maya region began as a highly localized phenomenon, probably with various small and isolated script communities. These different traditions may not yet have shared a standard repertoire of signs, nor did their writing systems share the same structures. Therefore it is possible that highly advanced systems (such as in Kaminaljuyu) existed side by side with less complex systems, such as those encountered on some Late Preclassic lowland script documents. In all cases, however, the first steps toward writing took place under similar social conditions. Writing did not develop parallel with the institution of kingship. There is a growing body of sculptural images of lords from both the lowlands and the central highlands, which clearly predates the first written messages (fig. 4). The discovery of Late Preclassic, or even Middle Preclassic stelae, with the images of kings at sites such as Nakbe, Cival, Actuncan, and Cahal Pech leaves little doubt that complex societies and divine kingship flourished centuries before writing in the Maya lowlands, and writing does not seem to have been an indispensable resource for early kingship (Hansen 2001; Awe and Grube 2001; Estrada-Belli et al. 2003). However, it is during the enormous transformations of Maya society during the end of the Late Preclassic period that the political influence of the dynasties grew, the institution of kingship expanded, and competition between dynasties increased. As soon as writing was discovered as a powerful means of communication, it became a tool for the legitimation of power. This is the reason why some of the earliest texts focus on kingship and accession: the El Portón stela, which describes a "seating in office"; the Dumbarton Oaks pectoral (cat. 90), with a text about the accession into kingship; and also the newly discovered San Bartolo murals. By the beginning of the Early Classic, writing had become associated with the institution of divine kingship. Writing was so firmly connected to the world of the royal court that the collapse of this institution in the ninth century reduced the use of the hieroglyphic system once again to a few isolated communities of scribes.

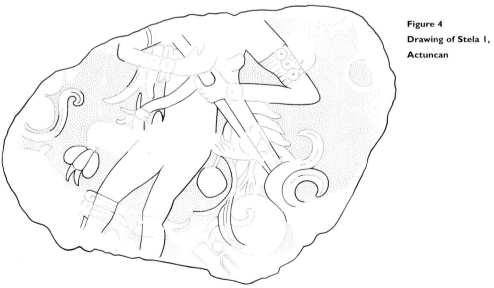

Figure 4
Drawing of Stela 1, Actuncan

Notes

1. For the recent debate regarding the decipherment of the Isthmian script, see Kaufman and Justeson (2001); Houston and Coe (2003). On Zapotec, see Urcid (2001).

2. On the Hauberg Stela, see Schele (1985); reevaluation of the date by Lacadena (1995); on early lowland writing in archaeological contexts, see also Reese-Taylor and Walker (2002).

3. For the development of hieroglyphic signs from iconography, see Justeson (1986); Justeson and Mathews (1991).

Figure 1

Street of the Dead, view from the Pyramid of the Moon, Teotihuacan

Strangers in the Maya Area:
Early Classic Interaction with Teotihuacan

Robert J. Sharer, University of Pennsylvania Museum, and
Simon Martin, University of Pennsylvania Museum

Interaction between the Maya and the great city of Teotihuacan (fig. 1) in Central Mexico is a defining characteristic of the Early Classic period, but its study has been plagued by outmoded views that distort our understanding. It is often assumed that Teotihuacan dominated relationships with the Maya, who are usually seen as passive recipients. According to materialist theory, Classic Maya polities were "secondary states" created by contact with Teotihuacan (Price 1978). Yet archaeological evidence is often ignored in these assessments, allowing theory to overwhelm data (Cowgill 2003). A balanced approach that incorporates archaeological and epigraphic data yields a more nuanced view of the complex and variable Teotihuacan-Maya relationship (Braswell 2003a; Martin 2001).

Evidence for Interaction

The evidence for Maya-Teotihuacan interaction comes mostly from obsidian, ceramics (see, for example, cats. 117, 119, 120), iconography, and architecture, along with at least one critical event suggested by epigraphy. The presence in the Maya area of green obsidian from the Pachuca source near Teotihuacan is a marker of trade with Central Mexico. Relevant ceramic ties include pottery manufactured in Central Mexico, most notably Thin Orange wares (produced in Puebla rather than Teotihuacan) (see cats. 123, 124), and distinctive Central Mexican forms along with elaborate modeled and mold-made effigy incensarios. These ceramic types and forms have been recovered in the Maya area as imports from Central Mexico and as locally produced emulations (Ball 1983). Iconographic ties are reflected in painted scenes on pottery, mirror backs, murals, incensarios, and as carved motifs on monuments and architectural elements. Distinctive talud-tablero-style building facades are a prominent architectural connection with Central Mexico, although the development of this style preceded its use at Teotihuacan (Gendrop 1984).

While most assessments of Teotihuacan connections are based on these criteria found in the Maya area, far fewer studies consider Maya obsidian, ceramics, iconography, and architecture found at Teotihuacan. Given the already noted Teotihuacan bias in such studies, it is hardly surprising that the Maya contributions to the Teotihuacan relationship have received far less attention, although several studies have begun to address this imbalance (Fialko 1988; Laporte 2003; Taube 2003a). Taube (2003a), for example, has examined Teotihuacan murals to show that elites adopted and manipulated Maya symbols, consistently connected with prestigious and valuable materials from this region. In addition, the appearance of Maya glyphs in some murals indicates that Maya people, or people literate in the Maya writing system, resided at Teotihuacan.

Motives and Meaning of Interaction

The postulated motivations for interaction have also focused heavily on Teotihuacan. While ideology likely played a role in Teotihuacan's entry into the Maya area, perhaps to proselytize its religion and cosmology (Coggins 1979), economic gain is usually cited as the major incentive

(Braswell 2003b). Contact with the Maya highlands provided Teotihuacan with access to mineral resources such as jade and obsidian (Brown 1977; Cheek 1977), while the Pacific plain supplied agricultural products such as cacao and rubber (Bove and Medrano Busto 2003; Parsons 1967–69). More direct economic and political control has also been proposed by the establishment of Teotihuacan colonies and enclaves within the Maya area—as at the highland capital of Kaminaljuyu—based primarily on the presence of *talud-tablero* architecture (Kidder et al. 1946; Ohi 1994; Sanders and Michels 1977). Explicitly or implicitly, such proposals suggest the existence of a Teotihuacan "empire" with strategically placed enclaves established to control resource extraction and administer subject Maya populations.

Tikal, a dominant Early Classic polity in the Maya lowlands, has been viewed as a Teotihuacan base for such economic and political control. But the archaeological, bioanthropological, and epigraphic evidence suggests alternative interpretations. Certainly the motives for Teotihuacan-Maya interaction were complex and variable, but proposals for Teotihuacan-managed political control from colonial enclaves at Kaminaljuyu, Tikal, and elsewhere find little support today (but see Bove and Medrano Busto 2003; Cowgill 2003).

We must also consider similar motives from the Maya perspective, since interregional interaction involves reciprocal relationships. As in earlier times of "Olmec influence," the Early Classic Maya were not passive recipients of "Teotihuacan influence." Rather, connections seen from architecture, artifacts, and iconography were products of two-way exchanges in which both partners in the relationship actively manipulated foreign goods and symbols for their own purposes. Thus, Maya rulers likely used exotic goods and symbols from Teotihuacan to reinforce their prestige and power in various ways across time and space (Schele and Freidel 1990). For example, very early in the span of contacts with Central Mexico, a single cache of Teotihuacan-style vessels and Pachuca obsidian was dedicated by a ruler of Altun Ha (in present-day Belize); but this connection was not exploited further (Pendergast 2003). *Talud-tablero* facades were apparently used to give certain Maya buildings explicit symbolic links with distant Central Mexico and its powerful capital (fig. 2). But this foreign architectural style took on distinct and localized variations throughout the Maya area, as has been documented at Kaminaljuyu (Cheek 1977), Copan (Sharer 2003a), Tikal (Laporte 2003), and Oxkintok (Varela Torrecilla and Braswell 2003). Furthermore, Maya elites manipulated not only Teotihuacan goods and symbols but also those from a range of external contacts and relationships with cities throughout Mesoamerica (Demarest and Foias 1993; Sharer 2003a, b).

The Preclassic Origins of Maya States

Contrary to theories proposing a Teotihuacan-inspired origin for Maya states, archaeological evidence supports an indigenous genesis for state-level polities in the Maya area well before the onset of interaction with Teotihuacan. Major diagnostics of divinely sanctioned rulership were present in the Maya area by the Late Preclassic period. Late Preclassic stelae in the highlands and on the Pacific plain featured the accomplishments of rulers in carved portraits, hieroglyphic writing, and Long Count dates. By the Late Preclassic, Kaminaljuyu possessed many characteristics of a state-level polity that evidently dominated the Maya highlands. Similar polity capitals were established on the Pacific coastal plain. Some of these same features were present in the Maya lowlands during the Late and Terminal Preclassic. The vast site of El Mirador is the key to understanding the emergence of state-level polities in the Maya lowlands (Hansen 2001). Its enormous size alone suggests that El Mirador was the most powerful Late Preclassic lowland capital. Carved lowland stelae with inscriptions appear in the Terminal Preclassic, with examples at El Mirador and several smaller sites. The Late Preclassic murals at the smaller site of San

Figure 2
East Plaza Shrine, Tikal

Bartolo include the portrait of a newly installed ruler, accompanied by a text with an *ajaw* (lord or ruler) glyph (Saturno 2002). Historical texts suggest the long-enduring Tikal dynasty was founded by AD 100 (Martin and Grube 2000).

The Emergence of Early Classic Maya States

Archaeology indicates that many Maya capitals declined or were completely abandoned at the end of the Preclassic period. The reasons for this collapse remain obscure, but the changes paved the way for the rise of new polities in the Early Classic period and the expansion of states throughout the Maya lowlands. These Early Classic lowland polities comprised a system of independent states, ruled by *k'uhul ajawo'ob* (holy lords), an institution derived from Late Preclassic predecessors. Since state organizations emerged during the Late Preclassic, the origin of these new Early Classic polities was not due to Teotihuacan intervention (Freidel 1979; Hansen 1990, 2001; Sharer 1992).

As in other preindustrial states, Early Classic Maya polities were headed by kings, royal families, and courts that formed a centralized, hierarchical government within each kingdom, while commoners (primarily farmers and part-time and full-time occupational specialists) made up the bulk of the population. Many socioeconomic and political distinctions are visible in housing, artifacts, and burials. But the most dramatic contrasts are in the exalted status of elites reflected in evidence for wealth, privilege, and supernatural connections. Classic period texts indicate that Maya rulers claimed a divine right to rule, similar to the supernatural identity enjoyed by kings in many early states of the Old World. Unlike ancient Egypt and China, however, the Classic Maya were never unified under a single king or emperor. At any given time there were numerous Maya kings, each ruling an ostensibly independent polity. Yet, at the same time, most polities were enmeshed in complex hierarchical relationships headed by a few especially dominant kingdoms, most notably Calakmul and Tikal (Martin and Grube 2000).

Teotihuacan Contacts with the Pacific Coast and Highlands

The evidence for Early Classic contacts between the Maya and Teotihuacan varies from region to region and changed through time. Some of the earliest contacts with Teotihuacan come from Guatemala's Pacific coastal plain and are demonstrated in pottery, elaborate effigy *incensarios*, and other artifacts derived from Central Mexico (Parsons 1967–69; Shook 1965) (fig. 3). Excavations at two of the largest sites on the Pacific plain, Balberta and Montana, provide a firm archaeological context for understanding Teotihuacan interaction in this region.

Research reveals Balberta reached its apex at the beginning of the Early Classic era (around AD 200–400), when it was apparently the capital of a large polity that interacted reciprocally with Teotihuacan and other areas of Mesoamerica (Bove et al. 1993). This interaction was economic, centered on the export of cacao. Artifacts recovered from the site include pottery decorated with cacao bean effigies, imported vessels from Central Mexico and the Gulf Coast, and obsidian from both Pachuca and Zaragoza in Puebla. These trade relationships contributed to Balberta's prosperity and boosted the prestige of its rulers. But there is no evidence that interaction with Teotihuacan was responsible for the development of a state system at Balberta.

After some two centuries of prosperity, Balberta rapidly declined; by AD 400 it was replaced by a new capital, Montana (Bove and Medrano Busto 2003). The monumental scale of Montana's Early Classic architecture is unrivaled on the Guatemalan Pacific Coast. Local versions of Teotihuacan pottery, effigy censers, and other items could suggest that colonists from Central Mexico resided in Montana and commissioned artisans to produce everyday and ceremonial artifacts modeled after prototypes from their homeland. Montana is seen as a Teotihuacan-controlled trading center to secure coastal products such as cacao, cotton, and rubber. Montana's location also suggests it was a staging area for trade with other Maya polities, including Kaminaljuyu, and sites in the Maya lowlands beyond.

In the highlands, between AD 200 and 400, a combination of factors led to a decline in prosperity and population at Kaminaljuyu (Valdés and Wright 2004). Trade was curtailed by a general decline throughout much of the region, and the source of its irrigation system dried up, severely reducing agricultural production. Even though commercial contacts with Teotihuacan date to this era at Balberta, it appears that Kaminaljuyu did not establish ties with Central Mexico until after AD 400, when it experienced a major revival, including elite trade with the Maya lowlands and the Caribbean, Pacific, and Gulf coasts. Teotihuacan was also among these new exchange partners, probably mediated by Montana, providing Kaminaljuyu's ruling elite with green obsidian, stuccoed pottery, and other prestige goods from Central Mexico. Kaminaljuyu's expanded power and prosperity was reflected in the rebuilding of its civic and ceremonial core in the *talud-tablero* style of Central Mexico. Excavation has revealed that some of these structures covered elaborate royal tombs and probably served as funerary shrines for Kaminaljuyu's rulers (Kidder et al. 1946).

Figure 3
Upper part of an *incensario*, **from El Manantial,**
Escuintla

These architectural changes and the appearance of Teotihuacan artifacts have been seen as evidence of a Teotihuacan takeover of Kaminaljuyu (Kidder et al. 1946; Sanders and Michels 1977). However, while Central Mexican *talud-tablero* facades appear on Kaminaljuyu's buildings, they were adapted to local materials and construction methods to produce a distinctive variant of this foreign style (Cheek 1977). Kaminaljuyu's Early Classic royal tombs contained the skeletons of elite individuals originally assumed to be foreign rulers from Teotihuacan, installed at Kaminaljuyu to control the lucrative trade in obsidian and other highland resources. But isotopic analyses reveal these buried elites were born and raised in the Maya highlands, and the bones of accompanying sacrificed retainers were from Maya lowland regions—probably war captives (Valdés and Wright 2004). Interestingly, the analyses of the bones of one presumed Kaminaljuyu ruler indicate he was locally born and raised but probably spent his adolescent years in Central Mexico, likely reflecting elite interaction based on reciprocal trade and residency. In fact, the presence at Teotihuacan of Maya artifacts, ceramics, images, and architecture (Fialko 1988) indicates widespread commercial contacts between Central Mexico and Maya polities in both the highlands and lowlands. Economic connections are probably not the only reasons for these contacts; doubtless the rulers of both Kaminaljuyu and Teotihuacan also reinforced their authority by adapting symbols associated with their distant and powerful foreign partners.

Teotihuacan Contacts with the Maya Lowlands

There is considerable evidence of outside contacts in the Maya lowlands during the Early Classic period. Pottery and other artifacts point to trade connections with the southern Maya area and more distant lands, including Teotihuacan. At the large and politically powerful Early Classic capital of Tikal, the most obvious foreign connection was with Central Mexico and Teotihuacan. Excavations in Tikal's Mundo Perdido Group documented a sequence of architecture inspired by the Central Mexican *talud-tablero* style that began by around AD 300 (Laporte 2003). In her study of Tikal's royal tombs, Coggins (1975) pointed to Burial 10 as exhibiting a pattern of offerings that was closely connected to the Early Classic tombs of Kaminaljuyu and Central Mexico, including several pottery vessels with stucco-painted decoration executed in Central Mexican style (see cat. 127). Burial 10 has been identified as the tomb of Tikal's fifteenth ruler, Yax Nuun Ayiin I, whose reign (AD 379–411) came in the midst of the period of *talud-tablero* architecture at Tikal—a connection that could reflect links to either Kaminaljuyu or Teotihuacan. But with more historical evidence provided by deciphered texts, the events surrounding Tikal's foreign contacts during this period are beginning to be better understood.

Based on records such as Tikal Stela 31, Proskouriakoff (1993) suggested that the demise of Tikal's fourteenth ruler, now identified as Chak Tok Ich'aak (r. AD 360–78), came at the hands of foreign conquerors armed with *atlatls* (spear-throwers) and other military paraphernalia from Central Mexico. Newly deciphered texts name the leader of this incursion as one Siyaj K'ak' and describe his "arrival" in AD 378 but do not record his origins. This event was followed in 379 with the installation of a new king, Yax Nuun Ayiin, by the new masters of Tikal. The foreign takeover scenario is strengthened by the name of Yax Nuun Ayiin's father, "Spear-Thrower Owl"—which has overt connections to the military symbolism of Central Mexico (fig. 4). Although Spear-Thrower Owl's kingdom remains unknown, Stuart (2000) makes a case for identifying it with Teotihuacan. The implication of these interpretations posit Tikal's political and economic destiny transformed by a foreign takeover in AD 378, either directly sponsored by Teotihuacan or indirectly mediated through Kaminaljuyu.

Yet the evidence for a Teotihuacan presence behind these events remains circumstantial, and alternative scenarios remain viable, including Coggins's (1975) original suggestion that the

Figure 4
Marcador of Tikal, back. See
also Valdés, this volume, fig. 4

new Tikal king came from Kaminaljuyu. It is also important to note that even if Siyaj K'ak' was foreign to Tikal, his Mayan name could suggest he was of Maya birth. Recent isotopic analyses of the bones from Burial 10, thought to be those of Yax Nuun Ayiin, indicate that he was of local (Tikal) origin (Valdés and Wright 2004). These lines of evidence suggest that, rather than being a foreign takeover, the political transition from Chak Tok Ich'aak to Yax Nuun Ayiin may represent the triumph and return to power of an exiled Tikal royal faction, as has been proposed by several scholars (Borowicz 2003; Braswell 2003b; Culbert 2004; Laporte 2003; Laporte and Fialko 1990).

Teotihuacan's role in these events remains obscure. Yet there is general agreement that Tikal and other Maya polities adopted Teotihuacan war symbolism to reinforce their own prestige and associate themselves with the military power of this great city and its war deities (Schele and Freidel 1990; Stone 1989; Martin 2001). It also seems clear that this Teotihuacan connection was especially successful for Tikal. After AD 378 the new rulers of Tikal embarked on a course of expansion that would see their kingdom become a dominant power in the central lowlands, seemingly bolstered by their association or alliance with Teotihuacan (Schele and Freidel 1990).

The evidence suggests that Tikal even extended its reach into the southeastern borderlands of the Maya area by establishing a new polity capital at Copan and a secondary center at Quirigua (in present-day Guatemala). Both archaeological and historical evidence suggests that in AD 426, Tikal orchestrated the takeover of Copan and the establishment of an intermediate center at Quirigua as Copan's subsidiary to control the Motagua Valley trade route. But while retrospective records of Copan's dynastic founding include hints of a Teotihuacan connection, the archaeological evidence recovered from the founding-era buildings and tombs of Copan's newly established royal center exhibit connections to an array of powerful Early Classic capitals. These include not only Teotihuacan, but also Tikal and Kaminaljuyu and the subsidiary center of Quirigua (Sharer 2003a, 2003b).

While the archaeological, bioanthropological, and epigraphic evidence offer examples of Teotihuacan-Maya interaction during the Early Classic period, their interpretation often remains equivocal. Overall, this evidence demonstrates widespread and varied interaction with Central Mexico over a span of some four hundred years. The most consistent theme suggested by the archaeological data is reciprocal interaction, including exchanges of goods and ideas that were used and manipulated by the elite rulers of both Teotihuacan and Maya states to reinforce and consolidate their power. Evidence for more direct contact, such as the establishment of colonies and military enclaves is sparse—although perhaps present in the case of Montana on the Pacific Coast. Recent evidence, however, casts doubt on Teotihuacan takeovers once proposed at the major Maya capitals of Kaminaljuyu and Tikal. The archaeological data from each site seem more consistent with long-term economically motivated relationships with local adoptions of Teotihuacan goods and symbols to reinforce established Maya dynasties. In the case of Tikal, the historical texts record a dynastic shift during the period from AD 378 to 379, but the motivation and authority that directed this change remain unidentified. Thus, a case can be made for either a foreign-inspired takeover, presumably directed by Teotihuacan, or a local dynastic dispute that saw a formerly exiled faction returned to power.

Regardless of these historical details, in a broader perspective it is clear that interaction between Teotihuacan and the Maya provided economic and political benefits to both parties in the relationship. In the Maya area and in Central Mexico, new products were introduced or made more widely available to many people by enhanced access to distant resources. At the same time, the greatest benefactors from this increased economic prosperity were the ruling elites who controlled most, if not all, of the long-distance trade between Central Mexico and the Maya area. These economic rewards were further magnified by the political benefits enjoyed by both Maya kings and the rulers of Teotihuacan that derived from this interaction.

In this way interaction with Teotihuacan increased the power enjoyed by Maya kings. New sources of wealth were tapped and new symbols of military and supernatural power were introduced and used by Maya rulers to reinforce their authority. But Maya kings, and the state organizations they headed, did not come from Teotihuacan. The archaeological evidence documents the origins of Maya states in the Late Preclassic period, well before indications of Teotihuacan interaction appear in the archaeological record. Thus, it is fair to conclude that Maya states were indigenous developments and were not derived from Central Mexico.

Dancing in the Footsteps of the Ancestors

Allen J. Christenson, Brigham Young University

According to the *Popol Vuh*, one of the most important Maya texts to have survived the Spanish Conquest, the ancient gods created the founding ancestors of the various royal families in the Maya highlands with extraordinary vision, whereby they could see all things:

> Perfect was their sight, and perfect was their knowledge of everything beneath the sky. If they gazed about them, turning their faces around, they beheld that which was in the sky and that which was upon the earth. Instantly, they were able to behold everything. . . . Thus their knowledge became full. Their vision passed beyond the trees and rocks, beyond the lakes and the seas, beyond the mountains and the valleys. (Christenson 2003, 197–98)

Although the creator gods eventually clouded this vision so that men could see only those things that were "nearby" (Christenson 2003, 201), the royal progenitors and their descendents who ruled after them nevertheless believed that they bore within their blood the potential for divine sight, enabling them to carry out sacred rituals as their ancestors had once done. Thus, Ruth Bunzel quoted a highland Maya priest from Chichicastenango: "And now this rite and custom belongs to the first people, our mothers and fathers. . . . This belongs to them; we are the embodiment of their rites and ceremonies" (Bunzel 1952, 232, 238).

In 2001, while conducting ethnographic research in Santiago Atitlán, Guatemala, I spoke with the son of a local traditionalist priest regarding his ancestors who had founded certain ritual prayers and practices performed during Day of the Dead observances in the community. During our discussion, I showed him a photograph of the principal elders of the town taken by Alfred P. Maudslay in the nineteenth century (fig. 1). He told me that these men were well known to him, although they had died long ago: "We all know them. They still visit us in dreams and in person. We know their faces, they are still very powerful—the soul of our town. These people live because I live, I carry their blood. I remember. They are not forgotten." In highland Maya languages, the word *na'* (to remember) also means "to feel," or "to touch." To remember someone who has died is to make them tangible and present to those who carry their blood.

In ancient Mesoamerica, political leaders based much of their legitimacy on their ability to manipulate the supernatural world through ritual activity. Rulers acted as intercessors between humans and gods as a primary focus of their divine kingship (Fields 1989, 9). Among the ancient Maya of the lowlands, kings donned the guise of the Maize God and performed a sacred dance replicating the creation of the world (fig. 2). These rulers did not consider their actions to be mere playacting; they were taking part in a genuine renewal of the cosmos by a deity acting through human mediation (Houston and Stuart 1996, 299–301). By reenacting the stages of divine creation through ritual established by ancestral precedent, kings could act as partners with deities in recharging the cosmos.

The kings of the highland Maya also conducted such dances prior to the Spanish Conquest as tokens of their authority. The *Título de Pedro Velasco*, a fragmentary early colonial K'iche' Maya manuscript bearing the date 1592, records that "each of the lineages had a house to hear the

Figure 1

Elders on the steps of the *cabildo*, Santiago Atitlán, 1881

Figure 2
**Vase of the Dancing Lords,
AD 750–800**

word and to carry out judgments. There the lords danced" (Carmack and Mondloch 1989, 161, 178). Following the conquest, authorities attempted to suppress such native dances, although in many areas local leaders continued to perform them in private houses (Gage 1958, 244–47; Chinchilla Aguilar 1963; Mace 1970; Estrada Monroy 1979, 57–59; Mendieta 1993, 140). Francisco Ximénez, the Dominican priest who discovered the original manuscript of the *Popol Vuh* in his parish at Chichicastenango at the beginning of the eighteenth century, wrote that the Maya preferred their own ancient dances to those composed for them by the early Catholic missionaries, and they continued to perform them in secret: "The ancient Fathers gave them certain histories of the Saints in their language, which they may sing to the accompaniment of the drum in place of those they sang in the days of their heathenism. Nevertheless, I understand that they sing these only in public, where their priest may hear them; yet in secret they carry out very lovely memories of their heathenism" (Ximénez 1967, 8; translation by author).

At the time of the Spanish Conquest, three major royal lineages ruled the Guatemalan highlands. The descendents of one of these ruling lineages, the Tz'utujil, continue to live on their ancestral lands along the southern and western shores of Lake Atitlán. The principal community of the Tz'utujils is Santiago Atitlán, founded in 1547 by the surviving residents of the ancient royal capital city whose ruins today lie across a small bay from the modern city. Despite centuries of social and political pressure to abandon core elements of their theology, a significant number of traditionalists maintain what they can of the ritual cycles once observed by their ancestors. When asked about the origins of certain traditional rituals, Tz'utujils frequently reply that they are as old as the world, far older than the coming of the Spaniards. They were first performed by their ancestors who had divine power (Christenson 2001, 22–23, 68; Mendelson 1965, 91).

At Santiago Atitlán, the most highly revered and powerful individual within the traditional Maya religious structure is a priest, called the *nab'eysil*, who is responsible for performing an annual ritual dance that "rebirths" the world. This dance is performed in honor of a deity called Martín, the principal patron of maize, rain, and life itself. The *nab'eysil* believes that ancestral personages who set the pattern for contemporary rituals continue to operate through him as a conduit at appropriate times and under appropriate circumstances. It is their sacred ancestral vision that allows him to "see" beyond the limits of time and distance as the ancient founders once did. The precise relationship between Martín and the *nab'eysil* is not clear, although the latter appears to be a corporeal manifestation of divine power (Mendelson 1958a, 124; 1958b, 6; 1965, 91). Once touched by this divinity through ritual, the *nab'eysil* never loses its presence, even in death. Living Tz'utujil-Maya priests often invoke a long list of dead *nab'eysils*, adding the name of Martín to each.

The deity invoked as Martín is represented by a large cloth bundle wrapped in green velvet called the *ruk'ux way, ruk'ux ya'* (heart of maize food, heart of water) (fig. 3). It contains a number of very old garments said to be the "skin" or clothing of Martín. Sacred bundles of the type worshiped in Santiago Atitlán were also used by ancient Maya kings to bear the tokens of their power and right to rule. The principal royal symbol of power among the ancient highland Maya was a bundle called the Pisom Q'aq'al (Bundled Fire/Glory). The *Título de Totonicapán*, an important K'iche' Maya document composed in 1554, asserts that the Pisom Q'aq'al was given to the royal progenitors of the highland Maya by Nacxit, the king of the legendary city of Tulan in the east. It was there that the progenitors received the power that gave them authority to rule (Carmack and Mondloch 1983, 175, 181–82).

Other sacred bundles contained similar objects of power, including the "skins" of their gods. Thus, the principal sign of Tohil, the patron deity of the K'iche' Maya, was the bloody skin

Figure 3
Martín bundle on the altar of Confraternity San Juan

Figure 4
Deer and jaguar dancers kneeling to the cardinal directions, Confraternity San Juan

of a deer slain in his name: "Set the skins of the deer aside and watch over them. . . . These will surely be our substitutes before the faces of the nations. When you are asked, 'Where is Tohil?' It will be this deerskin bundle that you shall show them" (Christenson 2003, 234–35).

Like the bundles of the ancient Maya, the Martín bundle is kept in a carved wooden chest so that it is seldom seen. The chest bears the image of a massive ear of maize with multiple split cobs. Tz'utujils often bring seed maize to the confraternity house to be blessed in front of the chest containing the Martín bundle to ensure an abundant harvest. Rows of split-cob maize ears adorn the rafters of the confraternity house, symbolizing the presence of Martín as Lord of Maize (see cat. 1). The bundle represents the tangible expression of Martín and his power to create and sustain life, much as the Maize God of the ancient Maya acted as the principal creator deity.

In preparation for the Dance of Martín, performed annually at midnight on 10 November, the *nab'eysil* priest removes the Martín bundle from its chest and lays it on a long wooden, benchlike altar, where other elders cense it with copal smoke, spray it with cologne (the preferred brand these days is Brut for Men), and sprinkle it with flower petals.

A Deer Dance is then performed by two young men wearing deer pelts with the head and antlers still attached (fig. 4). These pelts are manifestations of Martín. One of the elders told me that the deer pelts were the "skins and bones" of Martín and that those who wear them take on his power when they dance. Two other dancers wear nearly hairless animal pelts, which they associate with jaguars. These skins are normally kept on a table at the southern end of the confraternity house. The first jaguar impersonator carries a small stuffed squirrel called the *ral b'alam* (child of jaguar), which he uses to claw at the back of the principal deer dancer. The dancers consider the squirrel to be a small jaguar that hunts and kills the deer dancer. The dancers once used a stuffed mountain cat, an example of which also lies on the deerskin table, but these are hard to find now, and the head of the confraternity doesn't wish to have the old one damaged by overuse. Prior to the dance, the *nab'eysil* priest had blessed the deerskins used in the dance, addressing them as "King Martín, Lord of the Three Levels, Lord of Rain, Lord of Maize, and Lord of All the Mountains."

At the beginning of the Deer Dance, all four participants kneel in a line, the first deer at the head, facing the doorway to the east. To the beat of a split-log drum, the dancers call upon the power of that direction to aid them in their performance, naming a long list of deities, saints, mountains, and other geographic features located in the east. These are invited to be present and guide them in their steps. They also raise their heads to call on "Heart of the Sky" and kiss the ground while praying to "Heart of the Earth." The procedure is then repeated while

Figure 5
Nab'eysil in the garments of Martín

Figure 6
Nab'eysil receiving petitioners following the Dance of Martín

facing each of the other cardinal directions. Having invoked the power of the four directions, the performers then dance rapidly around the confraternity house, hopping from foot to foot and periodically whirling in place as they mark a generally clockwise course. As they dance, the jaguars make loud whistling sounds while roughly pawing at the backs of the deer with the little stuffed squirrel. The deer in turn cry out and try to escape from them.

The "death" of the deer occurs at about midnight, the hour when the Maya believe the power of the underworld is at its greatest. At this point, the dancers return their costumes to the table where they are normally kept, and the *nab'eysil* begins his portion of the ritual. First, all the doors and windows of the confraternity house are closed and bolted shut. Participants suggest that they cannot open the Martín bundle until they close the doors and windows, otherwise its power would rush out and destroy the world in a great windstorm (Mendelson 1965, 57). Having secured the room, the *nab'eysil* then opens the Martín bundle and removes one of several very old beige-colored garments. The top garment has a painted pattern resembling tufts of hair. The *nab'eysil* likened this design to the deer pelts used in the Deer Dance, but much older and more powerful. It is likely therefore that the *nab'eysil*'s dance represents a sacrificial act in which he replicates the actions of Martín in order to recharge the world with life-giving power.

Dressed in the garment of Martín, the *nab'eysil* priest kneels to each of the four directions in the same order and fashion as the deer and jaguar dancers. While kneeling, the *nab'eysil* invokes the power of Martín with a long series of titles, including Lord of Rain, Lord of Maize, Lord of the Sun, Lord of Clouds, Heart of the Earth, Heart of the Sky, Heart of the Mountains, and Heart of the Plains. The *nab'eysil* then dances several times around the confraternity house in the same clockwise course followed in the Deer Dance (fig. 5). While dancing, the *nab'eysil* holds his arms away from his body while taking short, purposeful steps from side to side, knees bent and head tilted toward the direction of movement. These steps are accompanied by a split-log drum played by the *xo'*, the wife of the head of the confraternity, although the *nab'eysil* doesn't follow the cadence of the drumbeats, which is very rapid. One of the purposes of the dance is to bring the first rains, and the thick cloud of incense within the room is symbolic of a rain cloud. As the *nab'eysil* dances, he seems to disappear periodically and then reappear from the darkness and smoke as if moving through clouds.

Having made several circuits around the interior of the confraternity house, the *nab'eysil* moves to the center and stands before a large table with his arms outstretched and his head bowed. Everyone in the room is then invited to approach the *nab'eysil* one at a time (fig. 6). Holding candles representing the renewal of light, each person kisses the Martín garment two or three times about the navel area. One confraternity member commented to me that the *nab'eysil* had been killed like Jesus Christ and that is why he holds his arms in the form of a cross. Yet Christ is also conflated with Martín as a maize deity. During a performance of the Martín Dance in 1952, the first jaguar dancer declared that "Jesus Christ and Mary are intertwined with King Martín, the Sacred World, the sky, the earth, and the sons of God" (Mendelson 1957, 215). This is consistent with a comment by a participant in the ritual who suggested to me that the pose of the *nab'eysil* doesn't represent a cross, but a maize plant as it grows out of the earth (Christenson 2001, 164–66). The position of the *nab'eysil*'s outstretched arms is also common in ancient Maya depictions of the Maize God as he emerges out of the underworld at the time of first creation, numerous examples of which may be found on painted ceramic vessels as well as carved stone monuments dating back many centuries prior to the Spanish Conquest (Quenon and Le Fort 1997, 893–95) (fig. 7).

Following a performance of the Martín Dance in 1997, the *nab'eysil* asked me if I had "seen the ancient *nuwals* [revered ancestors, including pre-Columbian Tz'utujil kings] giving birth to the world." He explained that "when I dance, I feel nothing but the great weight of Martín's garment. Only a *nab'eysil* can bear this weight. For others it would kill them. I don't see the people around me because I am filled with the power of Martín and the ancestors, and I dance in their world." For the *nab'eysil*, the dance is not a symbol of creation but a means of returning to the dawn of time itself in order to repeat the actions of deified ancestors and gods. As a result, and because he had danced in the garments of Martín, he declared that "everything is new again." This is akin to the actions of the ancestral kings among the highland Maya who once danced in the guise of deities at certain ritually appropriate times of the year in order to regenerate the world and endow it with life-sustaining power.

Figure 7
Drawing showing the rebirth of the Maize God with arms outstretched. Detail of carved panel, Lower Temple of the Jaguars, Chichen Itza

Catalogue

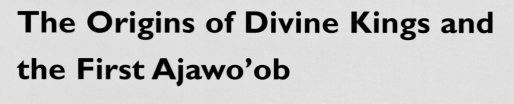

The Origins of Divine Kings and the First Ajawo'ob

Divinely sanctioned authority in Mesoamerica derived from the intimate relationship between maize agriculture and the propitiatory rituals performed by religious specialists to ensure its abundance. The success of maize agriculture by the Middle Formative period enabled the Olmec to develop an extensive trade network (Fields 1989, 7), circulating an innovative agricultural ideology in which precious objects of jadeite and shell symbolized the wealth of the maize surplus (Taube 1996). The earliest kings were portrayed wearing the regalia of the Maize God, embodying the sacred power that guaranteed abundant crops. The primary ritual action of kingship was to establish the quadripartite cosmos, symbolizing the *milpa*, or maize field, with the king in the guise of the maize deity as the central axis of the universe.

The royal crown of the first Maya kings, the headband marked with a trefoil in its center, also originated among the Gulf Coast Olmec during the Middle Formative period. The trefoil emblem signified the maize plant, originally found marking the forehead of the Olmec maize deity and later becoming the precious jewel, or *sak hu'unal*, that continued to identify Maya kings for more than one thousand years.

The title of *ajaw* (lord) is the other primary signifier of the earliest Maya kings. Initially found in a variety of iconographic and epigraphic contexts, one form of the title may represent the Maya version of a widespread Mesoamerican tradition of recognizing the king as "speaker," whose voice reflected not only his earthly authority but also his ability to communicate with supernaturals and ancestors (Fields 1989; Houston and Stuart 2001). Alternatively, the *ajaw* title may derive from an ancient root word for planting seeds, implying the preeminence of the role of "sower" (Mathews and Justeson 1984) and reaffirming that the power of the king derived from an agricultural source.

I

Nicolás Chávez Sojuel, born 1950s
Guatemala, Santiago Atitlán

Carved Wall Relief
1997
Wood
35¼ x 21 x 3½ in. (89.5 x 53.2 x 9 cm)
Courtesy of Allen J. Christenson

Symbolic elements of reenacting the creation of the cosmos are shown in this panel, carved by a traditionalist Maya artist, who presents the struggle between the life and death aspects of nature as played out in the worship of Martín and Maximon, two major deities of the town of Santiago Atitlán. The panel's central building has the typical thatched roof and stone walls of a traditional *cofradía* (religious brotherhood devoted to the veneration of a specific saint) house. The supporting poles, carved in a serpent pattern, represent the snakes that guard the entrance to Paq'alib'al, the local sacred cave, where the saints and

deities live and where rain clouds are born. The inverted vessel on the roof, a traditional feature of local homes and *cofradías*, signifies the earth; the building's interior is conceived as a sacred cave, equivalent to the earth's womb. Maize, cacao, fruits, and flowers hang from rafters, indicating that this is a place of abundance, where the life-giving powers of the earth are regenerated. The crosses atop each of the flanking structures conflate the Christian cross with the world tree that anchors the center of creation, identifying the structures themselves as center places.

Maximon dominates the central section, overseeing the symbolic sacrifice of dancers dressed as deer by another dancer dressed as a jaguar. Sacrifice is essential to maintain the equilibrium of the world, as expressed in this ritual dance. The man on the right plays a split-log drum to set the tempo of the dances, and the man on the left holds a noisemaker to announce the presence of the god. This scene occurs during Holy Week

(Easter), when Maximon's effigy is hung among tree branches placed in a Colonial-era chapel. Here he presides over the death of Christ and receives offerings. During the five-day period preceding Easter, traditionalists believe that Maximon holds all political and spiritual authority in the community while the "life deities" pass through the underworld of the dead.

The section on the right shows the resurrection of Martín, the patron deity of maize, mountains, and life itself. The *nab'eysil* (a Maya priest), dressed in the garments of Martín, performs a dance that conceptually gives birth to the world, signifying the ongoing centrality of the acts of creation in modern Maya life.

(Based on Allen J. Christenson's research in Santiago Atitlán, Guatemala; see also Christenson 2001 and his essay in this volume. The artist and his brother, Diego Chávez Petzey, were commissioned to carve replacement panels, such as this one, for the sixteenth-century altarpiece in Santiago Atitlán's church, which had suffered earthquake damage.)

2

Altar Cloth

Guatemala, Alta Verapaz, Coban, ca. 1950
Rayon, cotton, and synthetic fiber
80 x 14¼ in. (203.2 x 36.2 cm)
Los Angeles County Museum of Art, Costume and
Textiles Special Purpose Fund (M.2004.221)

3

Tzute

Guatemala, Huehuetenango, Colotenango, ca. 1950
Rayon, cotton, and synthetic fiber
28 x 38 in. (71.1 x 96.5 cm)
Promised gift to the Los Angeles County Museum of Art

The weaving of textiles in highland
Guatemala constitutes an enduring link
between ancient and modern Maya societies.
The process of weaving is symbolically tied
to the birth of children (Prechtel and Carlsen
1988) and to the creation of the world and
its cycles of time and regeneration (Schele
1997). The colors, designs, and forms of
clothing identify an individual's ethnicity and
social affiliations in Chiapas, Mexico, and
southern Guatemala. In *cofradías*, an image of
the patron saint, often dressed in clothing
typical of the community, is placed upon an
altar for veneration. The humans, deer, horses,
and plants on this richly woven altar cloth
represent the abundance of creation.

The *tzute* is a multipurpose cloth that may
be woven in a wide range of forms and sizes,
depending on the community (Asturias de
Barrios 1997). *Tzutes* can be slung over the
shoulder and used to carry objects, but this
tzute was worn as a headcloth by one of the
highest authorities within a *cofradía*. Women
also wear head coverings, and both are woven
on back strap looms. The beautifully brocaded
abstract chevron, zigzag, and diamond designs
may symbolize lightning and thunder (Altman
and West 1992, 97).

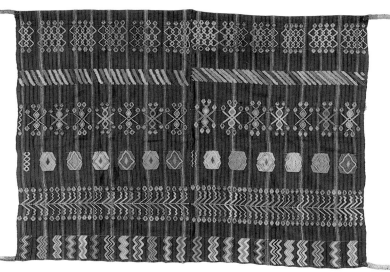

3

4

Seated Lord with Maize God Headdress (Monument 77)

Mexico, La Venta, north of Great Pyramid, 900–400 BC
Basalt
35⅞ × 28¼ × 30⁵⁄₁₆ in. (91 × 73 × 77 cm)
Instituto de Cultura de Tabasco, Dirección de
Patrimonio Cultural, Parque Museo de La Venta,
Villahermosa, Mexico

This seated figure portrays a human ruler in the guise of the Olmec Maize God, one of the earliest such portrayals. The cleft-headed mask of the Olmec Maize God may once have adorned the front of his headdress, such as that seen on San Martín Pajapan Monument 1 (see introduction, fig. 4). The back curving cleft cranium denotes young, growing maize (Taube 1996, 47–48), and the cleft pattern at the back of the headdress symbolizes the quadripartite shape of the cosmos. Creased paper bands, another characteristic of the Olmec Maize God, flank the ruler's face. He wears the crossed-bands pectoral and belt ornament that typically mark celestial phenomena. The cross-legged position established the format for later Maya kings, as seen on Late Classic period painted ceramics.

Other references:
Diehl 1990, 54–56; González-Lauck 1996, 172–73

4

5

Young Lord (catalogue only)

El Salvador/Guatemala, Pacific Coast, 900–400 BC
Serpentine with traces of cinnabar
25¹³⁄₁₆ × 4⁵⁄₁₆ × 2⅛ in. (65.5 × 11 × 5.4 cm)

The imagery incised on this figure reveals the
antiquity of combining cosmological and
political symbols as a unified expression of
royal power. The young lord poses as the
world tree at the center of the cosmos (see
Joralemon 1996b, 212–15; *Olmec World* 1995,
278–83). He holds two scepters in a manner
that presages the so-called crab-claw position
of Early Classic Maya kings (see cat. 66). The
scepters signify both vegetation, especially
maize, and the rituals practiced to ensure its
abundance.

5

6

Stela 11

Guatemala, Kaminaljuyu, 200–50 BC
Granite
78 × 26¾ × 7⅛ in. (198.1 × 67.9 × 18.1 cm)
Museo Nacional de Arqueología y Etnología, Guatemala
City (MNAE 3093)

Stela 11 portrays one of the earliest Maya
rulers dressed as a divine being. Similarities
to Izapan-style monuments can be seen in
features such as the basal panel and spiked
incense burners flanking the king (Norman
1976, 289–90; Parsons 1986, 65–66). A profu-
sion of bird and tree imagery surrounds the
figure. The Principal Bird Deity looks down
upon the figure, who also wears a bird mask,
above which is a creature whose forehead
sprouts the trefoil maize plant. The king
grasps the lightning axe of Chaak—illustrat-
ing his role as the divine being who breaks
open the earth for the resurrection of the
Maize God—and a curved scepter.

The branches of the king's headdress
express his personification as the world tree.
The ruler portrays himself as the pillar of
the cosmos and the bridge between the
underworld, symbolized by the gaping maw
of the earth creature below his feet, and the
heavens, implied by the bird at the top of the
monument. The composition first appeared
in the cave painting at Oxtotitlan, Guerrero,
where an Olmec ruler wearing a bird costume sits upon a zoomorphic throne (introduction, fig. 2).

The lobed and sprouting form on the
king's hipcloth resembles the early version of
the *ajaw* title (see cats. 22–26).

Other reference:
Clancy 1985, 108

7

Seated Female Figure with Mirror Ornament

Mexico, La Venta, Mound A-2, Columnar Tomb,
700–500 BC
Jade and hematite
3⅛ in. (8 cm)
CNCA-INAH, Museo Nacional de Antropología,
Mexico City (13-417)

8

Carved Mirror Ornament

Mexico, Southern Veracruz, AD 200–500
Slate, hematite, shell, and iron oxide pigment
7⁹⁄₁₆ in. (19.2 cm)
Los Angeles County Museum of Art, Gift of the Art
Museum Council (AC1998.89.1)

9 (catalogue only)

Kneeling Figure

Reportedly from the Tabasco-El Peten area of Mexico
or Guatemala, AD 500–600
Wood and hematite
14¾ in. (38 cm)
The Metropolitan Museum of Art, The Michael C.
Rockefeller Memorial Collection, Bequest of Nelson A.
Rockefeller, 1979 (1979.206.1063)

A rare depiction of a female in Olmec art,
the seated figure is also unusual for her
hematite mirror ornament. Her seated pose
and mirror, an emblem of political and
religious authority, convey her elite status.
Mirrors functioned as divination tools, providing symbolic access to other realms.

The front of the carved mirror is also
made of faceted pieces of hematite; a cave
saurian is depicted on the back, enveloped
in cloud scrolls and water vapor. The mirror
was once worn as a pendant, indicated by
the hole in the rim.

The extremely rare wooden figure may
once have held a square mirror, and the figure's pose suggests a trance state associated
with divination. His features and costume are
neither entirely Maya nor Olmec but rather
combine aspects of the two styles (Ekholm
1964).

Other references:
7: Diehl 1990, 59; Castro-Leal 1996, 216
9: Easby and Scott 1970, no. 182; Coggins 1998, 258–59

7

Front

Back

8

10
Transformation Figure

Mexico, Gulf Coast, Tabasco, 1000–600 BC
Serpentine with traces of cinnabar
4¼ x 3⅛ in. (10.8 x 7.9 cm)
Los Angeles County Museum of Art, Gift of Constance
McCormick Fearing (M.86.311.6)

11
Figure Holding Jaguar Cub

Guatemala, Alta Verapaz, Tamahú, 400–200 BC
Fuchsite
7¾ in. (20 cm)
Museo Nacional de Arqueología y Etnología (Dieseldorff
Collection), Guatemala City (MNAE 5095)

The figure with both human and jaguar features represents a religious specialist or divine
ruler who is transforming into his animal
companion spirit. The Mesoamerican spiritual
belief in these beings (referred to as *naguales*
or *wayob*) forms an enduring aspect of religion, and this figure attests to the antiquity
of this belief. *Naguales* assumed a variety of
animal and composite forms, although rulers
are most likely to be associated with jaguars.

Beneath his human form, the figure is a
jaguar: the skin and hair on his head have
been removed to expose his feline aspects.
The figure's otherworldly qualities were originally enhanced by glowing eyes of pyrite.

The features of the figure protectively
holding a jaguar cub in his right arm imply
a post-Olmec sculptural tradition (Easby and
Scott 1970, cat. 68). The figure was once
worn as a pendant.

Other references:
10: Reilly 1989; Benson 1996, 228–30; *Olmec World*
1995, 174
11: Coggins 1985, 105

10

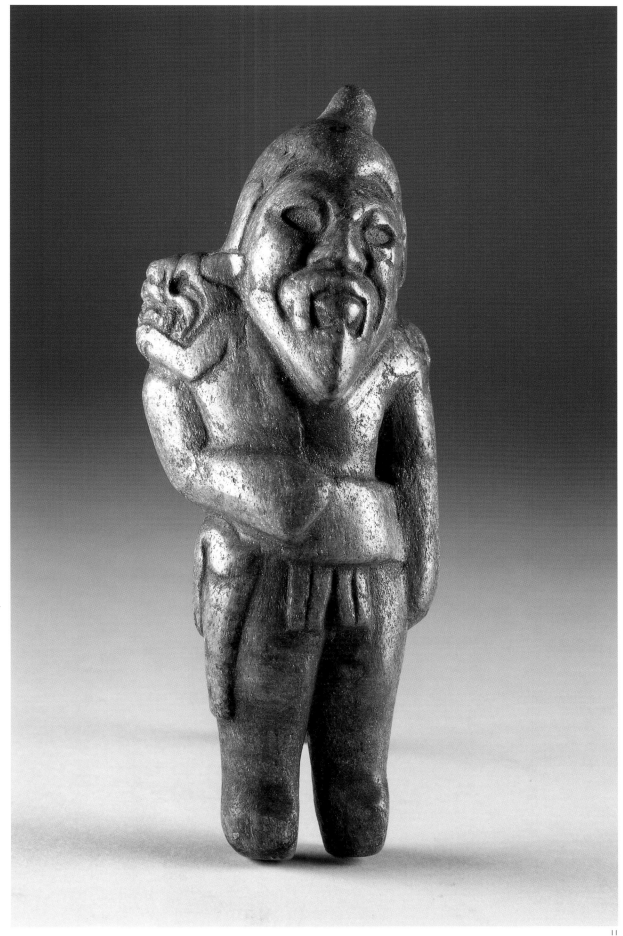

12

Carved Altar

Guatemala, Pacific Coast, 600–300 BC
Stone
Diam.: 31 ½ in. (80 cm)
Museo de Arte Precolombino y Vidrio Moderno,
Antigua, Guatemala (1.2.75.23)

This altar, reportedly found near San Antonio Suchitepéquez, features one of the most complex scenes of the well-known Mesoamerican acrobat figure. Here, a simply dressed man forms the circular border by grasping his ankles. The same man is also shown frontally,

his feet arched over his head, dressed as the Olmec Maize God (Taube 1996, 50). He wears the trefoil emblem atop his head, the personified Jester God headband, a tasseled ear of corn, and quetzal plumes. On his chest is a so-called spoon, which he possibly used to ingest hallucinogens that allowed him to enter into a trance state and manifest as the Maize God.

The crested raptor head hanging from the frontal figure's waist acts as the point of articulation between the two representations.

Other references:
Shook and Heizer 1976; Tate 1995, 62–63

13

Celt with Incised Profile

Mexico, Olmec, 900–600 BC
Jadeite
14⅜ x 3⅛ x ¾ in. (36.5 x 7.9 x 1.9 cm)
The Metropolitan Museum of Art, The Michael C.
Rockefeller Memorial Collection, Gift of Nelson A.
Rockefeller, 1963 (1978.412.5)

14

Headdress Ornament

Mexico, Guerrero, 900–600 BC
Jadeite
1¼ x ¾ x ⅜ in. (3.1 x 2 x 1 cm)
Promised gift to the Princeton University Art Museum
(L.1994.59.2)

15

Incised Maskette

Mexico, possibly Veracruz, 600–400 BC
Greenstone
7⅞ x 5⅛ in. (20 x 13 cm)
Peabody Museum of Archaeology and Ethnology,
Harvard University (22-23-20/C9596)

16

Seated Lord Wearing Headdress and Cape

Mexico, Veracruz, Arroyo Pesquero, 900–600 BC
Diopside
6⁷⁄₁₆ x 3¾ in. (16.3 x 9.3 cm)
Dumbarton Oaks Research Library and Collections,
Washington, D.C. (PC.B. 592)

17

Pendant

Guatemala, Peten, Tikal, Structure 5D-Sub-1-1st, Burial
85, 50 BC–AD 50
Fuchsite and shell
5 in. (12.3 cm)
Museo Sylvanus G. Morley, Tikal, Guatemala
(12p-98/78)

The potency of maize as a symbol of wealth is apparent by the Middle Formative period, when greenstone celts, symbolizing maize plants, were adorned with trefoil emblems emerging from the cleft heads of supernatural beings (Fields 1982; 1991). The trefoil defines the figure on this celt (far right) as the Olmec Maize God (Taube 1996). On a royal headband, the central maize icon would have been

flanked by a pair of jewels, such as the ornament seen below (cat. 14).

When rulers wear the trefoil crown, they signal their power to ensure agricultural fertility. In the Olmec heartland, such royal portraits are found on both monumental and portable sculptures. The incised maskette reveals an Olmec-style face covered with scrolled patterns on the cheek and a maize icon in the center of the forehead. The richly dressed figure of the Olmec lord resembles Monument 77 (cat. 4) with its similar headdress, belt, and cape. Above his headband he wears the cleft mask of the Olmec Maize God, above which sprouts the trefoil vegetation motif.

One of the earliest representations of a Maya king wearing the trefoil crown is the pendant from Tikal Burial 85, which was placed on the axis of the North Acropolis, the sacred mountain where many ancestral tombs are located.

Other references:
14: Joralemon 1996b, 267–68
15: *Olmec World* 1995, 251; Pohorilenko 1996, 250
16: Benson 1971
17: Coggins 1985, 105

14

13

15

16

17

18

Incised Mask

Mexico, Olmec, 900–400 BC; reused by the Maya,
AD 100–900
Serpentinite
5 × 4⅜ in. (12.5 × 11.2 cm)
Courtesy of the Trustees of The British Museum
(AM1938, 1021.14)

19

Headband Jewels

Belize, Cerros, Structure 6B, 400 BC–AD 250
Jadeite
Between 1⅝ and 2¼ in. each (4.1 and 5.7 cm)
Institute of Archaeology, Belmopan, Belize (35/203-
1:54, 55, 56, 52)

20

Cache Vessel Containing Jade and Shell Objects

Honduras, Copan, Conjunto 10J-45, Pozo Central Patio,
AD 500–600
Stone, jadeite, and shell
Vessel: 8 × 14 in. (20.3 × 35.6 cm); central figure:
5 in. (12.7 cm)
IHAH, Centro Regional de Investigaciones
Arqueológicas, Copan, Honduras

The five-part pattern known as a quincunx
appears in Olmec and Maya art and archaeology as a layered symbol of both the *milpa*
(maize field) and the cosmos: both are four-
sided and are defined by the central axis,
either the great world tree/maize plant or
the king in that guise. The incised mask is
Olmec in style but was found in the Maya
lowlands, undoubtedly a royal heirloom.
Here, the ruler's face appears at the center
of a quadripartite composition.

Quincunx-patterned dedicatory caches
composed of greenstone celts appear at a
number of Middle and Late Preclassic sites
(see Bauer, this volume), while at Cerros and
Copan, these offerings consist of royal jewels.
At Cerros, the cache containing the headband
jewels was found at the structure's summit
within a vessel layered with spondylus shells
and mosaic mirrors above the quincunx-
patterned carved jades (Freidel and Suhler
1995, 138).

The essence of the pattern and its corresponding symbolism is found in the cache
vessel discovered in the center of the plaza
of an outlying residential complex at Copan
(Nakamura 2004). The lidded stone container
held a quincunx-patterned offering of spondylus shells and carved jades oriented to the
cardinal directions. The centerpiece is a
jadeite figure of an Early Classic king wearing
a maize plant on his royal headband, signifying his role in centering the cosmos.

Other references:
18: McEwan 1994, 23
20: Schmidt 1998, 560

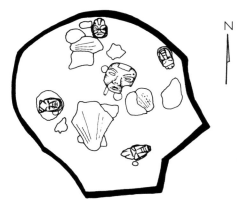

Cache recovered from Structure 6B, Cerros

19

Central figure of cat. 20

21

Plate Portraying Enthroned King

Maya Area, AD 200–400
Ceramic with pigment
Diam.: approx. 11 in. (28 cm)
The Art Institution, New York (1990.0264)

The king portrayed on this plate is dressed as the Maize God, denoted by the maize cob in his headdress, the trefoil leaves, and the maize silk hair. He is seated cross-legged, as are earlier rulers, and the foliated sign around his mouth may designate him as *ajaw* (lord, or ruler) (see also cat. 26). He holds an open bundle in his hands with an object that is also found among the symbols in the border encircling the king, which may represent the sacred paraphernalia of office. Similar icons are painted on the walls of Burial 48 at Tikal, which contained the remains of the Early Classic king Siyaj Chan K'awiil.

22
Maya-Style Belt Plaque Fragment

Discovered in Costa Rica, AD 200–350
Jadeite
5⅜ x 1³⁄₁₆ in. (13.7 x 3 cm)
Peabody Museum of Archaeology and Ethnology,
Harvard University (977-4-20/25516)

23
Earflare Inlay

Guatemala, Peten, Holmul, Group II, Structure B,
Room 2, AD 300–400
Shell with red pigment and traces of resin
1⅞ in. (4.7 cm)
Peabody Museum of Archaeology and Ethnology,
Harvard University (11-6-20/C5620)

22

24
Ceramic Fragment with Royal Title

Guatemala, El Mirador, 300–250 BC
Ceramic with slip
3½ x 2¾ in. (9 x 7 cm)
Museo Nacional de Arqueología y Etnología, Guatemala
City (MNAE 12,016)

25
Seated Figure of Lord

Maya Area, Central Lowlands, AD 250–450
Jadeite
7½ x 4½ in. (19 x 11.3 cm)
Promised gift to the Musées Royaux d'Art et d'Histoire,
Brussels

26
Stela 3

Guatemala, Takalik Abaj, 200 BC–100 AD
Stone
51¹⁄₁₆ x 27½ in. (130 x 70 cm)
Museo Nacional de Arqueología y Etnología,
Guatemala City

Ajaw (lord) or *k'uhul ajaw* (holy lord) were
among the highest titles carried by Maya
rulers. The title took a number of hieroglyphic forms during the Late Classic period
as both a prefix and fully rendered sign (see
Lounsbury 1973; Mathews and Justeson 1984).
Dated contexts for the earliest forms of the
ajaw title are rare; however, the brief texts at
San Bartolo, which conclude with the title and

23

are associated with accession scenes, date to
around 100 BC (Saturno and Urquizú 2004).

Ajaw also names the last day in the Maya
twenty-day cycle, and its appearance in calendrical contexts during the Early Classic reveals
that a common form at that time is indented
or lobed. A corresponding lobed form occurs
on royal paraphernalia as a title, often adorned
with the trefoil vegetal motif suggesting its
semantic equivalence with the Jester God
(Schele and Miller 1983, 37; Reents-Budet
and Fields 1987, 18). The belt plaque fragment (cat. 22), for example, depicts a
zoomorph wearing the foliated and lobed
ajaw as a title, possibly naming an early Tikal
ruler (Wanyerka 2001, 24). On the earflare
inlay (cat. 23), a profile face is shown wearing a beaded helmet with a zoomorphic form
of the Jester God at the front of the helmet;
the foliated and lobed form of *ajaw* adorns the
top (see also Florescano, this volume, fig. 1).

The ceramic fragment (cat. 24) depicts a
lobed *ajaw*, which can be dated to a clearly
Late Preclassic context (Matheny 1986, 338),
and whose characteristics suggest a possible
iconographic origin of the form. An oval
cartouche with a squared U-motif appears
within the lobed form, which is flanked by
leaflike scrolls. The cartouche has two squares
on its rim; a similar cartouche was painted
on the lower east mask facade of Cerros
Structure 5C-2nd, perhaps indicating a ruler's
name. A similar cartouche is found in the text
on the Izapan figure, although its meaning
in this context is uncertain (cat. 89:A2).

Detail of mask, lower east facade, Structure 5C-2nd, Cerros

The form of the *ajaw* on the ceramic fragment mirrors that of the cave mouth depicted in Chalcatzingo Monument 1 (Reilly, this volume, fig. 1). Although Chalcatzingo is located in eastern Morelos, many Middle Formative period monuments are framed by open-mouth shapes (Carrasco Vargas, this volume, figs. 3, 4). A corollary can be seen in the fragmentary Stela 3 (cat. 26), where a person stands on a basal panel, associated with the open mouth of an earth creature (see cat. 6). Here, the central element is the early form of *ajaw*, which also occurs hieroglyphically in the texts on cats. 89:B4 and 92:A6.

The heartland Olmec spoke a Mixe-Zoquean language, the source of many loan words describing significant aspects of Meso-american culture (Campbell and Kaufman 1976). In Popoluca de Sayula, a Veracruz-area Mixe language, the word for mouth is *ajw*, although *ajaw* may also derive from the early Common Mayan form *aj-a:w (he who shouts) (Houston and Stuart 2001, 59). The cave mouth/lobed form may have provided an early version for the Mesoamerican metaphor of ruler as "speaker" (Fields 1989, 75). The importance of orality in relation to the ruler continues through the Postclassic period, where a primary royal title was *tlatoani* (one who speaks, or great lord) (Fields 1989, 75; Houston and Stuart 2001, 51).

The identification of the oval cartouche with knobs and flanking leaves as a version of the *ajaw* title may be confirmed by the figure of the seated lord (cat. 25), who wears the lobed and foliated *ajaw* as Jester God. The figure's mouth is framed by the early *ajaw* title, designating his royal role as speaker.

27

Seated Figure of Lord

Guatemala, Peten, Uaxactun, Structure A-XVIII,
Cache A31, 200 BC–AD 100
Fuchsite with pigment
10 x 5 in. (25.5 x 12.5 cm)
Museo Nacional de Arqueología y Etnología, Guatemala
City (MNAE 924)

This figure was part of an offering that
included an array of stone "eccentrics,"
stone objects chipped in an unusual and non-
functional way, and fragments of obsidian.
The figure, seated in the cross-legged pose
of royal authority, is simply adorned with
Olmec-style cleft motifs incised on the sides
of his head, which may refer to corn tassels
(Taube 1996). A large k'in (sun) glyph adorns
each cheek, an early use of this identification
with solar phenomena by a Maya lord.

Other references:
Coggins 1985, 106; Fahsen 2001b, 364

28
Bar Pendant Depicting Lord

Belize, Nohmul, AD 250–450
Jadeite
5½ x 1 in. (14 x 2.5 cm)
Courtesy of the Trustees of The British Museum
(AM1938, 0708.1)

The depiction of the Pax God on this pendant closely resembles that on the pendant from Copan (cat. 80). The faces on both pendants have the square eyes of K'inich Ajaw, the Sun God, and both wear the headband with the lobed and foliated *ajaw* of the Jester God. The crossed bands in the mouth, however, are a primary characteristic of the Pax God. Read phonetically, *pax* is *te'* (tree), reinforcing the concept of the wearer of this pendant as the world tree.

Reference:
Schele and Miller 1986, 81, pl. 20

28

The Cosmos and the King

Maya kings reigned over a cosmological domain comprising three vertical levels: the celestial upper world, associated with supernatural beings and ancestors; the earthly middle world, the place of human existence; and the watery underworld, which could be entered through caves or still bodies of water. Linking the levels of the cosmos was a great world tree, commonly represented by the ceiba but sometimes by a maize plant. The horizontal earthly plain, surrounded by a primordial ocean, was four-sided in form and oriented to the cardinal directions with the central axis mundi defining a fifth cardinal direction. Mesoamerican societies shared similar concepts of the physical structure of the universe, first conceived by the Olmec and elaborated by the Maya and other, later civilizations. The tri-level cosmogram was the conceptual stage on which divine kings played a seminal role, reenacting sacred events to ensure the continuity of the universe.

Maya rulers commemorated their ritual actions through art and monumental architecture. Kings utilized architecture to replicate the topography of the universe; that is, a pyramid was recognized as a sacred mountain (*witz*), while flanking plazas were perceived as symbolic bodies of water (*naab'*). On a smaller scale, Maya kings employed objects as symbols of the physical world and divine universe, conveying cosmic principles through a rich iconographic repertoire.

29

Crocodile

Guatemala, Pacific Coast, 900–400 BC
Greenstone and shell
6 x 6⅜ x 19 in. (15 x 16 x 48 cm)
Museo de Arte Precolombino y Vidrio Moderno,
Antigua, Guatemala (1.2.75.339)

The crocodile represented the surface of the earth floating in the primordial sea. This figure has the spiny back and crested brow that characterize the Mesoamerican caiman, and the shell disks on its sides also denote its connection to water. Human beings occasionally wear the crested brow and pelt of the caiman, as demonstrated by the Atlihuayan figure (at right), an Early Formative portrayal of a man in a trance state.

30

Carved Bowl

Mexico, Las Bocas, 1200–900 BC
Ceramic with traces of red pigment
4 x 9⅛ in. (10.2 x 23.2 cm)
Los Angeles County Museum of Art, Gift of Camilla
Chandler Frost (M.2002.13)

The creature known as the Olmec Dragon may take the form of a celestial being, as the deeply carved image on this bowl illustrates. While not from the Olmec heartland, the bowl carries distinctive motifs of the Olmec art style.

The defining features of the celestial dragon—the crossed bands and the upturned paw-wing—are conveyed in the characteristic *pars pro toto* manner of Olmec-style art (see Reilly, this volume, fig. 3). To both the Olmec and Maya, these bands symbolized the sacred location of the center of the sky, a reference to the crossing point of the ecliptic and the Milky Way, a region over which this supernatural being presided.

30

31

Carved Blackware Vessel with Lid and Water Lily–Shaped Handle

Maya Area, Central Lowlands, AD 250–450
Ceramic
11 x 12½ in. (28 x 31.8 cm)
Denver Art Museum Collection, purchased in honor of
Jan and Frederick R. Mayer with funds from 2001
Collector's Choice (DAM 1998.35a, b)

32

Lidded Vessel with Crested Water Bird

Reported to have been found in Tabasco, Mexico,
AD 350–450
Ceramic with slip
9⅜ x 10¹⁵⁄₁₆ in. (24 x 27.5 cm)
The Brooklyn Museum (64.217a, b)

33

Quadrupod Vessel with Peccary Feet and Lid with Cormorant and Fish Handle

Guatemala, AD 250–400
Ceramic with slip
10¾ x 10¾ in. (27.3 x 27.3 cm)
Yale University Art Gallery, Gift of Peggy and Richard
Danziger, L.L.B. 1963 (2001.82.1a, b)

Water lilies, associated with still water, symbolize agricultural fertility due to their presence in canals that sustain raised fields. On the lid of this vessel (cat. 31), stylized fish and birds invoke the watery context of the underworld, as do the scrolls on the vessel's body. The features of the unusual crested water bird (cat. 32) imply an otherworldly being, because its beak has a rounded knob marked by a quatrefoil, an ancient emblem that often designates portals to the supernatural realm.

Elegant long-necked cormorants raising fish from the surface of the water are a common theme on Early Classic vessels. Here, the vessel (cat. 33) rests on four naturalistic peccary heads, another aspect of such tetrapods (see cat. 138). Peccaries are associated with the pillars supporting the four directions of the cosmos (Schele and Miller 1986, 280) or with the constellation Gemini (Freidel et al. 1993, 82).

Other references:
32: Easby 1966, 104; Coggins 1985, 112

31

32

33

34

Lidded Turtle Shell Vessel

Maya Area, Central Lowlands, AD 350–450
Ceramic
8½ x 16 in. (21.6 x 40.6 cm)
Promised gift to the Fine Arts Museums of San Francisco
(L03.59)

Turtles play a significant role in the mythology of creation and the resurrection of the Maize God. The body of the turtle corresponds to the surface of the earth from which the Maize God is reborn (Freidel et al. 1993, fig. 2:4). A human head emerges from either side of the vessel's lid, one wearing a helmet associated with the quetzal (k'uk') and the other wearing a helmet associated with the macaw (mo'). The composition may refer to the personified location Mo' Witz (Macaw Mountain), found on ceramics from Río Azul and in hieroglyphic texts at Copan and Tres Islas.

Other reference:
Miller and Martin 2004, 87

34

35

Cache Urn

Guatemala, AD 250–450
Ceramic
18¹¹⁄₁₆ in. (47.5 cm)
Fundación Televisa A.C., Mexico City (R21 P.J. 180)

36

Cache Urn

Guatemala, AD 250–450
Ceramic
19¼ in. (49 cm)
Fundación Televisa A.C., Mexico City (R21 P.J. 181)

These lidded vessels were placed as caches during building-dedication rituals, and their iconography resembles the architectural facades of the Late Preclassic and Early Classic periods (Coggins 1985, 126–27). One vessel (cat. 35) portrays a deity from the Palenque triad designated as GI, whose characteristic features include a central shark's tooth and fish fins. A mythological bird rests on the deity's head; above the bird is the icon known as the quadripartite badge (Robertson 1974), an offering bowl containing precious objects.

The other vessel portrays an unknown deity whose mouth is covered by a woven mat from which hangs a trident motif. Freidel et al. (1993, 420) suggest that the deity may be a version of Chaak, the Maya god of rain, whereas Taube (2003a, 297–98) associates the knot-over-mouth motif with representations of dead persons and underworld gods (see below).

**Cache Vessel Depicting Supernatural Beings,
AD 250–450**

35, 36

37

Bone Handle

Maya Area, Central Lowlands, AD 100–350
Human bone
5⅛ x 1¼ in. (13 x 3.2 cm)
American Museum of Natural History (30.3/2504)

38

Bar Pendant Depicting Lord

Belize, Altun Ha, Tomb B-4/6, AD 584
Jadeite
8 x 2⅝ x ¾ in. (20.2 x 6.7 x 1.9 cm)
Institute of Archaeology, Belmopan, Belize, courtesy of
the Royal Ontario Museum, Toronto (RP 256/3)

These objects reveal the manner in which
kings were aligned with supernatural locations. In the elaborately rendered image on
the bone handle, a stepped pyramid marked
with a k'an cross may signify the Mountain of
Sustenance. The handle may have held a sacrificial implement that a ruler utilized to attain
a trance state.

The pendant depicts a king seated upon
the personified cleft-headed mountain with
the Sun God emerging from the cleft. A cacao
tree, symbol of abundance and wealth, climbs
up behind the seated king, and an ancestral
figure floats above him, providing supernatural sanction for his royal position. The text
on the reverse marks a war event in AD 569
and the king's accession to office in AD 584.
The pendant formed part of a lavish late-
seventh-century burial of a young lord.

References:
37: Schele and Miller 1986, 285
38: Mathews and Pendergast 1979; Coggins 1985, 148

37

Front

Back

Supernatural Patrons

Various supernatural beings, who were critical to the definition of divine king-ship, presided over the Maya world and its inhabitants. Kings acted in concert with gods and other spiritual beings, who bestowed supernatural faculties on Maya rulers. Some deities, such as the Maize God, played seminal roles during the creation of the cosmos. Equally important to the earliest Mesoamerican kings was a supernatural avian creature, the so-called Principal Bird Deity, known to the sixteenth-century K'iche' Maya as Wuqub' Kakix. A version of the PBD appeared as early as the Middle Formative period among the Olmec and played a major role during the Late Preclassic on both the Pacific slopes and in the highlands of Guatemala. Later Maya kings often incorporated the name of the Sun God, K'inich Ajaw, into their royal titles, invoking the protec-tion of this powerful patron deity.

Maya kings frequently depicted themselves in the guise of supernatural beings or wore elements of costume that illustrated a divine association. The title *k'uhul ajaw* (holy lord), which came into use sometime after AD 400, con-veys the relationship between kings and their patron deities. Through divination rites and their patron gods, kings embodied sacred energy, *ch'ulel*, the life force possessed by all animate and inanimate beings in the universe, and this served as the basis for their claim to sacred status.

39

Architectural Medallion Depicting Maize God

Maya Area, 100 BC–AD 100
Limestone stucco
6½ x 3¼ in. (16.5 x 8.3 cm)
Los Angeles County Museum of Art, Gift of Constance
McCormick Fearing (AC1998.209.50)

40

Earflare Depicting Supernatural Beings

Belize, Pomona, 50 BC–AD 50
Jadeite
Diam.: 7⅛ in. (18 cm)
Institute of Archaeology, Belmopan, Belize, courtesy
of the Trustees of The British Museum (AM1950,
Loan 03.1)

41

Fluted Tripod Vessel

Guatemala, Southern Highlands, AD 400–600
Ceramic with red slip
5¾ x 4½ x 4½ in. (14.5 x 11.5 x 11.5 cm)
Fine Arts Museums of San Francisco, Bequest of
Leroy C. Cleal (2002.84.1.33)

42

Plate with Maize God

Guatemala, AD 500–600
Ceramic with slip
16⅝ x 3¾ in. (42.2 x 9.5 cm)
Promised gift to the Museum of Fine Arts, Boston

To the Maya, the human life cycle mirrored that of maize, and episodes of the Maize God's life were commemorated in art and reenacted by kings during ritual performance. The architectural medallion portrays a version of the Maize God with features derived from both Olmec-style and Isthmian-style representations (Taube 1996, 59). Comparable early depictions include the Maize God figure of the San Bartolo murals (below) and the *sak hu'unal* (headband jewel) seen on Nakbe Stela 1 (see Hansen and Guenter, this volume, fig. 2).

The Pomona earflare, found in a tomb chamber with four small jadeite figures, contains the earliest representations of the Maize God and Sun God in hieroglyphic form. Justeson et al. (1988, 116) point out the analogous quincunx positioning of jadeite heads in a cache at Cerros (see cat. 19), suggesting that this earflare might have been surrounded by the four figures. This pattern may provide a context for understanding the hieroglyphic inscription, which is also laid out in a quadripartite pattern. The grammatical sequence of the inscription is not well understood, although the component parts can be identified as deities, including the Principal Bird Deity.

The carved vessel portrays a king in the guise of the Maize God, who is dancing, a primary form of ritual expression among the Maya.

Commissioned by the Naranjo king K'inich Tajal Chaak in the early sixth century, the painted plate portrays an anachronistic version of the head of the Maize God. The face is framed by a series of beads (see cat. 63), and the mouth is the elongated version of early Maize God forms (see cat. 39). The maize cob, trefoil vegetation, and silken hair in this portrayal resemble those on cat. 21.

Other references:
40: Kidder and Ekholm 1951; Schele and Miller 1986, 79
42: Reents-Budet et al. 1994, 326; Martin and Grube 2000, 70; Grube and Martin 2004, II-13

Detail of the first segment of San Bartolo mural, discovered in 2001, showing Maize God and attendants

39

40

43
Carved Bowl Depicting K'inich Ajaw

Discovered in Mexico, San Juan Teotihuacan,
AD 400–550
Ceramic
5¼ x 8⅛ in. (13.2 x 20.5 cm)
CNCA-INAH, Museo de Sitio de Teotihuacan, Mexico
(10-262408)

44
Carved Bowl Depicting K'inich Ajaw

Guatemala, San Agustin Acasaguastlan, AD 400–600
Ceramic
Diam.: 9⁹⁄₁₆ in. (24.3 cm)
National Museum of the American Indian, Washington,
D.C. (NMAI 207626.000)

45
Maya-Style Incised Mirror-Back Ornament

Discovered in Costa Rica, San Carlos, La Fortuna,
AD 200–400
Slate and pigment
6¾ x ¾ in. (17 x 2 cm)
Museo Nacional de Costa Rica (29267)

The characteristic feature of K'inich Ajaw, the Sun God, is the four-petaled flower that is read as k'in (sun, day). A personified version of K'inich Ajaw appears on this carved Maya vessel (cat. 43). A winged serpent-bird sprouts from the head of the Sun God; arching over the scene is a boa constrictor with gaping jaws, the great sky saurian. A lobed and foliated ajaw is attached to the tail of the serpent. The representation here has no known analogy in the Maya lowlands, although the vessel is typical of pottery from the Peten and is unquestionably carved in Early Classic Maya style. Its discovery in Central Mexico provides further evidence

of interaction between the elite of the Maya area and Teotihuacan.

An analogous and richly carved vessel is from the upper Motagua River valley of southern Guatemala (cat. 44). This vessel apparently replicates in ceramic the tradition of gourd and wood carving, of which few examples survive. The central figure in the guise of the Sun God commemorates a trance state or ritual performance, signaled by the two Vision Serpents held in his arms. Blood scrolls, sacrificial implements, and the presence of mythical creatures associated with the different levels of the cosmos reinforce the essence of ritual performance.

Glyphic forms of the Sun God's name appear on the mirror back, signaling the god's patronage over the month of Yaxk'in in the Maya calendar. The Sun God's name occurs twice more in this abbreviated text, which commemorates a king who crowned himself as the ninth successor of his lineage.

References:
44: Schele and Miller 1986, 193–94
45: Schmidt et al. 1998, 628–29

43

44

45

46

Lidded Bowl Depicting Mam

Mexico, Campeche, Calakmul, Structure IV-B, Tomb 2,
AD 350–450
Ceramic
4¾ x 7½ in. approx. (12 x 19.3 cm)
CNCA-INAH, Museo Histórico Fuerte de San Miguel,
Baluarte de San Miguel, Campeche, Mexico (10-397991)

Vessel lid with turtle knob

Underside of vessel

46

47

Lidded Vessel Depicting Mam and Turtle Shell

Honduras, Copan, AD 400–550
Ceramic and pigment
10 x 5 in. (25.4 x 12.7 cm)
IHAH, Centro Regional de Investigaciones
Arqueológicas, Copan, Honduras (CPN-C-1797)

An aged deity variously known as God N, Mam, or Pawahtun is often shown emerging from conch shells or turtle carapaces. Four Pawahtuns serve as the pillars that support the world, and the Maya perceive the surface of the world as the back of a turtle. The vessel (cat. 46), from the same Calakmul tomb as cat. 150, is unique in having its bottom modeled as a portrayal of Mam, while the turtle appears on the lid as its knob.

48

Lidded Vessel Depicting Itzamnaaj on Back of Peccary

Maya Area, AD 400–600
Ceramic
9½ x 8 in. (24.1 x 20.3 cm)
Dallas Museum of Art, Dallas Art Association purchase
(1972.10.a–b)

Itzamnaaj, another aged deity, is one of the most important in the pantheon of the ancient Maya. In his headband he wears a flower marked with the *ak'ab'* (darkness) glyph. As a central deity in the acts of creation, he is associated with the sky. Here he rides on the back of a peccary, manifested in the night sky as the constellation Gemini.

48

49

Carved Blackware Vessel Depicting
Itzamnaaj and Principal Bird Deity

Maya Area, Central Lowlands, AD 250–450
Ceramic
Diam.: 13 in. (33 cm)
Denver Art Museum Collection, purchased in honor of
Jan and Frederick R. Mayer with funds from 2001
Collector's Choice (1998.34 a, b)

On the lid of this vessel, an aged figure sits
on a disk representing a *k'in*/flower symbol.
He is borne on the back of the Principal Bird
Deity, which wears the flower headband of
Itzamnaaj; this portrays the PBD as the *way*, or
spiritual companion, of Itzamnaaj. The vessel's base is decorated with profile saurian
and water symbols. The vessel and its contents, placed in the earth during an important
event, embodied the three-dimensional
cosmogram, with the celestial reference of
Itzamnaaj on top, the earth offerings
within, and the water symbols
signifying the underworld.

49

50

Dish Depicting Itzamnaaj as Principal Bird Deity

Guatemala, Peten, AD 500–600
Ceramic with slip
9 x 4½ in. (22.9 x 11.4 cm)
Staatliche Museen zu Berlin, Preussischer Kulturbesitz,
Ethnologisches Museum, Berlin (IV Ca 50116)

A modeled head of Itzamnaaj in his manifestation as the Principal Bird Deity is attached to the front of this vessel, whose unusual shape reflects the greater freedom of potters and painters in the Early Classic period. The vessel's sides are decorated with incised representations of the PBD.

The bird's tail can be removed so that the hieroglyphic text inscribed on it can be read more easily. Below the tail are two modeled heads, and the upper has the stone axe of the god K'awiil protruding from it. The modeled heads are in essence the pictorial version of the name of Siyaj Chan K'awiil II, who reigned at Tikal from AD 411 to 456 as the sixteenth king in the dynasty.

The eight glyphs on the tail confirm the proposed attribution to Tikal. The glyphs begin with a day name followed by a verb. The next two glyphs relate titles associated with the Sun God. The fifth glyph shows the name of Chak Tok Ich'aak II, followed by the emblem glyph for Tikal, identifying the ruler as a holy king of the city. The final two glyphs are titles, including one which may be freely translated as "great artist." The vessel may have been commissioned by Chak Tok Ich'aak to make an offering to his deceased grandfather, Siyaj Chan K'awiil. He may also have dedicated the vessel to Itzamnaaj, a god of great importance to his grandfather.

Reference:
Grube in press

Detail of "tail" showing glyphic text

51

Double-Chambered Vessel Depicting Principal Bird Deity and Hero Twin

Maya Area, Central Lowlands, AD 350–550
Ceramic
12 x 8 in. (30.5 x 20.3 cm)
The Metropolitan Museum of Art, The Michael C.
Rockefeller Memorial Collection, Gift of Nelson A.
Rockefeller, 1963 (1978.412.90a, b)

52

Lidded Tripod Vessel

Guatemala, AD 300–400
Ceramic with stucco and pigment
11½ in. (29.2 cm)
Kimbell Art Museum, Fort Worth, Texas (AP1997.01)

The Principal Bird Deity as Wuqub' Kakix, the false sun of an earlier creation, appears in the opening chapters of the K'iche' Maya creation epic, the *Popol Vuh*. The Principal Bird Deity head as seen on the censer stand (p. 6) resembles those found on Late Preclassic temple facades (see Freidel, this volume, fig. 2). This censer stand once sat on a bowl or brazier containing hot coals, which heated the surface of the vessel. The dish on top of the PBD's head supported a handled openwork incense burner, which contained copal. The warmed copal released the aroma and clouds of smoke that are important components of Maya ritual.

The double-chambered vessel (cat. 51) shows Wuqub' Kakix moments before Junajpu, one of the Hero Twins, shoots him with a blowgun, taking away the dazzling powers previously represented in his glittering eyes and teeth.

On the body of the lidded vessel (cat. 52) are four manifestations of Itzamnaaj in his bird form with clawed feet, tail, and wings. The cylinder tripod vessel form is associated with Teotihuacan, but the taller and more slender shape and the human head effigy knob are typically Maya. The text on the lid is too eroded to read but has components of a dedication phrase.

51

53

Lidded Vessel with Cormorant Handle

Guatemala, Central Peten, AD 350–450
Ceramic with slip
14¾ x 15⅜ in. (37.5 x 38.5 cm)
Museo Popol Vuh, Guatemala City (0414)

The integral role of the great avian supernatural with kingship in Mesoamerica can be seen as early as the Middle Formative in the cave painting at Oxtotitlan, Guerrero (see introduction, fig. 2). The king, portrayed on this vessel (detail at right), arrayed in a bird costume and dancing in ritual performance in the company of underworld supernaturals, wears the trefoil crown, designating his royal status and authority. He also wears the necklace of the PBD; the pectoral here is a woven mat (see also cats. 82, 149, 150).

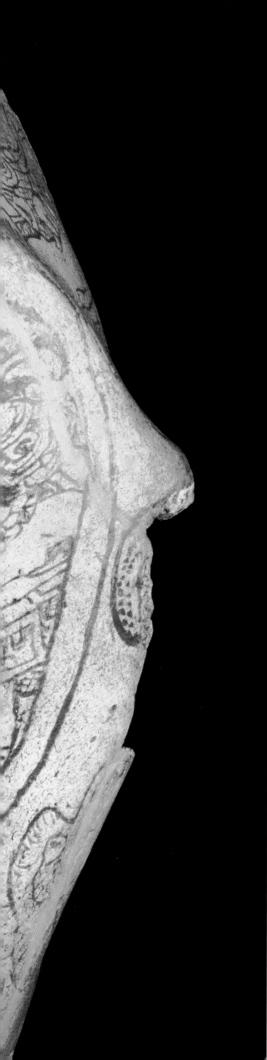

Religious Duties of the King

Royal responsibilities were concerned with not only social, economic, and political affairs but also ritual performance. For the Maya, ritual dance was, and continues to be, not merely a symbolic act but rather a means by which humans transform themselves into supernatural beings in order to replicate their actions. Painted images and hieroglyphic texts on Late Classic period vessels attest to the importance of *wayo'ob'*, or protective spirit companions that often take the form of animals and are invoked during rituals of transformation. Maya kings commonly associated themselves with the jaguar, which lives in caves and moves easily on land and in water (all cosmologically significant places in Mesoamerican thought), thus conveying enormous power.

These transformations might also be induced by methods such as blood sacrifice or the ingestion of hallucinogenic substances. In these trance states, Maya kings encountered divine forces, summoning ancestors and other supernatural beings to the earthly realm to assist with human concerns. Kings also performed conjuring rituals using mirrors as divining tools. The process of conjuring otherworldly spirits might also bring forth an apparition known as the Vision Serpent, from whose open mouth emerged the invoked sacred being, either a deity or an ancestor.

54

54

Perforator

Mexico, Olmec, 900–400 BC
Jadeite
15 x 1⅛ in. (38 x 3 cm)
Courtesy of the Trustees of The British Museum
(AM1907, 0608.3)

55

Incised Ritual Object

Guatemala, Pacific Coast, 900–400 BC
Jadeite
3⅝ x 11⅜ in. (9.3 x 29 cm)
Museo de Arte Precolombino y Vidrio Moderno,
Antigua, Guatemala (1.2.75.288)

The nature of religion in the Americas focuses on the importance of reciprocal actions in which sacrifice and ritual are performed to nourish the gods and ensure their benefi-cence. The sacrificial rite of bloodletting was the method by which a ruler provided suste-nance to the gods, because blood represented the most precious form of reciprocity; it was also a way to enter a trance state. This early perforator, undoubtedly a symbolic tool that was not actually used for bloodletting, attests to the antiquity of this practice in Meso-america.

The figure incised on the ritual object is in the guise of the Olmec Maize God. Such figures are frequently found on Olmec-style celts and "spoons," enigmatic ritual objects related to religious rites and political author-ity. Formerly known as "swimmers," these more likely represent trance states in which the figure appears to float or to be in a posi-tion of supernatural flight (Taube 2000, 306–7).

Other reference:
54: McEwan 1994, 23

56
Stela

Maya Area, 3rd–4th century
Limestone
33 in. (83.8 cm)
The Princeton University Art Museum (1999–232)

This stela illustrates a vision quest by the
Maya ruler B'ak-T'ul, who wears the headband of kingship on his forehead, perhaps
indicating that the quest was part of his
accession rituals. Rendered in the guise of a
deity, he has let blood and brought forth the
Vision Serpent, which twists around his body.
Four supernaturals climb the serpent's body,
while a scalloped band, likely representing
a stream of blood, falls behind his right
shoulder (Schele and Miller 1986, pl. 66).

The king faces a hieroglyphic text that
records the date and nature of the event illustrated, although the date's unusual format
has hindered its decipherment. The date is
followed by a bloodletting verb, and the text
ends with the personal name of B'ak-T'ul
and an unidentified emblem glyph that may
reveal the site ruled by B'ak-T'ul and his
descendant, who commissioned this retrospective monument.

Other references:
Easby and Scott 1970, cat. 169; Lacadena 1995, 250–62

56

57 (image unavailable for publication)

Lidded Vessel with Image of Deceased Lord

Mexico, Campeche, Becan, Structure IX, AD 250–450
Ceramic with pigment
20¼ x 8⅝ in. (51.5 x 22 cm)
CNCA-INAH, Museo Histórico Fuerte de San Miguel,
Baluarte de San Miguel, Campeche, Mexico
(10-568677 0/2)

Under the floor of a temple in Structure IX, archaeologist Luz Evelia Campaña V. discovered a vaulted chamber. There were no skeletal remains among the many precious objects, including fifteen ceramic vessels, that had been placed in the chamber. The vessels were decorated with representations of animals and motifs that symbolize the levels of the Maya cosmos. The most spectacular is this lidded dish decorated with a modeled and painted iguana. The iguana, like the jaguar, was a powerful animal spirit companion or *way*; the iguana here wears the belt of Maya rulers, complete with the head of the Maize God and three pendant plaques, implying that it was the *way* of a Maya lord (Boucher et al. 2004, 385–86). The half-skeletal human head in the iguana's mouth is linked allegorically to the Maize God's decapitation. Three sacrificed figures surround the iguana, their bodies cut in half and gushing blood; their headdresses may signal personal names or have symbolic associations.

Both the lid's imagery and that of the stela (cat. 56) likely make reference to related sacrificial beliefs. These images recount the king's role as the world tree and perpetuator of the cosmic order through personal blood sacrifice to ensure fertility, regeneration, and cosmic renewal.

Other reference:
Campaña V. and Boucher 2002, 64–69

58

Divination Figure

Maya Area, AD 150–350
Limestone
10⅜ x 9⅜ in. approx. (26.4 x 23.8 cm)
Promised gift to the Museum of Fine Arts, Boston

This figure, although incomplete, has a forward-leaning pose and staring eyes that suggest a trance state. His jaguar ears imply a ruler's transformation into his *way*, because kings and jaguars were closely linked as powerful beings. The figure's hipcloth is marked with crossed bones, and on his back he wears a belt head resembling the Principal Bird Deity with pendant plaques, further confirming his royal status. The partial square frame at the front indicates that the figure may once have held a mirror, a divination tool. A brief text on the frame's back features squared glyphic signs that resemble the little-known Isthmian script, although the details of each sign identify the text as lowland Maya. The text currently eludes decipherment.

Back of Divination Figure

59 (catalogue only)

Tripod Lidded Vessel with Toad

Maya Area, Central Lowlands, AD 400–600
Ceramic
10 x 8 in. (25.3 x 20.2 cm)

60

Carved Vessel Depicting Vision Serpent

Maya Area, Central Lowlands, 200 BC–AD 100
Stone
5⅝ x 4¾ in. (14.2 x 12 cm)
Dumbarton Oaks Research Library and Collections,
Washington, D.C. (PC.B. 593)

61

Incised Peccary Skull

Honduras, Copan, Tomb I, AD 580
Bone with red pigment
8½ in. (21.5 cm)
Peabody Museum of Archaeology and Ethnology,
Harvard University (92-49-20/C201)

One means of entering a trance state involved ingesting hallucinogenic substances, including those derived from nerve toxins found in the glands of a specific toad. The toad here, whose glands are indicated by the spotted elements behind its eyes, seems to emerge from the water's surface depicted on the vessel's lid. The small stone cup depicting two Vision Serpents may have held such a hallucinogen. The apparition of a Vision Serpent materialized as a result of the trance state; here, the serpent's mouth emits a sacred liquid.

The incised peccary skull was recovered from a tomb excavated by George Gordon (1896, 29–32). While the tomb dates to the Late Classic, the skull is Early Classic in style, an heirloom commemorating a ritual event that took place in AD 376. The scene depicts two seated figures framed by a quatrefoil cartouche, implying that they are in a cave or other sacred location. They face each other with a personified altar and bound stela between them. *Wayo'ob'* surrounding the quatrefoil also substantiate an otherworldly context for the scene. A similar composition appears on the Motmot floor marker (Fash et al. 2004, 70), in which K'inich Yax K'uk' Mo' and his successor commemorate an event. On the peccary skull, K'inich Yax K'uk' Mo' has been identified as the figure on the left (Stuart 2004, 223) based on his macaw (*mo'*) headdress, although the date recorded on the skull occurs fifty years before his accession to office in AD 426.

Other references:
60: Schele and Miller 1986, 192
61: Longyear 1952, 111; Coggins 1985, 170; Fash 1991, 52; Wanyerka 2001, 30–32

59

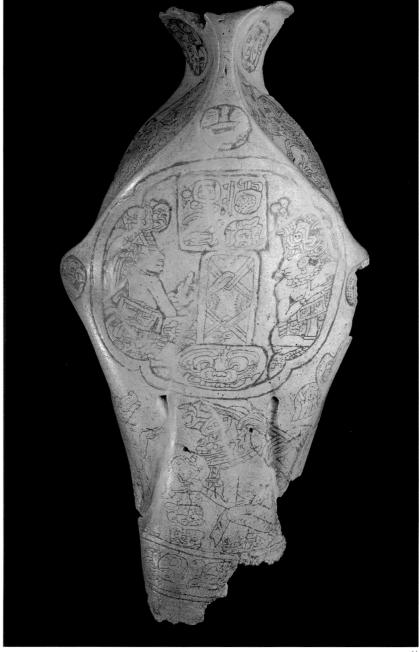

60

61

Royal Portraits

The development of the divine status of Maya kings prompted numerous innovations in media, pictorial compositions, and representational styles. Artists transformed Preclassic concepts of royal portraiture into fully idealized narratives denoting supernatural sanction and divine powers as the basis for rulership. Early portraits maintain the idealized rendering of the emblems of sacred kingship while the features of the portrayed kings convey individuality. This aesthetic development derives from the evolution of royal patronage. Artists, who were often of noble status, were important members of the royal court, playing a major role in supporting the king through their richly designed expressions of his stature.

To convey divine status, artists depicted rulers wearing elaborate headdresses and costumes and carrying emblematic objects that identified the king with various deities, often obscuring the boundaries between deity and human to the eyes of the modern viewer. When kings impersonated deities in the course of ritual performance, they essentially assumed the identities of these supernatural beings and wielded divine powers. Rulers are shown in a variety of poses holding objects of power appropriate to the artwork's expressive intent and social function. Royal paraphernalia was often made from perishable materials such as cloth, paper, feathers, and wood; since these no longer survive, the only record of them is found in these royal portraits.

62

Facade Mask

Mexico, Southern Campeche, AD 100–300
Stucco and pigment
37¾ x 27½ in. (96 x 70 cm)
CNCA-INAH, Museo Nacional de Antropología,
Mexico City

The Late Preclassic in the Maya lowlands saw the development of pyramids with monumental stucco masks on their facades, and this phenomenon is closely tied to the emergence of kingship. The masks served as emblematic names of the historical individuals who acceded to office (Stuart 2002). The beads seen around the face of this mask may be of jadeite and are found in many early portrayals of Maya kings (see cat. 63). They signify preciousness and power through the symbolic link of jadeite to water and fertility.

62

63

Tripod Vessel with Seated King

Guatemala, AD 350–400
Ceramic with slip
13⅜ x 5½ in. (34 x 14 cm)
The Art Institution, New York (1191.0050a, b)

In this royal portrait, an unnamed king sits upon a double-headed jaguar throne, which rests upon the personified mountain of creation. He wears the headdress of the Principal Bird Deity with the jewel of Itzamnaaj, and his face is encircled by beads. The belt head of the king represents the Maize God, and from it hang three belt plaques associated with maize fertility. The king carries a double-headed serpent bar, symbolizing the sky and his ability to access ancestors and supernatural beings. A double-entwined rope falls from the back of his headdress, and at its end is a trussed deer with a skeletal head. Related imagery associated with ancestors among contemporary Maya suggests that this king may be calling on his ancestors to sanction his royal authority.

Detail of back of headdress

64

Censer with Seated King

Guatemala, AD 350–450
Ceramic with slip
33 × 12½ in. (83.8 × 31.8 cm)
The Metropolitan Museum of Art, Gift of Charles and
Valerie Diker, 1999 (1999.484.1a, b)

The veneration of ancestors was an important
function of censers, which portray individual
kings (see cat. 113). Censers have two parts:
the top depicts the king seated in a royal
pose; the bottom forms the container for
coals and incense. This king wears a headdress
with a mirror as its central jewel, and feather
panaches cascade from each side in a style
reminiscent of Teotihuacan formal dress. He
holds a tray for an offering; the divination
mirror in front of him refers to his ritual
responsibilities.

64

65

Pectoral Depicting Ruler Seated on Throne

Mexico, Quintana Roo, Dzibanche, Templo del Buho,
AD 350–550
Shell, jadeite, pyrite, and mother-of-pearl
9⅞ x 7⅞ in. (25 x 20 cm)
CNCA-INAH, Museo Nacional de Antropología,
Mexico City (10-57117)

During the Early Classic, the Templo del Buho was the most important building at Dzibanche. Excavations in 1994 by archaeologist Luz Evelia Campaña V. revealed a stairway leading down to two burial chambers. One contained a seated individual accompanied by a rich array of precious objects. The seated individual wore jade earflares and a shell bead and jade necklace, and had a jade bead in the mouth, a widespread Mesoamerican burial custom. The most spectacular item was this inlaid-shell pectoral incised with an image of a king seated on a throne with woven mat borders. The king carries a double-headed serpent bar and wears the trefoil crown and a jaguar-pelt kilt, and plaques hang from his belt and throne. Because there are no hieroglyphic inscriptions in the tomb or on Dzibanche's monumental sculptures, the name of the person buried in the tomb is unknown.

Reference:
Campaña V. 1995

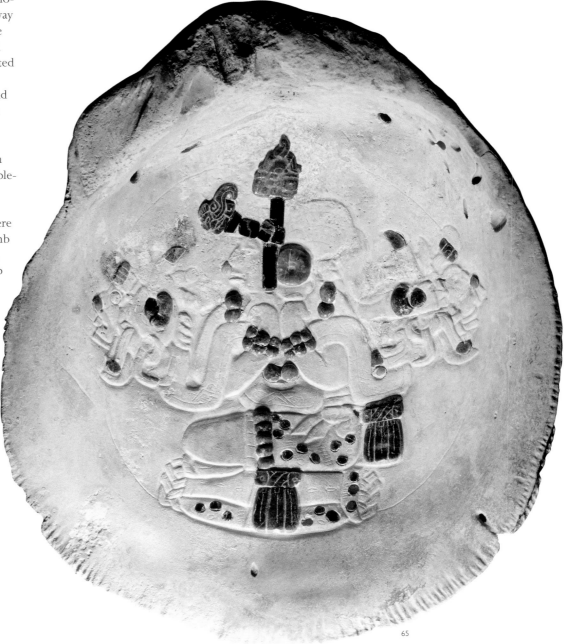

65

66
Figure of a Lord

Honduras, Copan, Hieroglyphic Stairway, AD 300–500
Jadeite
5¾ x 5¹⁵⁄₁₆ x 1⅝ in. (14.5 x 15 x 4 cm)
IHAH, Centro Regional de Investigaciones
Arqueológicas, Copan, Honduras (CPN-J-185)

Part of a dedicatory cache found beneath the altar at the foot of the Hieroglyphic Stairway, this figure and another with it were heirlooms at the time of the offering. The cache dates to the reign of K'ak' Yipyaj Chan K'awiil in the mid-eighth century, but the figure's Early Classic style is revealed in its pose: slightly bent legs, and the so-called crab-claw position of the arms. Although simply dressed, the figure has large earflares and a necklace as well as the headband worn by rulers, which together connote a person of status.

Reference:
Fash 1998, 284

66

67

Cache Vessel with Carved Lid
Portraying King

Guatemala, Tikal, Mundo Perdido, AD 350–450
Ceramic
4⅞ x 9⅞ in. (12.3 x 25 cm)
Museo Nacional de Arqueología y Etnología, Guatemala
City (MNAE 11,129A, B)

68

Lidded Vessel with Royal Portraits

Guatemala, Peten, AD 250–550
Ceramic
11⅞ x 15½ in. (30.2 x 39.5 cm)
The Museum of Fine Arts Houston, Gift of Mr. and
Mrs. George R. Brown (77.48.A, B)

Artists also carved royal images on ceramic
vessels. On the Tikal vessel the king's head
emerges from the open mouth of a saurian,
invoking a supernatural context. The large
earflare on the saurian is a typical Early
Classic quincunx version with a central U
surrounded by four dots.

The supernatural context of the profile
heads on the lidded vessel is the watery realm
of the underworld, implied by the water
lily–shaped knob on the lid. The faces, surrounded by the beads seen in other portrayals
(cats. 62, 63), may represent deified ancestors
floating on the surface of the underworld. The
headdresses, one portraying the Principal Bird
Deity with Itzamnaaj's flower headband and
the other with a water lily jaguar, may represent the names of the individuals, a characteristic pattern of royal costume during the Early
Classic period.

67

Personal Instruments of Power

Kings used regalia made of rare materials such as jadeite and shell, demonstrating their power to obtain precious objects from distant places. Royal portraits carved on stone monuments or painted on ceramics illustrate the lavish use of accoutrements, which included heirloom jewels and badges of office received during rites of accession. These objects of adornment linked the king to his community's history, to his deified ancestors, and to the gods themselves, and they are characterized by their rich materials, superb craftsmanship, and diversity of form and decoration.

69

Lidded Bowl

Guatemala, Peten, ca. AD 300–500
Ceramic and slip
Lid: 4½ x 14 in. (11.4 x 35.6 cm); bowl: 5½ x 14 in.
(14 x 35.6 cm)
Los Angeles County Museum of Art, purchased with
funds provided by the Forman Family Fund through the
1990 Collectors Committee (M.90.104a–b)

Ceramics used during royal feasts often were decorated with imagery that sanctioned social hierarchy and rulership. This vessel is unusual for its narrative scene, which is more akin to Late Classic painted vessels. Here, rulers dressed in jaguar-pelt kilts and elaborate headdresses sit on jaguar-pelt pillows. They hold opened bundles, suggesting ritual activity involving the use of sacred objects, and they are accompanied by members of the court.

70

Eccentric Flint

Honduras, Copan, Structure 10L-16, AD 450
Flint with traces of textile
17 in. (43 cm)
IHAH, Centro Regional de Investigaciones
Arqueológicas, Copan, Honduras (CPN-P-4)

71

Cache Urn Depicting Supernatural Beings

Guatemala, Central Peten, AD 350–450
Ceramic with pigment
20⅛ x 14⅜ in. diam. (51 x 36.5 cm)
Museo de Arte Precolombino y Vidrio Moderno,
Antigua, Guatemala (1.2.75.276)

72 (catalogue only)

Scepter with Image of K'awiil

Maya Area, Central Lowlands, AD 500–800
Slate
19⅜ x 7⅛ x 1 in. (49.2 x 18 x 2.5 cm)

This flint formed part of a cache of sacred
objects found in the Rosalila Temple. The
cache contained nine flints and other offerings, which were wrapped in blue cloth
(Fash 1991, 100). A master artist knapped this
flint into a delicate and detailed rendering of
K'awiil, a deity more prominent during the
Late Classic period as a patron of royal dynasties, and whose name is carried by many
kings as part of their official titles. Characterized by the smoking flint knife or torch that
protrudes from a mirror on his forehead,
K'awiil was associated with lightning. Full-
length versions of K'awiil reveal his serpent
leg and foot, which represent his *way* (animal
spiritual companion) (Freidel et al. 1993, 196).

The cache urn lid portrays an early and
unusual frontal version of K'awiil on its
upper section, and his zoomorphic face is
framed by large earflares. The lower section
features the Palenque triad deity GI, who
wears the quadripartite badge associated with
sacrifice as his headdress.

The elegant scepter portraying K'awiil was
once carried by a king or queen, as demonstrated by royal portraits at Machaquilá,
Palenque, and Quirigua.

70

72

73

Two Carved Femurs

Mexico, Chiapas, Chiapa de Corzo, Mound I, Tomb I,
100 BC–AD 100
Human bone
Lengths: 9¼ in. (23.5 cm); 10⁷⁄₁₆ in. (26.5 cm)
CNCA-INAH, Museo Regional de Chiapas, Tuxtla
Gutiérrez, Mexico (10-222063; 10-222062)

From the same tomb as the spouted vessel
(cat. 104), these carved femurs were found
paired with two uncarved bones. Long bones
such as these appear in funerary contexts as
relics of venerated ancestors and may have
been used in commemorative ceremonies.
Bones 1 and 3, seen here, apparently came
from the same individual (Agrinier 1960, 3)
and were carved with elaborate designs referring to cycles in the life of the Maize God.
The profile head of the Isthmian-style Maize
God appears on both bones, with minor variations. Both profiles are framed by the same
vegetal motif wrapped around the chin that is
seen in the architectural medallion (cat. 39).

Other references:
Lowe 1990, 85–86; Christenson 1996; Schmidt et al.
1998, 606

74

Three Carved Bones

Maya-style, discovered in Michoacán, Mexico,
AD 300–400
Jaguar bone
Lengths: 8½ in. (21.5 cm); 7¼ in. (18.5 cm); 8½ in.
(21.5 cm)
The University Museum, University of Pennsylvania,
Philadelphia (68-32-2a; 68-32-3; 68-32-2b)

The two femurs are carved in a manner resembling the stacked supernaturals seen on cache vessels (see cat. 71). One depicts the beaded face of the king, whose head-dress comprises the Principal Bird Deity surmounted by a jaguar, both wearing the diadem of Itzamnaaj. The youthful face of the Maize God appears at the top. The other femur also portrays a king, and his headdress features two images of the PBD and the zoomorphic form of the Jester God at the top. On the reverse of each femur is a stack of four supernatural beings.

74

75

Shell Trumpet

Maya Area, Central Lowlands, AD 250–400
Conch shell with traces of cinnabar
11⁹⁄₁₆ x 5⁵⁄₁₆ in. (29.3 x 13.4 cm)
Kimbell Art Museum, Fort Worth, Texas (AP1984.11)

Throughout Mesoamerican history, conch shells were modified and used as trumpets. On this trumpet, the face of a king is shown wearing a large quincunx-patterned earflare with personified knots. His headdress incorporates a water lily jaguar sign, which also occurs as his name in the brief text adjacent to the profile head, which states that he is the owner of the trumpet (Schele and Miller 1986, 83–84).

Other reference:
Wanyerka 2001, 80–81

Ball Game Model, detail of musician playing shell trumpet, 200 BC–AD 500, Mexico, Nayarit

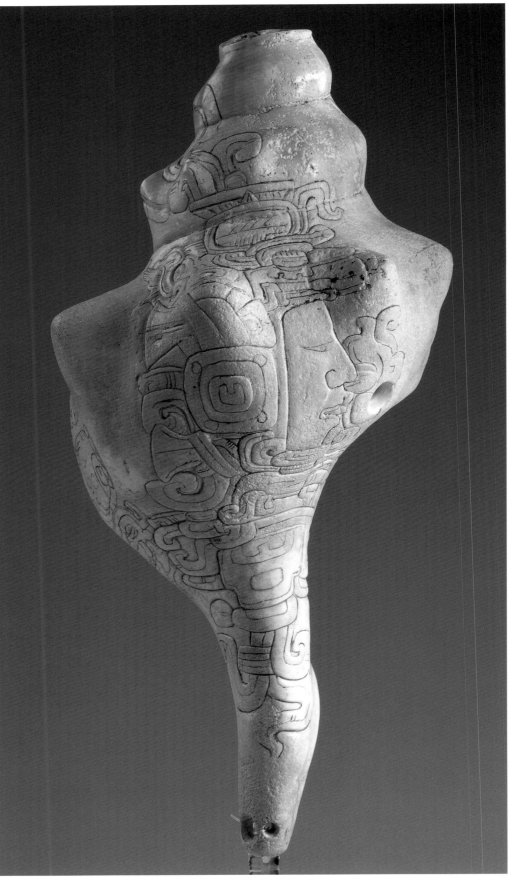

76

Royal Belt Ornament

Maya Area, Central Lowlands, AD 500–700
Jadeite
5⅛ × 6⅝ × 1⅝ in. (13 × 16.8 × 4.1 cm)
Dallas Museum of Art, The Nora and John Wise
Collection, gift of Mr. and Mrs. Jake L. Hamon, the
Eugene McDermott Family, Mr. and Mrs. Algur H.
Meadows and the Meadows Foundation, and Mr. and
Mrs. John D. Murchison (1982.W.2)

77

Three Belt Plaques

Mexico, Calakmul, Structure III, Tomb 1, AD 350–500
Jadeite
4 × 2⅜ in. (10.2 × 6 cm); 4¹⁄₁₆ × 2⅜ in. (10.3 × 6 cm);
4⅛ × 2½ in. (10.4 × 6.2 cm)
CNCA-INAH, Museo Histórico Fuerte de San Miguel,
Baluarte de San Miguel, Campeche, Mexico (10-342887;
10-342888; 10-342889)

The earliest components of Maya royal costume included the headband crown marked with a Maize God emblem, and a belt with a central jadeite element that typically portrayed the Maize God, a patron deity, or deified ancestor. Three jadeite plaques hung from the belt head and, since Olmec times, they symbolized the maize plant (Joralemon 1988, 38) (see Hansen and Guenter, this volume, fig. 2). This belt head has the square eyes and forehead mirror of the Sun God; however, these characteristics may also refer to the partitioning of the cosmos into earth, sea, and sky (Freidel et al. 1993, 140). The belt plaques each contain a two-glyph text within a cartouche. Although the glyphs can be read phonetically, they do not convey a meaningful statement in terms of current understanding of Early Classic inscriptions.

Other references:
76: Easby and Scott 1970, no. 192
77: Carrasco Vargas 1998, 628

76

77

78

Olmec-Style Pendant

Discovered in Mexico, Quintana Roo, Cozumel,
San Gervasio, AD 600–900
Pendant: 900–400 BC
Jadeite
2⅝ x 2¼ in. (6.8 x 5.5 cm)
CNCA-INAH, Museo Regional de Yucatan "Palacio
Cantón," Merida, Mexico (10-152738)

79

Bar Pendant with Mat Motif

Honduras, Copan, Structure 10J-45, Burial 36,
AD 350–450
Jadeite with traces of cinnabar
8 x 1⅜ x ¾ in. (20.1 x 3.5 x 1.9 cm)
IHAH, Centro Regional de Investigaciones
Arqueológicas, Copan, Honduras (CPN-J-827)

80

Bar Pendant with Image of Pax

Honduras, Copan, Structure 10J-45, Burial 36,
AD 350–450
Jadeite
9⅜ x 1¹⁄₁₆ in. (23.8 x 2.7 cm)
IHAH, Centro Regional de Investigaciones
Arqueológicas, Copan, Honduras (CPN-J-828)

The pendant with its distinctive Olmec-style
face (cat. 78) came into the possession of
a Late Classic period Maya king, who was
subsequently buried with this royal jewel. As
an heirloom, the pendant underscored the
importance of ancestors, a primary source
of authority for the ruler.

The bar pendants were found in a royal
tomb in an outlying residential area of
Copan. One pendant is carved with a woven

mat pattern, associating the jewel with the
title that signifies *aj pohp* (he of the mat). The
other is richly carved with an image of the
Pax God as the axis mundi (Taube 2001) (see
cat. 28). The burial may be that of a mid-
sixth-century Copan king, either the eighth
or ninth in the recorded dynasty (Nakamura
2004).

Other references:
78: Pohorilenko 1996, 252–53; Schmidt et al. 1998, 578

78

79

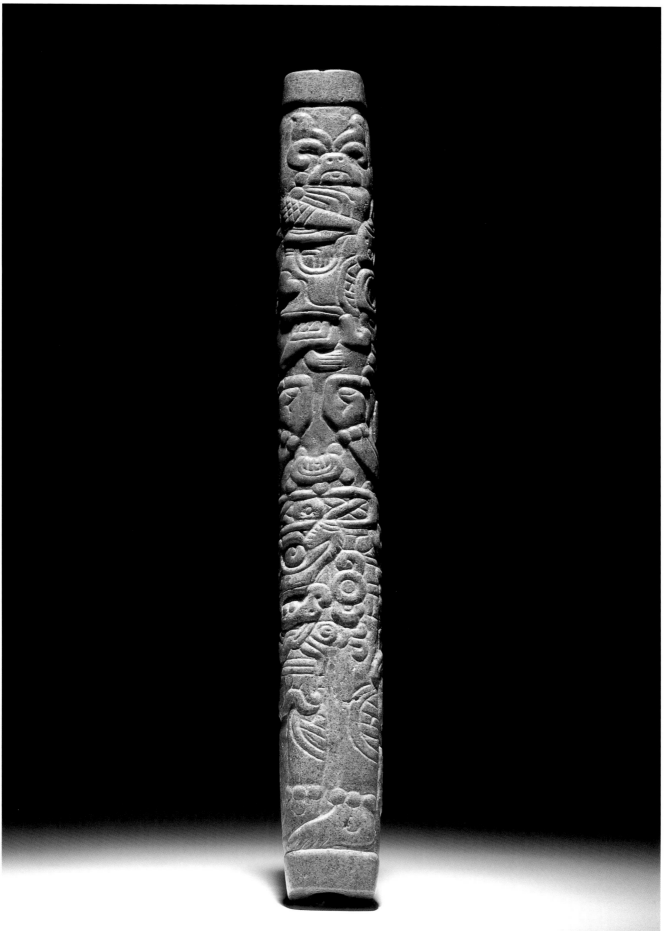

81

Earflare Inlay

Maya Area, Central Lowlands, AD 400–550
Shell and cinnabar
3¾ x 4 x 1 in. (9.5 x 10.2 x 2.5 cm)
Fine Arts Museums of San Francisco, Bequest of Leroy
C. Cleal (2002.84.1.20)

The kneeling figure seen here appears to offer
an icon of royal power, the Jaguar God of
the Underworld, to the person wearing the
earflare. Other precious objects surround the
figure, including shells and ear spools. The
figure's belt head and pendant plaques attest
to his own elite status.

81

82

Earflare Depicting Principal Bird Deity

Guatemala, Río Azul, AD 300–400
Jadeite
3 x ¼ in. (7.5 x 2 cm)
Museo Nacional de Arqueología y Etnología, Guatemala
City (MNAE 12,044)

83

Pair of Flower-Shaped Earflares

Maya Area, AD 350–550
Jadeite
3 x ⅜ in. (7.5 x .95 cm)
The Princeton University Art Museum (2003-25 a, b)

84

Pair of Earflares

Belize, Altun Ha, Tomb A-1/1, AD 400–500
Obsidian with cinnabar
1¾ x 1¾ in. (4.4 x 4.4 cm)
Institute of Archaeology, Belmopan, Belize, courtesy of
the Royal Ontario Museum, Toronto (RP 200/1a, b)

Earflares, worn with a protruding central
cylinder and counterweights dangling down
the back, symbolized flowers (Stuart 1992),
and they are integral components of royal
costume. The earflare from Río Azul is incised
with an image of the Principal Bird Deity
wearing its characteristic necklace (see cat.
53); the wings and tail cover the surface of
the flare. Above the bird is another avian head
resembling the verb for accession to office,
affirming the importance of the PBD to early
Maya kingship.

The fluted earflares from Altun Ha were
made from obsidian, a material rarely used
by Maya artists for jewelry; their hieroglyphic
text, which conveys an ownership statement,
revealed an important function of early texts
(Mathews and Pendergast 1979).

Other references:
82: Muñoz Cosma et al. 1999, 184
84: Coggins 1985, 121

82

83

84

The Origins of Writing

Writing first appeared among ancient Sumerians and Egyptians about five thousand years ago. It developed independently in the Americas, and by 700 to 600 BC calendrical notations were being recorded on monuments in southern Mesoamerica. The precise origins of writing among the Maya are unknown, but the concept of arranging symbols systematically in a vertical format can be seen on Olmec objects dating to around 600 BC. Later, Olmec-style objects were occasionally inscribed with early Maya texts, relating the names and titles of rulers who inherited these heirlooms.

In Mesoamerica, writing was always an important component of a system that expressed elite power and prestige, and the narrative quality of Maya art provided the ideal condition for the development of writing. The earliest Maya hieroglyphic texts appear as captions, documenting the ruler's ownership of precious regalia, his accession to office, and his titles.

Between AD 250 and 900, Maya writing developed into one of the most complex scripts ever invented. Highly pictorial, the hieroglyphs are arranged in the same order as a literary form of spoken Mayan, which facilitated decipherment in the latter part of the twentieth century. Today it is possible to read the nuanced expressions of the historic and dedicatory actions performed by numerous Maya kings and queens, and members of their court.

The onset of writing among the Maya was accompanied by the appearance of a new calendrical system known as the Long Count. The much older Calendar Round measured the endlessly repeating cycles of time based on a 260-day sacred cycle and a 365-day solar year. The Long Count, however, measured time from a fixed point (in 3114 BC), enabling the Maya to measure historical time and reckon genealogical descent, a significant aspect of documenting status and legitimacy to the throne.

85

Tablet with Incised Inscription

Mexico, Guerrero, Ahuelican, 900–500 BC
Greenstone
3½ x 3½ x ¾ in. (8.9 x 8.9 x 1.9 cm)
Dallas Museum of Art, Dallas Art Association purchase
(1968.33)

The incised signs on this tablet are read from top to bottom and illustrate the cosmic order of the world; the greenstone represents the primordial ocean. The plaque also symbolizes a plaza, with the edges of its four platforms surrounding the open plaza space. The symbol at the top is the mythological sky-house of the north. Below this is the world tree, here in the form of a maize plant, with four seeds marking the cardinal directions. Below the maize plant appears an incurving earth sign with a stepped mountain. The maize plant/world tree bridges the three realms of the universe and sustains the cosmic structure. The three dots represent the three stones of the cosmic hearth where the gods erected the maize/tree at the center of creation.

Reference:
Olmec World 1995, 234

85

86

86 (catalogue only)

Plaque with Maya Hieroglyphic Text

Mexico, Campeche, Isla Piedras
Front: Olmec-style, 800–500 BC; back: Maya-style,
50 BC–AD 200
Jadeite
3¼ x 4¾ x 1⅛ in. (8.4 x 12.1 x 2.9 cm)

87

Ritual Object with Maya Hieroglyphic Text

Mexico, Olmec, found in Costa Rica, Guanacaste
Province, 700–400 BC
Text: Lowland Maya, AD 100–300
Jadeite
2¹⁄₁₆ x 7⁵⁄₁₆ in. (5.2 x 18.5 cm)
Museo del Jade, Instituto Nacional de Seguros, San José,
Costa Rica (INS 6726)

88

Ornament

Mexico, Gulf Coast, 900–400 BC
Text: Lowland Maya, AD 100–250
Jadeite
4³⁄₁₆ x 4⁵⁄₁₆ in. (10.5 x 10.9 cm)
Courtesy of the Trustees of The British Museum
(AM1929, 0712.1)

89

Jaguar Figure with Hieroglyphic Text

Mexico, Tabasco, 150 BC–AD 150
Steatite
6¾ in. (17.1 cm)
Peabody Museum of Natural History, Yale University
(YPM 236866)

The majority of heirloom objects are elite items used for adornment or rulership rituals, such as these portable sculptures, pectoral jewels, and so-called spoons. Many spoons have cord holes drilled into them and were worn suspended around the neck; they may have held hallucinogens that helped induce trance states (see cat. 12).

The Maya treasured these objects and inscribed them with hieroglyphic texts. The beginning of this spoon's upper phrase is eroded, but it ends with the regal title, "divine lord of the night," which also concludes the second phrase. The lower part begins with a statement dedicating the spoon; this is followed by the object's name, which

87

identifies it as a symbolic maize ear (Mora Marín 2002, 16). The last three glyphs represent the owner's name and titles.

Known Preclassic signs record information about rulers and their ritual activities. Examples of a short text composed of a personal name and regal titles are the Olmec face plaque (cat. 86), which was acquired by a Maya lord more than six hundred years after it was made, and the ornament (cat. 88). The text on the back of the plaque begins with the verbal statement u-*bah* (it is the image of), followed by the name of the lord and two titles, including a version of sacred or holy primogenitor (see Fahsen and Grube, this volume, fig. 3). The ornament, once worn as a pectoral, bears two name glyphs (McEwan 1994, 22).

The text on the were-jaguar figure opens with a dedication expression (see also cat. 87:A4). Although the syntax is uncertain, an early version of the *ajaw* title appears at B4 (see also cat. 92:A6), and a seating expression may occur at B7 (see also cat. 90:A5). The progenitor title at B2 echoes that on the face plaque (cat. 86). The two-glyph compound at A3-B3 may mean "sun-stomach jaguar" and appears to name the *way* depicted by this tiny sculpture.

Other references:
86: Schele and Miller 1986, 150–51, pl. 45
87: Graham 1998, 52
89: Coe 1973, 25; Coe and Kerr 1997, 69

88

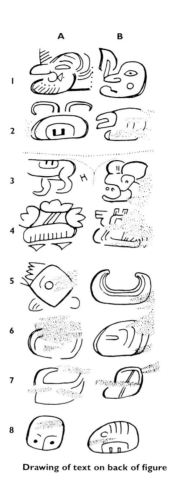

Drawing of text on back of figure

89

90

Flanged Pectoral with Maya Hieroglyphic Text

Mexico, Olmec, reportedly found near Merida, Yucatan,
1000–600 BC
Text: Lowland Maya, AD 100–300
Quartzite
3½ × 10½ × 1⅛ in. (8.9 × 26.7 × 2.8 cm)
Dumbarton Oaks Research Library and Collections,
Washington, D.C. (PC.B. 538)

91

Ceremonial Axe

Belize, Kendal, AD 200–300
Jadeite
8⅝ × 2½ × 1¼ in. (22 × 6.4 × 3 cm)
Merseyside County Museums, Liverpool

The appearance of longer texts coincides with
the consolidation of the office of divine kingship, and most of these longer texts focus on
accession to office. The flanged pectoral, once
worn by an Olmec ruler, later came into the
possession of a Maya king. The text opens with
four glyphs that usually comprise dedication
phrases on monuments and painted ceramics:
the introductory glyph *ALAY-ya* (here/here is)
is followed by the verbal compound *t'ab-ey*
(was dedicated). Two glyphs (A3-B3) may
name the object. The text describes a Maya
lord's seating in office (A5) followed by an
early *ajaw* and his name, which appears both in
the text (A6-B6 and C2-D2) and is inscribed
in his portrait above his left shoulder.

The axe was found in an elite tomb in
northern Belize with other royal jadeite jewelry (see Schele and Miller 1986, pls. 10, 19,
90). The axe form symbolized a maize plant
to the Olmec, a concept that may have been
well known to the Maya. The image dominat-
ing the top of the axe is the deity known as
GI of the Palenque Triad, or Chaak-Xib-Chaak,
whose costume includes shell earflares. This
tomb contained a jadeite version of a shell
earflare (Schele and Miller 1986, pl. 10), suggesting that Chaak-Xib-Chaak was the ruler's
patron. The brief glyphic text describes the
accession to office of the ruler, whose personal name concludes the inscription.

References:
90: Coe 1966; Schele and Miller 1986, 119–20; Benson
1996, 254; Wanyerka 2001, 79–80
91: Schele and Miller 1986, 227

Front

Back

90

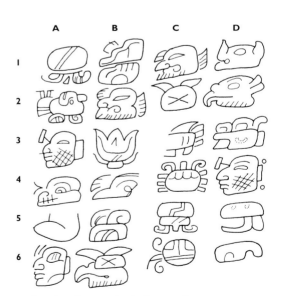

Drawing of text on back of pectoral

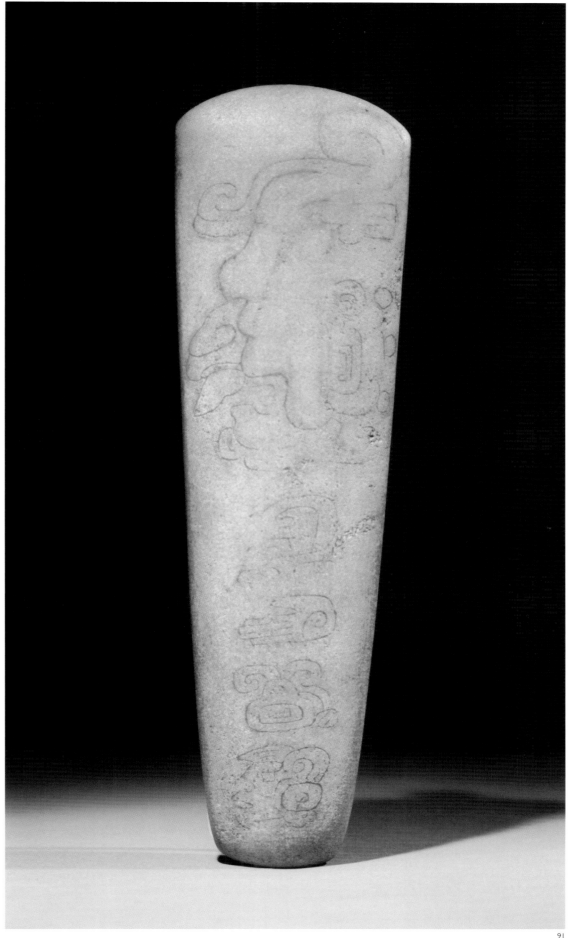

92

Belt Plaque Fragment

Maya Area, AD 250–400
Jadeite
4⅝ x 2⅛ in. (11.7 x 5.4 cm)
Dumbarton Oaks Research Library and Collections,
Washington, D.C. (PC.B. 586)

93

Belt Plaque Fragment

Maya Area, Central Lowlands, found in Guanacaste
Province, Costa Rica, AD 300–400
Jadeite
8⅞ x 1⅛ in. (22.6 x 2.9 cm)
Museo del Jade, Instituto Nacional de Seguros, San José,
Costa Rica (INS 4442)

94

Belt Plaque Fragment

Maya Area, Central Lowlands, found in Guanacaste
Province, Costa Rica, AD 300–400
Jadeite
8⅞ x 1¼ in. (22.5 x 3.1 cm)
Museo del Jade, Instituto Nacional de Seguros, San José,
Costa Rica (INS 4441)

These jadeite plaques, often incised with the
king's portrait and a hieroglyphic text, were
part of the belt assemblages worn by rulers.
During Maya dynastic upheavals, the victors
may have demonstrated their power by dis-
persing symbols of divine kingship such as
these three plaques, which were transported
to Costa Rica sometime between AD 350 and
600. The Costa Ricans changed the plaques'
orientation to mimic those worn by their
own elite: they cut the plaques in half and
drilled holes so the plaques could be suspended horizontally around the neck.

The Maya ruler shown on the trimmed
plaque (cat. 92) wears a wide belt with a
zoomorphic head. From the head hang three
plaques incised with a sign denoting "wind."
The text commemorates the completion of a
calendrical time period and the ruler's accession to power. The two eroded glyphs (A5-
B5), signifying a toad or saurian head, and a
profile human head resembling the Maize
God may represent the ruler's name. The final
glyphs are titles: the *ajaw* at A6 is identical to
that on cat. 89 (B4), and two titles (A7-B7)
are associated with primogeniture (see cats.
86 and 89).

92

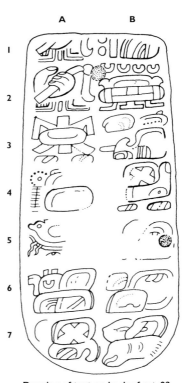

Drawing of text on back of cat. 92

Two of the plaques have been cut in half vertically, and only one column of the original two-column text and half of the incised figure can be seen. One fragment (cat. 93) shows the left side of a standing ruler. He holds a ceremonial bar; emerging from its lower end is a jaguar head surmounted by a foliated *ajaw*, a possible reference to Foliated Jaguar, an important but little-known person associated with Copan (Martin and Grube 2000, 193, 201).

The hieroglyphic text relates two dates and two events; all personal names were lost when the plaque was bisected. The first event is the conjuring (A3) of an unknown supernatural, followed by the sacred or holy primogenitor title. The second event is the ruler's accession to office (A5-A6). The last glyph is the head of the Sun God functioning as the title *k'inich ajaw* (sun-eyed lord). The ruler's mother is mentioned (A7-A8), although only the "child of mother" statement and the jaguar head part of her name survive.

Portions of the date and verbal statements on the other plaque (cat. 94) survive, but the names of the king and his parents are lost. The cartouches each originally contained four glyphs. The upper cartouche begins with a partial date; the middle cartouche recorded the king's mother (A3-A4); and the bottom cartouche likely recorded the king's name and titles. One glyph (A5) may be a deity name, often used in the names of Maya kings. The title at A6 is composed of the head of the Maize God, prefixed by the number 4, and followed by *k'inich*.

References:
92: Schele and Miller 1986, 82–83, pl. 22; Graham 1998, 51
93: Balser 1974, 33–35; Fields and Reents-Budet 1992
94: Balser 1974, 31; Fields and Reents-Budet 1992

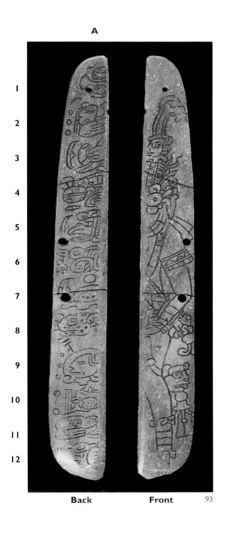

A

1	
2	
3	
4	
5	
6	
7	
8	
9	
10	
11	
12	

Back   **Front**   93

A

1
2
3
4
5
6

94

95

Lidded Vessel with Day Names

Guatemala, Tikal, Mundo Perdido, AD 300–450
Ceramic with slip
8 x 4 in. (20.3 x 10.2 cm)
Museo Nacional de Arqueología y Etnología, Guatemala
City (MNAE 11,138a, b)

96

Carved Bowl with Feathered Serpents

Maya Area, AD 539
Ceramic with stucco and pigment
6¾ x 9¼ in. diam. (17.2 x 23.5 cm)
The Metropolitan Museum of Art, Purchase, Fletcher
Fund and Arthur M. Bullowa Bequest, 2000 (2000.60)

The lidded vessel was found in Temple
5D-84, the northernmost shrine atop the
platform of Structure 5D-86, the E-Group
complex in Tikal's Mundo Perdido royal
compound. A woman was entombed there
with eight ceramic vessels, including the
cache dish with the portrait of a deified
ancestor (see cat. 67). The vessel here is
embellished with a sequence of day names,
including Imix and Ajaw, the first and last
days of the 260-day ritual calendar. The quality of the vessel's painting and modeling
indicates the highest level of artistic production, underscoring its owner's nobility.

The carved blackware bowl is decorated
with a complex tableau featuring two Vision
Serpents from whose open maws emerge
figures that may be the Hero Twins. This
serving bowl is unusual for the Long Count
date (9.2.15.4.16 1 K'ib 14 Sip; or 1 June
539) incised on its inside rim. The meaning
of this bowl's date is now lost, although
many sites, including Calakmul, Mexico, have
examples of incised death or resurrection
imagery on ceramics or tomb walls, inscriptions made by mourners and those entrusted
to close the tomb.

References:
95: Laporte and Fialko 1987; Reents-Budet et al. 1994,
327; Laporte 2000

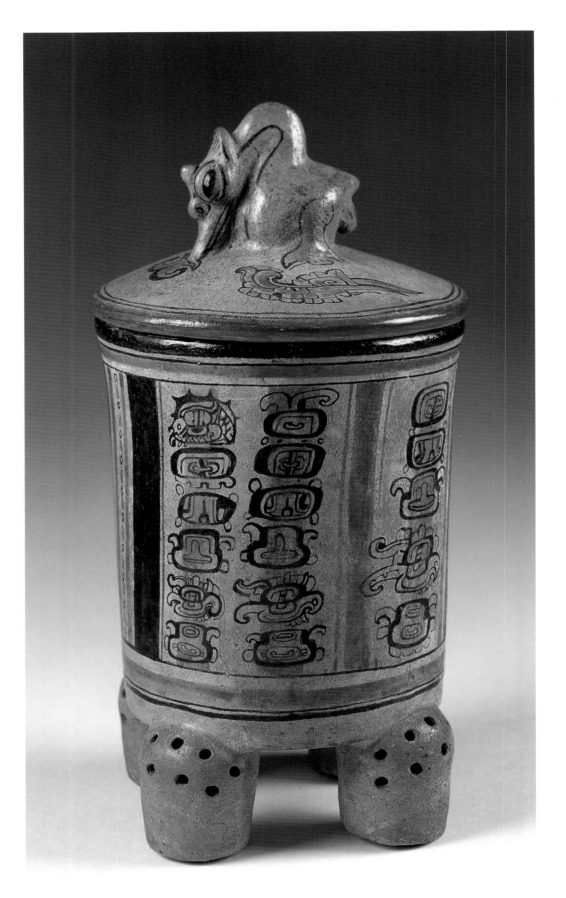

96

97

Stela 20

Belize, Caracol, AD 400
Limestone
31½ in. (80 cm)
Institute of Archaeology, Belmopan, Belize

Stela 20 was broken into many pieces in antiquity; its surviving sections graced the main entrance stairway of Caracol's E-Group complex. The lower section, excavated in 1950, depicts two people seated facing each other, one on an elaborate throne that has an overarching zoomorphic top (which may symbolize a sacred cave) and sprouting vegetation. The portrayed location may be a direct reference to Caana, a massive ceremonial building topped by three temples, which represents Caracol's mountain of creation.

The upper part of Stela 20, shown here, was excavated in 2002. It portrays a Caracol ruler, who became king in AD 400, standing atop the sacred mountain. A hieroglyphic text next to his head relates his name (eroded) and notes his title, Ux Witz Ajaw (Lord of the Three-Mountain Place). The stela's main text opens with a Long Count date, written with bar and dot numbers and the earliest full-figure variants of the period glyphs, that may be reconstructed as 8.18.4.4.14 12 Hix 2 Mol (19 September 400). The rest of the text has not survived on the retrieved fragments of the stela. The king's reign fits between those of two known rulers, but little information is available on Caracol's early history because few Early Classic monuments survive.

The portrait here depicts icons associated with the king's divine power, including the belt with anthropomorphic and zoomorphic heads, and the jadeite belt plaques. In front of his nose is a stylized flower, perhaps a reference to the king's breath soul. He holds a double-headed ceremonial bar that issues streams of sacred liquid marked with celestial signs. Deities and jaguarlike supernaturals float in the sacred waters, and the king is portrayed as the agent who brings forth these divine beings.

References:
Beetz and Satterthwaite 1981, fig. 81; Martin and Grube 2000, 100–115; Grube and Martin 2004, 14–16

98

Spouted Vessel with Hieroglyphic Text

Maya Area, 50 BC–AD 200
Indurated limestone with red veins
5⁵⁄₁₆ x 6⁵⁄₁₆ in. (13.5 x 16 cm)
The Metropolitan Museum of Art, Gift of Charles and
Valerie Diker, 1999 (1999.484.3)

99

Carved Dish

Guatemala, AD 250–450
Ceramic
5⅛ x 10¾ in. (13 x 27.3 cm)
Houston Museum of Natural Science, R. H. Wilson Jr.
Collection, museum purchase made possible by the Lillie
and Roy Cullen Endowment Fund (4443)

The spout of the limestone jar may indicate that the vessel was used to froth cacao liquid at the moment of serving, with the limestone helping to maintain a steady temperature. Two beings floating in smoke or mist are carved on the exterior; images such as this often portray deified ancestors or gods, and here they are suspended below a "sky" band marked with *ik'* signs that refer to wind, breath, and soul-force. These figures embody the dyad *k'in* and *ak'ab'* (sun/daylight and darkness/underworld). Maya spiritual beliefs often express the unseeable as cosmic oppositions symbolized by pairs of supernaturals or gods. Here, the figure with the squinting square eye may be the Jaguar God of the Underworld, his zoomorphic manifestation appearing below his feet. The human figure rides atop a long-snouted head whose eye recalls that of the Principal Bird Deity.

The short hieroglyphic text inscribed on the jar spout begins with a dedication phrase (A1-A2), followed by what may be an accession (A3) and stela-binding or divination rite (A4). It ends with the name or title of the text's protagonist (A5).

The text on the dish describes it as an *uk'ib kakaw* (vessel for drinking cacao) and gives its owner's name and titles. Three cartouches are incised with profile representations of individuals, perhaps deified ancestors whose names are rendered by the icons in their headdresses, their nominals including the Jester God, a divination mirror emerging from an *ajaw* glyph, and a compound comprising a jaguar head, paw, and tail, plus a bird wing.

Reference:
98: Coe 1973, 26–27

Royal Feasting

Feasting and gift-giving were integral to Mesoamerican social and political events, including heir designation and accession ceremonies, war victory celebrations, marriages, and religious observances. Kings established and maintained personal and political relationships by providing generous quantities of fine food and drink for their guests, and by giving gifts, thus openly conveying power and success. By participating in such feasts, guests accepted future obligations to provide economic and political support to the ruler, further solidifying his power.

Vessels developed from relatively simple forms in the Formative period to elaborate sculpted forms in the Early Classic. Vessels used during sumptuous feasts included basins, large platters, covered dishes, cylindrically shaped drinking vessels, and effigy forms, such as the serving vessel in the form of a deer (cat. 106). The Maya created many different drinks based on cacao, which was the preferred beverage of the royal court and a prized commodity in Mesoamerica from the Middle Formative period.

100

Squash Effigy Vessel

Mexico, Yucatan Peninsula, Acanceh, AD 450–550
Ceramic with orange slip
5½ x 6⅞ in. (14.1 x 17.5 cm)
CNCA-INAH, Museo Regional de Yucatan, "Palacio
Cantón," Merida, Mexico (10-426169)

101

Carved Bowl

Mexico, Yucatan Peninsula, AD 400–600
Limestone
3⅜ x 6¼ in. (8.6 x 15.9 cm)
Dumbarton Oaks Research Library and Collections,
Washington, D.C. (PC.B. 208)

The earliest food-serving container in
Mesoamerica was the gourd or calabash. It
pre-dates the domestication of maize (prior
to 5000 BC) and remains in use throughout
Mexico. During the Preclassic and Classic periods, artisans carved and painted containers

made from gourds and calabashes, although
these organic objects usually do not survive
in the Mesoamerican archaeological record.
Classic period artists also made replicas from
ceramic and stone, such as these two examples. The ceramic vessel, decorated with orange
slip, has an incised hieroglyphic text stating
that it is a drinking vessel for b'ukutz kakaw,
a chocolate-based drink served at feasts and
offered to the gods. The text ends with an
emblem glyph or place name of Akankeh,
the Yucatecan town today known as Acanceh.

The color and shape of the limestone
bowl mimic drinking vessels made from the
calabash. The incised images include hieroglyphic texts separating three cartouches,
each containing a figure and text. One cartouche features the god of cacao, his body
sprouting cacao pods, who points to a jar
likely filled with cacao drink. The text in front
of his face confirms his identity as ixim te'
(maize tree), a name found in texts painted
on many Classic period drinking vessels

that record their contents as ixim te'el kakaw
(maize-tree-like cacao). This underscores
the close relationship between cacao and the
Maize God. Maize was the principal food of
the Maya and cacao the preferred food of
the gods, and Classic and Postclassic period
beliefs indicate that the Maize God was resurrected from, variously, a maize plant, a calabash tree, or a cacao tree.

References:
100: Schmidt et al. 1998, 630; Miller and Martin 2004,
144, pl. 74
101: Miller and Martin 2004, 78–79, pl. 33

102

Censer Lid in Form of Female Holding Cacao

Guatemala, South Coast, AD 250–450
Ceramic
12⅗₆ x 16½ in. (32 x 42 cm)
Museo Nacional de Arqueología y Etnología, Guatemala City (MNAE 15,958)

103

Vessel in Form of Cormorant

Guatemala, Peten, AD 250–450
Ceramic with pigment
11 in. (28 cm)
Courtesy of David T. Owsley, via the Dallas Museum of Art

One of the most highly valued crops of the Pacific slopes of southern Guatemala was cacao. Representations of cacao are preserved in ceramics from this region, often in the form of incense burners or lidded cache vessels. This lid is modeled in the form of a young woman who holds a small bowl filled with cacao pods. She emerges from a pile of cacao beans, once used as a form of currency.

The Maya elite served a frothy cacao drink during feasts. The importance of these gatherings dictated the use of elaborate service vessels such as this unusual lidded container in the form of a cormorant with a tiny turtle attached to its breast. The text here begins with *y-uk'ib* (his drinking vessel), followed by a description of the vessel's contents. The artist has written the name of the cacao god rather than using the word for cacao. The text ends with the vessel owner's name and that of his father. The owner's name is incised on the disk attached to the back of the cormorant's head.

References:
102: Schmidt et al. 1998, 562
103: Emmerich 1984, cat. 50

102

103

View of text on back of vessel

104

104

Spouted Vessel

Mexico, Chiapas, Chiapa de Corzo, Mound 1, Tomb 1,
100 BC–AD 100
Ceramic with Usulutan resist decoration
8¼ x 7⁵⁄₁₆ in. (21 x 18.5 cm)
CNCA-INAH, Museo Nacional de Antropología,
Mexico City (10-000132)

105

Vessel

Guatemala, Tikal, Structure 5D-Sub-1-1st, Burial 85,
50 BC–AD 50
Ceramic with slip
16½ x 12¹⁵⁄₁₆ in. (42 x 32.8 cm)
Museo Nacional de Arqueología y Etnología, Guatemala
City (MNAE 9964)

106

Vessel in Form of Deer

Honduras, Copan, Structure 16, Hunal Tomb,
AD 430–435
Ceramic with slip
9¹³⁄₁₆ x 15⅜ in. (25 x 39 cm)
IHAH, Centro Regional de Investigaciones
Arqueológicas, Copan, Honduras (CPN-C-1761)

107 (catalogue only)

Lidded Vessel and Stand

Guatemala, Río Azul, Structure C-1, Tomb 19, AD 480
Ceramic with stucco and slip
13¾ x 6¾ in. (35 x 17 cm)
Museo Nacional de Arqueología y Etnología,
Guatemala City

Cacao had a prominent place at feasts, lending prestige to the feast's host and giving pleasure to his guests. It was created by mixing ground cacao beans, water, flavorings, and a sap-based foaming agent, and then pouring the liquid from vessel to vessel to produce a heady froth. During the Preclassic, spouted jars (cat. 104) and tall cylinder vessels (cat. 105) likely were used during feasts to prepare and serve cacao drinks.

Vessels filled with cacao also were placed in tombs to provide sustenance for the deceased in the afterlife. One such vessel (cat. 107) was found in the burial of an aristocratic man at Río Azul. This tomb was dug into bedrock underlying the platform that supported an early funerary temple perhaps

105

211

associated with Río Azul's tenth ruler. This globular lidded vessel has a hieroglyphic text stating that it was for cacao (see first glyph on lid at right), and the vessel itself contained powdery residue of a cacao beverage.

Pinole is made from cacao and ground maize, and the residue of both were discovered inside the deer effigy vessel (cat. 106) from the tomb of Yax K'uk' Mo', the founder of Copan's ruling dynasty (McNeil et al. in press). The vessel contained a delicate shell scoop in the shape of a human hand, which was stained reddish brown from the contents and the powdered cinnabar ritually scattered over the tomb's contents.

Other references:
104: Lowe 1990, 83; Schmidt et al. 1998, 572
105: Coe and McGinn 1963
106: Sharer 1999; Reents-Budet et al. 2004a, 172–73
107: Hall et al. 1990; Adams 1999, 53, 122, 129, 144, pl. 5

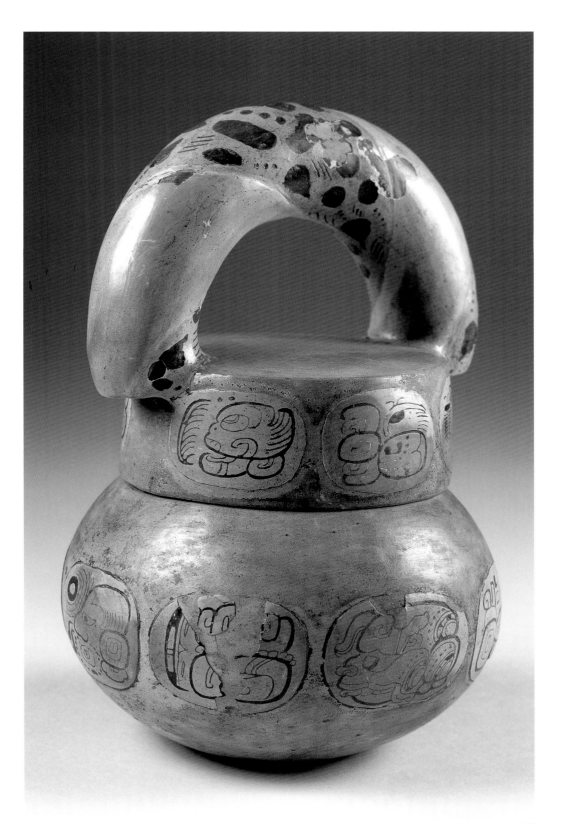

107

108

Tetrapod Vessel

Guatemala, Central Peten, 50 BC–AD 200
Ceramic with slip
9⅞ x 5½ in. (25 x 14 cm)
The Art Institution, New York (1990.0447)

109

Lidded Tripod Vessel with Hieroglyphic Text

Maya Area, Central Peten, AD 250–400
Ceramic
6 x 3 in. (15.2 x 7.6 cm)
Promised gift to the Fine Arts Museums of San Francisco

110

Plate

Guatemala, Tikal, Mundo Perdido, AD 150–300
Ceramic with slip
15 x 5¼ in. (38 x 13.4 cm)
Museo Nacional de Arqueología y Etnología, Guatemala City (MNAE 11,130)

111

Lidded Dish with Bird-Head Knob

Guatemala, Tikal, Mundo Perdido, AD 250–400
Ceramic with slip
7¾ x 6½ in. (19.6 x 16.5 cm)
Museo Nacional de Arqueología y Etnología, Guatemala City (MNAE 11,131a, b)

112

Lidded Dish Depicting Macaw

Guatemala, Central Peten, AD 250–400
Ceramic with slip
Diam.: approx. 20 in. (50.8 cm)
The Art Institution, New York (1991.0089a, b)

During the Early Classic period, artists eschewed the elaborately modeled, monochrome painted shapes of the Preclassic period in favor of more simplified forms intricately embellished with incised and, especially, painted imagery. These austere shapes, mostly cylinders and plates, provided an uninterrupted surface for images and texts, the latter being a particularly effective marker of prestige.

The change from complex modeling to intricate surface decoration was gradual, its first manifestations combining Preclassic

108

109

View of text on back of vessel

110

111

features (tall, mammiform supports or "feet," and modeled knobs) with the simpler Early Classic forms (cylindrical vases and wide plates with flat bottoms) that were then painted with complicated, symbolic designs. Early Classic artists continued making lidded vessels in the shapes of animals (cat. 112), although painted decoration now predominated.

Artists also developed individual painting styles that conveyed distinction and status to both the regal patron and the gift recipient. Often, the name and noble parentage of the patron or recipient was recorded on the vessel (cat. 109). Here, the text begins by noting that the vessel is for cacao, and ends with a long title sequence naming the patron/owner

and his father, who carries the regal title "west" *kaloomte'*.

Two vessels were among the offerings found in two burials at Tikal's Mundo Perdido complex, which was the residential and administrative center of Tikal until AD 378. The large plate (cat. 110) came from a rich cache of pottery vessels and greenstone artifacts (PNT-010) below the floor in Room 3 of Structure 5D-86, the group's central structure. Archaeologist Juan Pedro Laporte suggests that the cache came from the royal tomb (PNT-021), which was sacked during the fourth century. The four-footed dish with bird-effigy lid (cat. 111) was found in the burial of an infant, who was adorned with

greenstone jewelry; the burial was below the floor of Structure 5D-84, the northernmost shrine of the complex's E-Group, an assemblage of buildings associated with ancestral veneration rites.

References:
110: Laporte and Fialko 1987; Laporte 1995, 21; Schmidt et al. 1998, 644
111: Laporte and Fialko 1987; Schmidt et al. 1998, 575; Laporte 2000, 14–15

International Relations

Social, political, and economic relations among Maya cities as well as more distant powers are reflected in the artifacts found as offerings in building-dedication caches and elite tombs. Beautifully painted ceramic vessels were widely exchanged within the Maya region, while international relations are implied by the presence of royal Maya jadeite jewelry in ancient burials in northwestern Costa Rica and the highlands of Mexico.

During the fourth century, the Maya came into close contact with the powerful city of Teotihuacan in highland central Mexico. Named by the Aztecs one thousand years after its demise, Teotihuacan, or the City of the Gods, was the second largest city in the world in AD 350. Mutually beneficial commercial interests likely were a prime impetus for interaction, focusing on commodities such as obsidian (especially the green obsidian from the Pachuca source near Teotihuacan), cacao, cotton, spondylus shell, tropical bird feathers, and jadeite and other precious stones.

Maya hieroglyphic texts and works of art from this period suggest that powerful individuals aligned with Teotihuacan came to the Maya region, where they apparently held positions of authority in Maya courts, married into local royal families, and introduced new religious and political concepts. This prompted Maya rulers to portray themselves in Teotihuacan-style clothing and to furnish their tombs with objects made either by Teotihuacan artists or by Maya artists in Teotihuacan style. While scholars initially thought the direction of exchange was from west to east, it appears that the interaction was reciprocal as revealed in Burial 5 from the Pyramid of the Moon at Teotihuacan (see cats. 130–33).

113

Censer Lid Portraying Yax K'uk' Mo'

Honduras, Copan, Structure 26, Burial XXXVII-4,
AD 600–700
Ceramic with traces of post-fire pigment
27⅜ x 11⅝ in. (69.5 x 29.5 cm)
IHAH, Museo Arqueológico de Copan, Honduras
(CPN-C-1489)

114

Tripod Vessel with Image of Warrior Dressed as Tlaloc

Mexico, Teotihuacan, AD 550–650
Ceramic with red, green, white, and ochre slip
5½ in. (14 cm)
Los Angeles County Museum of Art, Gift of Constance
McCormick Fearing (AC1993.217.16)

Early Classic Maya rulers often used Teotihuacan icons and architectural styles to convey their authority, based on actual or perceived connections to that powerful metropolis. Artists interwove Teotihuacan motifs with traditional Maya elements on objects for personal use as well as on monumental architecture and public sculpture, fashioning a new visual language of political power.

Yax K'uk' Mo' (r. AD 426–ca. 437), the founder of Copan's ruling dynasty, is always shown with large rings around his eyes, ornaments that typify the Central Mexican storm god, who is also associated with warfare (see cat. 114). Portraits of Yax K'uk' Mo' often include his name rendered in his headdress by a quetzal (k'uk') with the eye of a macaw (mo'); on the censer lid this is implied by long feathers. It had been thought that Yax K'uk' Mo' came from Teotihuacan, but chemical analyses of his skeletal remains and pottery from his tomb suggest that he was of

Maya origin and came from somewhere between Copan and Tikal.

This is one of twelve censer effigy lids portraying the first twelve kings of Copan; all were found guarding a tomb entrance beneath the famous Hieroglyphic Stairway, on which is carved the longest Classic period stone text, a chronicle of the ruling dynasty of Copan. The tomb was thought to be that of a royal scribe given its contents, which included a decayed codex, ten paint pots, and a dish decorated with the image of a painter/scribe. However, the large quantity of royal accoutrements, the matting wrapped around the body, and the fact that the stairway above the tomb is named "the steps of Smoke Imix"—Copan's twelfth ruler—suggest that this might be his burial.

Reference:
113: Fash 1991, 79–84, 106–11

115

Tripod Vessel with Human Figure

Mexico, Campeche, Becan, Structure XIV, Room 3,
AD 450–550
Ceramic
6½ x 7⅛ in. (16.5 x 18 cm)
CNCA-INAH, Museo Regional de Yucatan, "Palacio
Cantón," Merida, Mexico (10-251140 0/41)

This vessel was part of a dedication cache deposited during the construction of a new building atop the ruins of an older building. The figure incised on the vessel resembles the Maya rain god Chaak. He sits in front of the sacred "jade mountain," the origin of precious things such as rain. When it was found, the vessel contained a Teotihuacan-style hollow figure. The figure had broken and spilled its contents, which included ten solid figurines, six of which portray Teotihuacan warriors. Two others portray non-Teotihuacan-style men, and two wear the Teotihuacan-like mosaic headgear with chin strap adopted by the Maya.

Archaeologist Joseph Ball, who excavated the cache, interprets it as a "victory offering" or a gift associated with funerary visitation. Both the cache and the construction of a new building coincide with ceramic changes at Becan that imply that the site shifted its focus from northern Yucatan to the Peten lowlands in the south during the sixth century. It is tempting to suggest that this cache is a reflection of political changes in the Maya lowlands after the fall of Teotihuacan as a major power, and that the Maya-style vessel was symbolically "containing" Teotihuacan's military might.

References:
Ball 1974; Ball 1977, 172–73; Clancy 1985, 118–19

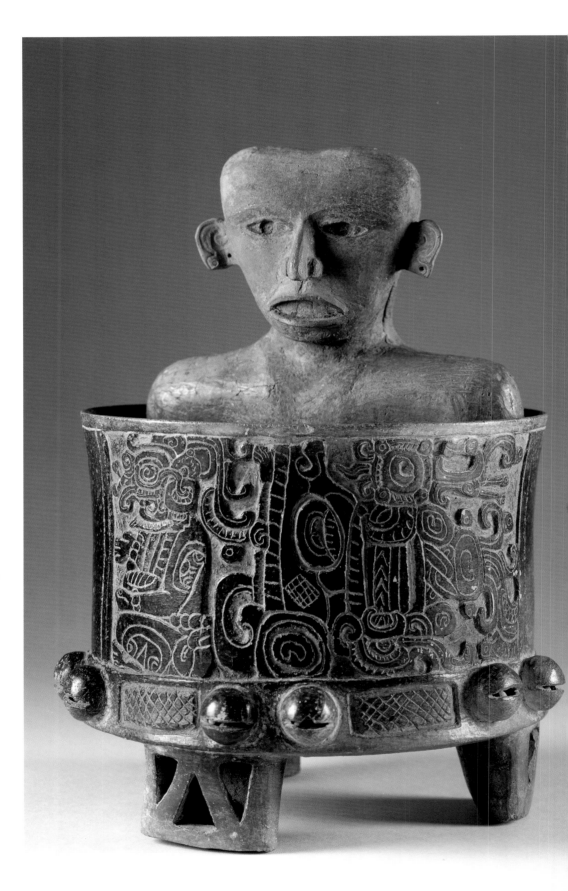

116

Figurine (La Muñeca)

Mexico, Yucatan, Yaxuna, Tomb 2, AD 350–450
Ceramic and slip
8⅞ x 5¹⁵⁄₁₆ x 2¾ in. (22.5 x 15 x 7 cm)
CNCA-INAH, Museo Regional de Yucatan, "Palacio
Cantón," Merida, Mexico (10-490149)

This hollow painted figurine was found cradled in the arms of a young woman interred at Yaxuna, a site near Chichen Itza in northern Yucatan. The tomb contained the remains of eleven other individuals—men, women, and children—perhaps members of the site's Early Classic ruling family who may have been assassinated. The burial's primary male had been decapitated, the usual sacrificial method for battle captives and deposed rulers. The young woman holding the figurine was one of two young women wearing the jadeite jewelry of royalty; she was also surrounded by the greatest number of grave goods, including accoutrements usually associated with male rulers. Archaeologists David Freidel and Charles Suhler, who excavated the tomb, suggest she was the heir apparent to the Yaxuna throne.

The ceramics in Tomb 2 include local wares as well as vessels from the Puuc area to the west, which are similar to ceramics from Oxkintok, a Maya site with numerous ceramic and architectural indications of links with Teotihuacan. This figurine was made in Yucatan, perhaps even at Oxkintok, although its Maya artisans followed Teotihuacan models for figural representation and ornamentation. The effigy's style and its placement by Yaxuna's usurpers in the arms of the heir apparent clearly signaled their appropriation of the right to rule.

Reference:
Ardren 2002, 81–87

116

117

Tripod Vessel

Guatemala, Kaminaljuyu, Mound A, Tomb A-I,
AD 400–500
Ceramic with slip and red pigment
7⅝ x 8¼ in. (19.5 x 21 cm)
Museo Nacional de Arqueología y Etnología, Guatemala
City (MNAE 2401)

118

Tripod Vessel

Mexico, Teotihuacan, AD 400–600
Brown terra-cotta with red burnished slip
5¾ in. (14.6 cm)
Los Angeles County Museum of Art, Gift of Constance
McCormick Fearing (M.83.217.33)

119

Lidded Tripod Vessel

Guatemala, Kaminaljuyu, Mound B, Tomb B-II,
AD 400–500
Ceramic with stucco and pigment
11⅝ x 6 in. (29.5 x 15.2 cm)
Museo Nacional de Arqueología y Etnología, Guatemala
City (MNAE 2574)

120

Lidded Tripod Vessel

Guatemala, Kaminaljuyu, Mound B, Tomb B-II,
AD 400–500
Ceramic with stucco and pigment
11¼ x 5½ in. (28.6 x 14 cm)
Museo Nacional de Arqueología y Etnología, Guatemala
City (MNAE 2575)

121

Carved Mirror Back

Guatemala, Kaminaljuyu, Mound B, Tomb B-I,
AD 400–500
Slate with pigment
7½ in. (19.2 cm)
Museo Nacional de Arqueología y Etnología, Guatemala
City (MNAE 3187)

122

Tripod Vessel with Image of Two Plumed Jaguar Heads

Maya Area, AD 400–650
Ceramic with stucco and pigment
Diam.: 8 in. (20.3 cm)
The Princeton University Art Museum (y1969-15)

Artifacts from Kaminaljuyu's Mounds A and B imply intimate contact with Teotihuacan during the latter decades of the fourth century. This interaction had a significant although short-lived impact on local architectural styles and elite burial patterns. Evidence suggests that most of the individuals interred in the thirteen tombs in these two mounds were Maya who adopted and adapted highland Mexican behaviors as a statement of political power. The few artworks from these tombs that were made in the Mexican highlands suggest that Teotihuacan individuals married into Kaminaljuyu's ruling dynasty to solidify their position within this powerful Maya center.

118

The incised tripod vessel (cat. 117) was found in a tomb, which had been created inside Mound A during a rebuilding phase that featured Maya-style architecture and burial traditions. The tomb chamber was used for many decades, and it contained at least eight individuals. The last person interred was a woman, the only female among the thirteen tombs. Around her were numerous objects, including this incised vessel. This tripod form is associated with Teotihuacan ceramic traditions (compare cat. 118), yet its elegant out-curving walls and decorative program are Maya in style and narrative content. This woman may have been joined in a royal marriage between Kaminaljuyu and Teotihuacan's ruling elite.

Two tombs in Mound B epitomize a new burial pattern that recalls that of Teotihuacan, in which the interred were usually placed in a seated position. Burial offerings included both local and foreign artifacts from other Maya areas, Veracruz, and Central Mexico. New types of offerings, which also recall Teotihuacan, include offering bowls (instead of the Maya-style cache vessels), dog skeletons, shell eye rings, and mosaic disks. Tomb B-I is the most "Teotihuacan" of the thirteen burials. The tomb contained three individuals dressed as Teotihuacan warriors, with Tlaloc-like shell rings on their foreheads or over their eyes. The Veracruz-style mirror (cat. 121), which was worn by Skeleton 2, depicts two figures facing each other across a vessel that may contain offerings of food or copal.

Although Tomb B-II resembles Tomb B-I, only two of the six stucco-and-painted tripod vessels found in the tomb were decorated in Teotihuacan style; the other four were embellished with Maya motifs and narratives (cats. 119, 120). One vessel (cat. 120) renders a king in the guise of the Maize God emerging from the mouth of the Vision Serpent. He holds the headband of royal office and faces the sacred mountain of creation. A saurian head, with a U-shaped *ajaw* symbol on its forehead, is on the vessel's lid. The other vessel (cat. 119) shows a king seated on a throne. Though dressed in Teotihuacan style, with spangled headdress, back mirror, and feather panache, the figure wears Maya-style jadeite jewelry.

This hybrid aesthetic is particularly well represented by the stucco-and-painted tripod vessel (cat. 122). Although the vessel's shape and tripod supports indicate that it likely originated in a Maya workshop, it is decorated with a Teotihuacan-style supernatural jaguar devouring a human heart and surrounded by life-giving water/blood.

References:
118–22: Smith and Kidder 1943; Kidder et al. 1946; Santley 1983; Wright 1998; Reents-Budet and Culbert 1999; Reents-Budet et al. 2004b

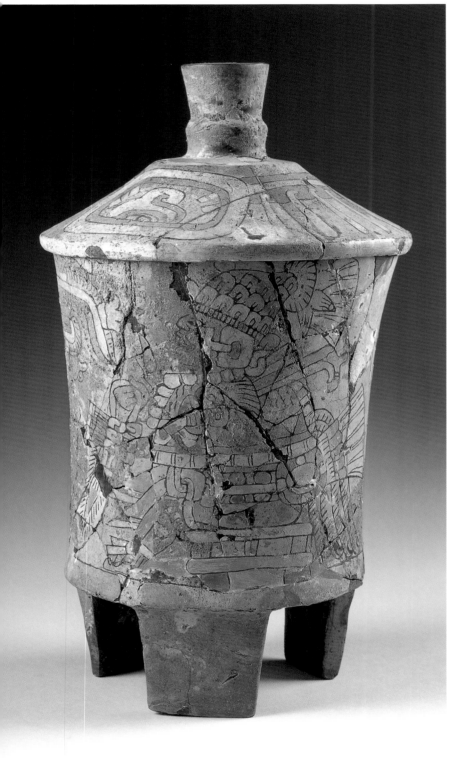

119

120

121

122

123

Vessel in Form of Dog

Guatemala, Kaminaljuyu, Mound A, Tomb A-III,
AD 400–500
Thin Orange ceramic
3¼ x 7½ in. (8.4 x 19 cm)
Museo Nacional de Arqueología y Etnología, Guatemala
City (MNAE 2439)

124

Vessel in Form of Dog

Mexico, Teotihuacan, AD 400–500
Thin Orange ceramic
2⅞ x 5⁵⁄₁₆ in. (7.3 x 14.2 cm)
Los Angeles County Museum of Art, Gift of Constance
McCormick Fearing (AC1998.209.18)

Thin Orange, a hallmark of Teotihuacan pottery, has a characteristic orange color and very thin walls. Chemical analysis has identified its origins in the state of Puebla, to the east of Teotihuacan. Thin Orange pottery has been found in late-fourth-century burials at a number of Maya sites, including Kaminaljuyu, Copan, and Tikal, although some of these are local reproductions. The burials from Kaminaljuyu's Mounds A and B that most closely follow Teotihuacan funerary patterns contained dog skeletons (Tombs A-VI, B-I, B-II) or a Thin Orange ceramic dog effigy (Tomb A-III; cat. 123). Among the Aztec and other highland Mexican peoples, dogs guided souls on their journey through the underworld. The similarity between the Kaminaljuyu canine effigy and that from the Mexican highlands (cat. 124) suggests it was imported from Mexico.

References:
123: Kidder et al. 1946, figs. 179f, 207c; Rattray and Harbottle 1992; Neff 2000

125
Lidded Tripod Vessel

Honduras, Copan, Sub-Jaguar Tomb, AD 525
Ceramic with stucco and pigment
9 x 4½ in. (22.9 x 11.4 cm)
IHAH, Centro Regional de Investigaciones
Arqueológicas, Copan, Honduras (CPN-C-1513)

126
Lidded Tripod Vessel

Honduras, Copan, Sub-Jaguar Tomb, AD 525
Ceramic with stucco and pigment
9⅝ x 4⅝ in. (24.4 x 11.7 cm)
IHAH, Centro Regional de Investigaciones
Arqueológicas, Copan, Honduras (CPN-C-1512)

127
Lidded Tripod Vessel

Guatemala, Tikal, Structure 5D-34, Burial 10, AD 404
Ceramic with stucco and pigment
9⅝ x 3½ in. (24.4 x 8.8 cm)
Museo Nacional de Arqueología y Etnología, Guatemala
City (MNAE 10,029a, b)

128
Tripod Vessel with Maya Hieroglyphs

Honduras, Copan, Sub-Jaguar Tomb, AD 525
Ceramic with stucco and pigment
11 x 11⅞ in. (27.9 x 30 cm)
IHAH, Centro Regional de Investigaciones
Arqueológicas, Copan, Honduras (CPN-C-1517)

129
Tripod Vessel with Teotihuacan Hieroglyphs

Honduras, Copan, Sub-Jaguar Tomb, AD 525
Ceramic with stucco and pigment
10¹¹⁄₁₆ x 11½ in. (27.2 x 29.2 cm)
IHAH, Centro Regional de Investigaciones
Arqueológicas, Copan, Honduras (CPN-C-1516)

Evidence of interaction with Teotihuacan is especially noted in late-fourth-century royal burials at Copan and Tikal, which were furnished with Teotihuacan-style ceramics. At Tikal, Burial 10 contained the remains of Yax Nuun Ayiin I, who took the throne in AD 379 and died on 17 June 404. His body lay upon a wooden litter or funerary bier, and at least nine sacrificed young men accompanied him to the underworld. Jade jewels, five turtle

125

carapaces, and many stuccoed-and-painted ceramic vessels were in the tomb, including the lidded tripod vessel (cat. 127). Its form and decorative technique recall Teotihuacan ceramics, while its imagery and hieroglyphic texts are Mayan. The vessel's chemical composition implies that it was made in a Tikal workshop that produced wares for an exclusive clientele.

The Sub-Jaguar Tomb, found beneath the Jaguar Stairs at Copan, may be the burial of Ruler 8, a mid-sixth-century ruler. The interred individual had a shell spangle headdress like that worn in death by Yax K'uk' Mo' (see Bell, this volume, and Agurcia Fasquelle, this volume). There were twenty-eight ceramic vessels in the tomb, of which sixteen were made in the vicinity of Quirigua, an important site in the nearby Motagua River Valley that in later years would become a formidable adversary of Copan. The pottery in the Sub-Jaguar Tomb, however, indicates that relations were friendlier during the sixth century.

Stucco was applied over the original carved-incised and slip-painted surfaces of the pair of lidded tripod vessels (cats. 125, 126). The post-fire painted imagery, which depicts a feathered feline devouring a human heart, recalls Teotihuacan iconography, while the curvilinear image style, human portrait head knobs, and profile saurian heads on the lids are all from Maya artistic canons. In addition, the chemical composition of the paste on both vessels is nearly identical to that of ceramics produced at Quirigua.

The two lidless tripod vessels might also have been made as a pair, and likely in a Quirigua workshop. Both depict water or sacred liquid motifs, one with Maya-style (cat. 128) and the other with Teotihuacan-style imagery (cat. 129). The Maya-style vessel is decorated with four saurian heads in cartouches. The vessel with Teotihuacan-style images is embellished with three images of a feather-encircled star with water issuing from its lower edge.

Other references:
125–26, 128–29: Bell et al. 2004b, 151–54; Reents-Budet et al. 2004a, 181–90, fig. 9.14
127: Coggins 1975; Coe 1990; Culbert 1993, fig. 19c; Martin and Grube 2000, 29–33

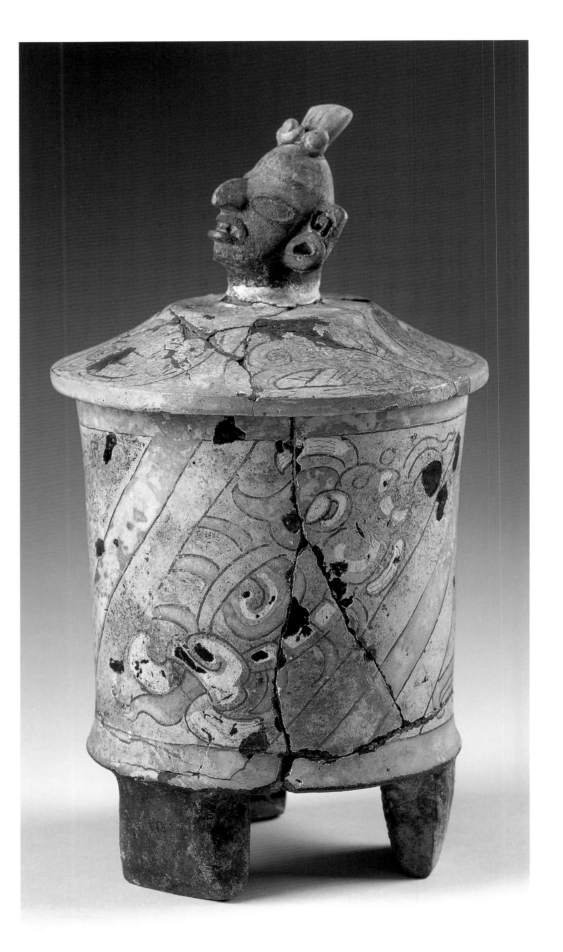

128

129

130 (bottom)

Necklace, Pectoral, and Earflares

Mexico, Teotihuacan, Pyramid of the Moon, Burial 5,
Individual 5B, AD 400–500
Jadeite
Pectoral: 4⅛ x 1⅜ in. (10.5 x 3.5 cm); earflares: diam.
1½ x 3 in. (3.9 x 7.6 cm)

131 (top)

Seated Figure with Pectoral, Necklace, and Earflares

Mexico, Teotihuacan, Pyramid of the Moon, Burial 5,
AD 400–500
Jadeite
Figure: 4⅞ x 3¼ x 2¼ in. (12.3 x 8.2 x 5.7 cm); earflares:
1½ x 2¼ in. (3.9 x 5.7 cm)

130–31

132 (bottom)

Necklace, Pectoral, and Earflares

Mexico, Teotihuacan, Pyramid of the Moon, Burial 5,
Individual 5A, AD 400–500
Jadeite
Pectoral: 4³⁄₁₆ in. (10.4 cm); earflares: diam. approx.
2⅞ in. (7.3 cm)

133 (top)

Standing Figures

Mexico, Teotihuacan, Pyramid of the Moon, Burial 5,
AD 400–500
Obsidian
Largest: 8⅝ in. (22 cm)

Proyecto Pirámide de la Luna (INAH/Aichi Prefectural
University/Arizona State University)

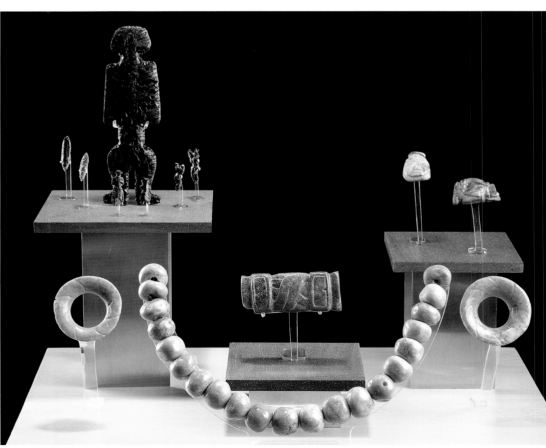

132–33

134

Plaque Portraying Seated King and Attendant

Maya Area, found near Teotihuacan, AD 600–800
Jadeite
5½ x 5½ in. (14 x 14 cm)
Courtesy of the Trustees of The British Museum
(AM1938, 1021.25)

Several tombs and burials have recently been found inside the Pyramid of the Moon, the dominant building at the north end of Teotihuacan's so-called Avenue of the Dead. Burial 5, discovered by archaeologists Rubén Cabrera and Saburo Sugiyama, contained three high-ranking individuals. Isotopic analysis of their skeletal remains indicates they were from the southern highlands of Guatemala. They were buried in a seated position, and the form and iconography of the jewelry they wore indicate a Maya origin and substantiate the isotopic signatures.

The richness of the objects in the tomb, its location inside one of Teotihuacan's most important ritual buildings, and the foreign origins of the interred individuals provide a counterpart to similar Teotihuacan remains found in the Maya region. Together, these point to a symbiotic relationship between the two cultures, rather than one of Teotihuacan dominance.

The burial's Individual 5A, likely a man between fifty and sixty years of age, was adorned with jadeite jewelry, including a necklace, a pectoral with a crossed-bands motif, and earflares with an incised decoration (cat. 132). Individual 5B, a man between forty-five and forty-nine years of age, wore jewelry (cat. 130) similar to that of Individual 5A. Individual 5C, the tomb's principal occupant, was heavily adorned with finely made jewelry, including jadeite and shell.

A cache in the center of the tomb contained a seated jadeite figurine (cat. 131) wearing a pectoral, two greenstone bead necklaces, and earflares; freshwater and marine shells; obsidian figurines; and decayed organic remains. The figurine, which likely held a scepter or standard, replicates the seated position of the individuals and probably played a symbolic role. Other offerings filled the tomb chamber, including animal skeletons, shells, greenstone adornments,

projectile points, stone disks, and obsidian blades and figures (cat. 133).

The portrait plaque (cat. 134) was found in a field near Teotihuacan in the 1930s. It depicts a sacred king, who wears a Jester God jewel and is seated on an altarlike throne. The plaque was probably a royal jewel, and its presence at Teotihuacan implies high-level contact between the two cultures, much like that indicated by Burial 5. The plaque's edges were re-carved in antiquity and a new suspension hole was drilled through its upper end.

References:
130–33: Sugiyama and Cabrera 2003, 42–49
134: Schele and Miller 1986, 122, pl. 34; McEwan 1994, 41

134

Death and Apotheosis

According to Maya cosmology, the gods initially made humans from a variety of substances before they created successful humans from a mixture of yellow and white maize, preserved in a sacred cave inside the primordial Mountain of Sustenance. Through the personal blood sacrifice of the gods, humanity was infused with life. The life cycle of humans was intimately tied to the life cycle of maize, reflected in the corollary stages of planting, germination, harvest, death, and regeneration.

Rich layers of symbolism surrounded Maya conceptions of the breath soul, the animated life force of the body, which was linked to the aroma of flowers and to beautiful sounds, especially music (Taube 2001, 272). Death was defined as the expiration of the breath soul, when the journey after death began, expressed metaphorically in ancient texts as *och b'ih* (he enters the road). Upon his demise, the king passed into the underworld, where he endured ordeals at the hands of the Lords of the Underworld. After defeating these lords of death, as the Hero Twins did in mythic time, the king was reborn in the guise of the Maize God, ultimately becoming a deified ancestor venerated by his successors.

135

Mosaic Funerary Mask

Mexico, Campeche, Calakmul, Structure II-D, Tomb 1,
AD 200–600
Jadeite, shell, and obsidian
7½ x 5⅞ in. (19 x 15 cm)
CNCA-INAH, Museo Histórico Fuerte de San Miguel,
Baluarte de San Miguel, Campeche, Mexico (10-397992)

136

Tripod Vessel with Burial Scene

Guatemala, AD 400–450
Ceramic
6 x 8 in. (15.2 x 20.3 cm)
Staatliche Museen zu Berlin, Preussischer Kulturbesitz,
Ethnologisches Museum, Berlin (IV CA 49845)

137

Tripod Vessel with Mythological Scene

Guatemala, AD 400–450
Ceramic
8⅛ x 12 in. (20.5 x 30.5 cm)
Miho Museum, Shigaraki, Japan

The expiration of the king's breath soul is portrayed on the mosaic funerary mask by the white shell curls on each side of the mouth. This remarkably naturalistic mask was worn by a member of the Calakmul elite, whose tomb was located below the floor of a building atop the first tier of Structure II, the site's largest pyramid.

The two incised blackware vessels are similar in shape and formal decorative features, suggesting they may have come from the same area if not the same workshop in the Peten lowlands. The burial scene vessel (cat. 136) depicts the entombment of a lord. His cloth-wrapped body rests on a stone bier, and he wears the headband of Itzamnaaj. The hieroglyphs on the supports record his name and describe his death sojourn as "entering the road." The tomb is symbolically located in the sacred maize mountain, which appears behind the bier. Six young women stand in the underworld waters, mourning his death. The vessel's second scene depicts the lord's resurrection in the company of his deified parents, represented by three anthropomorphic trees growing from his skeletal body. The center tree, a cacao, is the lord, and his name glyph is atop his head. His father is portrayed as a calabash tree and his mother as a tree

with vinelike serpents in its branches. Their bent arms and sinuous fingers resemble the paws of the crocodilian world tree on the other incised blackware vessel. The tomb's encasing pyramid is superimposed over the maize mountain, here marked with *ak'ab'* (darkness) icons and a sprouting maize seed at its summit.

The other incised vessel (cat. 137) depicts a complex mythological scene that has been interpreted as a portrayal of the Maya afterlife or "flower mountain of paradise." Two musicians play maracas and a drum, and the scene is graced by flowers and birds. A Vision Serpent surrounds the vessel, his body entwined with various cosmic entities, including the crocodilian world tree. The tree is rendered both vertically and horizontally (under the Vision Serpent), and both have rippled digits. K'awiil emerges from the underworld along the trunk of a ceiba tree, and the head of the wind god can be seen below the vertical crocodilian world tree. The Vision Serpent's tail encircles the location's name (6-wind sky-cave/enclosure), which comprises the names of many underworld locations. The two-column hieroglyphic text notes that this was the drinking vessel of a lord of Ucanal (*k'an-witz-nal*), who was subordinate to Siyaj Chan K'awiil II (r. AD 411–456), the sixteenth king in the Tikal dynasty established by Yax Ehb' Xook.

References:
135: Carrasco Vargas 2000, 16–17; García-Moreno and Granados 2000, 28
136: Entry compiled by Dr. Maria Gaida, Staatliche Museen zu Berlin, Preussischer Kulturbesitz, Ethnologisches Museum, Berlin. Taube 2004b; Martin in press
137: Freidel and Schele 1988b; Zender 2004, entry 34; Berjonneau et al. 1985, 218–19

136

Rollout view

Rollout view

138

Lidded Vessel with Figure of Canoer

Maya Area, Central Lowlands, AD 300–500
Ceramic
12 x 9¼ in. (30.6 x 23.6 cm)
Dallas Museum of Art, The Roberta Coke Camp Fund
(1988.82.A–B)

139

Cache Vessel Lid

Maya Area, Central Lowlands, AD 350–500
Ceramic
2¼ x 14⅛ in. (5.7 x 35.9 cm)
Courtesy of The Cleveland Museum of Art

The lidded vessel depicts a figure, or soul, seated in a canoe and paddling through the underworld's black waters. A fish perches on the back of the figure, whose head and back are incised with the sign k'in (sun). These markings connect the figure with the Sun God and the sun itself, whose diurnal journey provided a metaphor for human life. In Maya belief, the sun accompanied dead souls on their journey and the two became a single entity. The vessel's four supports are modeled as peccary heads; the star sign above their eyes identifies them as the constellation Gemini.

The life cycle of the maize plant also provided a metaphor for life after death. It was expressed in the allegorical life cycle of the Maize God, who was decapitated by the Lords of the Underworld. His sons, the Hero Twins, retrieved his bones and resurrected him, and he danced out of the underworld through a split in the earth's surface. On the incised cache dish lid, the Maize God's head rests on an offering plate shaped like a canoe. This plate makes reference to the gods' personal blood sacrifice, which created the cosmos. Three tools of sacrifice—an obsidian blade, a stingray spine, and a flint blade—float above the Maize God's face; these tools were also used by the Maya to undertake vision quests. Here, the underworld's watery realm is represented by blood, underscoring the Maize God's sacrifice.

References:
138: MacLeod and Puleston 1980, 71–78; Schele and Miller 1986, 270–71
139: Schele and Miller 1986, 195; Freidel et al. 1993, 217; Christenson 2003

138

139

140

Lidded Dish

Guatemala, Holmul, Group II, Building B, Room 2,
AD 400–550
Ceramic with stucco and pigment
8⁵⁄₁₆ x 11 in. (21.1 x 28 cm)
Peabody Museum of Archaeology and Ethnology,
Harvard University (11-6-20/C5576)

Many Early Classic slip-painted vessels were
decorated with post-fire stucco and paint.
The decoration was used to coat the vessel in
fields of color, such as the red and green seen
on this lidded dish from Holmul, or to create
pictorial imagery, iconic motifs, and hieroglyphic texts. Most of the vessels seem to have
been redecorated just before they were placed
in burials, although the reasons for this are
unknown. The process recalls the white stucco repainting of the polychromed exterior of
Copan's Rosalila temple, before it was buried
underneath new construction. This ritual

embalming of the temple resembles modern
practices among the Ch'orti Maya who dress
corpses and images of their death god in
white cloth (Agurcia Fasquelle 2004, 101–2).

This dish was found in a burial in
Building B, a monumental, acropolis-like
construction in the heart of Holmul. Later
additions to the building's pyramid covered
the earlier structures, which were transformed into tomb chambers. Rooms 1 and 2
held the remains of numerous individuals,
and the bodies were adorned with shell bead
necklaces and a mosaic of jadeite, shell, and
mica. Skeleton 13, at the eastern end of Room
2, was accompanied by five lidded dishes,
including the one shown here.

Other reference:
Merwin and Vaillant 1932, 20–35

141

Lidded Tripod Vessel with Carved Decoration

Honduras, Copan, Structure 16, Hunal Tomb, AD 435
Ceramic with slip
8⅜ x 8½ in. (21.2 x 21.5 cm)
IHAH, Centro Regional de Investigaciones
Arqueológicas, Copan, Honduras (CPN-C-1796)

142

Vessel

Honduras, Copan, Structure 16, Hunal Tomb, AD 435
Ceramic with red and orange slip, stucco, and paint
8³⁄₁₆ x 7¹³⁄₁₆ in. (20.8 x 19.8 cm)
IHAH, Centro Regional de Investigaciones
Arqueológicas, Copan, Honduras (CPN-C-1796)

143

Pendant

Honduras, Copan, Chirmol Structure, AD 450–550
Shell and jadeite
Diam.: 6 in. (15.2 cm)
IHAH, Centro Regional de Investigaciones
Arqueológicas, Copan, Honduras

The Hunal tomb was discovered beneath Structure 16, a primary pyramid and temple in Copan's acropolis and the focus of rituals of ancestor veneration throughout the Classic period. The skeletal remains of K'inich Yax K'uk' Mo' (see cat. 113) were found deep inside the structure, in vaulted tomb chambers. The remains indicate he was five feet, six inches tall, and was between fifty-five and seventy years old when he died. The body was placed on a large stone slab and wore a headdress of cut shell spangles, and jadeite, shell, and bone ornaments. There were many objects on the tomb's floor, including the remains of painted gourds and twenty-one ceramics of varied form, decoration, and origin (although most were locally made). This finely carved, lidded tripod and tall vase were among the pottery vessels. Both were made far from Copan. The tripod came from a workshop in the central Peten lowlands, most likely Tikal. The tall vase, decorated with post-fire stucco and paint, was from a workshop in the Mexican highlands, perhaps at a site in the modern state of Puebla, where Teotihuacan's characteristic Thin Orange pottery was made. The shell pendant resembles

one found in the Hunal tomb. Both were made from a Pacific Coast mollusk; this one is inlaid with shell and jade to form a portrait of the Principal Bird Deity.

References:
141–42: Grube 1990b; Rattray and Harbottle 1992; Sharer et al. 1999; Sharer 2003b; Bell et al. 2004, 132–36; Reents-Budet et al. 2004a, 179–80
143: Bell at al. 2004b, 136–41

141

142

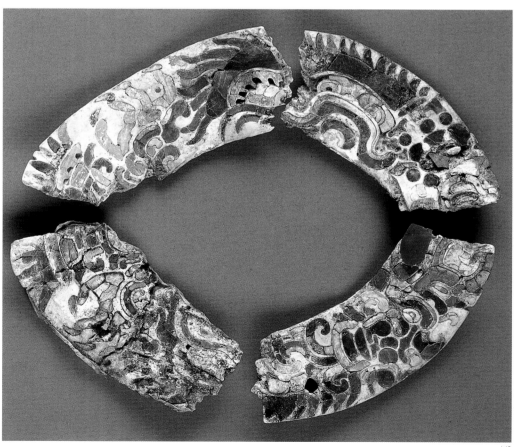

143

144

Lidded Tripod Vessel

Honduras, Copan, Structure 16, Margarita Tomb,
AD 450–500
Ceramic with stucco and pigment
7⅝ x 9⁵⁄₁₆ in. (19.5 x 23.7 cm)
IHAH, Centro Regional de Investigaciones
Arqueológicas, Copan, Honduras (CPN-C-1532)

145

Basal Flange Dish

Honduras, Copan, Structure 16, Margarita Tomb,
AD 450–500
Ceramic with slip
3¾ x 7½ in. (9.5 x 19.2 cm)
IHAH, Centro Regional de Investigaciones
Arqueológicas, Copan, Honduras (CPN-C-1527)

146

Basal Flange Dish

Honduras, Copan, Structure 16, Margarita Tomb,
AD 450–500
Ceramic with slip
3³⁄₁₆ x 9⁵⁄₁₆ in. (8.1 x 23.7 cm)
IHAH, Centro Regional de Investigaciones
Arqueológicas, Copan, Honduras (CPN-C-1526)

147

Pectoral

Honduras, Copan, Structure 16, Margarita Tomb,
AD 450–500
Jadeite and pigment
1½ in. (4 cm)
IHAH, Centro Regional de Investigaciones
Arqueológicas, Copan, Honduras

The Margarita tomb, discovered near the tomb of Yax K'uk' Mo' (see Agurcia Fasquelle, this volume, fig. 1), housed a royal woman thought to be his wife and the mother of the next ruler, K'inich Popol Hol. Her tomb and its adjacent offering chamber compose the richest female burial yet discovered in the Maya region. Her body lay upon a stone bier and was adorned with pectorals, anklets, and other jewelry made from more than ten thousand pieces of jadeite. She wore a massive jade, shell, and pearl necklace, its innermost strand comprising four carved jade pectorals representing a vulture, a supernatural fish, and two anthropomorphic heads, one of which wears the trilobed *hu'unal* headband.

Painted organic containers and eighteen pottery vessels, some filled with food offerings, were placed in the tomb and the antechamber. One of these, the appropriately named "Dazzler Vase" (cat. 144), was made in highland Mexico. It appears to depict the Hunal Platform underlying Structure 16; the goggle-eyed figure inside the temple may be Yax K'uk' Mo' (see cat. 113). Most of the ceramic vessels from the Margarita tomb and its antechamber were made locally; however, two of the unusually large polychrome dishes imply connections with other regions. One dish was made in the Guatemalan highlands (cat. 145), and the other is from the Peten lowlands (cat. 146). Although the vessels are similar, their shapes and decorative patterns reflect the aesthetics of their respective regions, and their presence in the Copan tomb serves as evidence of the long-distance relationships and sociopolitical power of this regal woman. The tomb also contained a number of objects associated with Teotihuacan, most notably two slate and pyrite divination mirrors.

References:
144: Sharer et al. 1999; Sharer 2003b; Bell et al. 2004b, 136–43; Reents-Budet et al. 2004a, 179–80; McNeil et al. in press
145–46: Reents-Budet et al. 2004a, 176–78
147: Bell at al. 2004b, 136–41

147

148

148

Lidded Vessel

Mexico, Campeche, Calakmul, Structure III, Tomb 1,
AD 375–450
Ceramic with slip
5¾ x 14⅝ in. (14.5 x 37 cm)
CNCA-INAH, Museo Histórico Fuerte de San Miguel,
Baluarte de San Miguel, Campeche, Mexico (10-290540)

149

Lidded Vessel with Portrait of King

Mexico, Campeche, Calakmul, Structure III, Tomb 1,
AD 375–450
Ceramic
15 x 8⅝ in. (38 x 22 cm)
CNCA-INAH, Museo Histórico Fuerte de San Miguel,
Baluarte de San Miguel, Campeche, Mexico (10-342805
1/2)

Tomb 1 was a vaulted chamber under Room
6 of Structure III, Calakmul's primary Early
Classic regal residential compound. A 9-meter-
(29½-foot-) long "psychoduct," a tube facili-
tating the passage of the soul from the tomb,
exited on the north side of the building. In
the tomb, the cloth-wrapped body of a male
at least thirty years old had been placed on
a woven mat. The body wore objects typical
of Maya rulers, including three jadeite-and-
shell mosaic masks. One portrait mask was on
his face; a jaguar mask with three incised pendant plaques (see cat. 77) was on his chest,
and another mask and pendant plaque were
attached to his belt. More than eight thousand
shell beads and thirty-two jadeite beads were
found. Five decorated ceramic vessels surrounded the body, including the painted lidded dish (cat. 148), which contained a food
offering. Its decoration refers to the realms
that the soul traverses on its journey. The dish's
basal flange is marked with water icons and
the adjacent exterior walls are painted black;
a squared-nosed saurian symbolizes the earth
floating in the underworld's dark waters. The
lid depicts two images of a celestial saurian
resembling the Vision Serpent and represents

the heavens. The decoration on the lid's knob
represents the four quadrants of the universe
and is surrounded by a circle painted to
resemble a jaguar pelt.

Funerary imagery on the blackware vessel
(cat. 149) includes its four supports, which
are modeled to resemble peccary heads, and
two Vision Serpents incised on its body. Both
motifs recall the decoration on the vessel
with the canoer (see cat. 138). The lid's modeled head and incised decoration depicts a
human figure, likely the deceased lord, his
upper arms marked with crossed-band symbols of death and the underworld. He wears
the pectoral and jadeite bead necklace of the
Principal Bird Deity, and his headband of
rulership features an elderly face, which may
represent a deified ancestor or tutelary deity
of the lineage.

References:
148–49: Pincemin Deliberos 1994; Dominguez Carrasco
1994; Folan et al. 1995, 320–25; Martin and Grube 1995;
Carrasco Vargas 1998a, 382

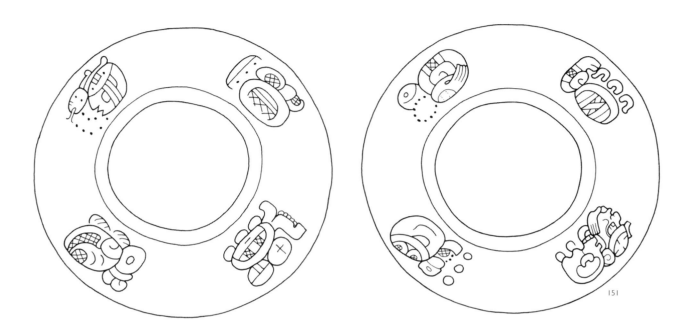

150

Lidded Vessel with Principal Bird Deity and Figure

Mexico, Campeche, Calakmul, Structure IV-B, Tomb 2,
AD 500–560
Ceramic
11¹³⁄₁₆ x 5⅚ in. (30 x 13.5 cm)
CNCA-INAH, Museo Histórico Fuerte de San Miguel,
Baluarte de San Miguel, Campeche, Mexico (10-397992)

151

Pair of Earflares with Hieroglyphic Texts

Mexico, Campeche, Calakmul, Structure II, Tomb 4,
ca. AD 695
Jadeite and red pigment
Diam.: 3¹⁵⁄₁₆ in. each (10 cm)
CNCA-INAH, Museo Histórico Fuerte de San Miguel,
Baluarte de San Miguel, Campeche, Mexico
(10-566760 0/2)

Archaeologist Ramón Carrasco, who excavated Structure IV, describes it as a place for rituals invoking ancestors and supernatural beings. Its central building is spanned by a carved stone lintel portraying the king as the Maize God dancing at (or out of) the *witz* mountain. The structure was sanctified by many ritual caches that included human sacrifices and symbolic groupings of stones and shells. In Structure IV-B Carrasco discovered a tomb thought to be that of the king Tuun K'ab' Hix, who died sometime before AD 560. He was a powerful regent who extended Calakmul's influence far into Quintana Roo and the Peten lowlands, even presiding over the accession of Naranjo's king Aj Wosal in AD 546. His lavishly furnished tomb contained some of the most elaborately modeled blackware pottery ever produced at Calakmul. The Principal Bird Deity seen atop the tripod vessel is a recurring theme on these funerary ceramics, suggesting that this avian supernatural had special symbolic meaning for the site and its ruling dynasty.

The earflares, incised with a short hieroglyphic text, were heirloom jewelry found in the tomb of Calakmul's esteemed king Yuknoom Yich'aak K'ak', whose rule began on 3 April 686. The mud-plaster walls of his tomb, deep inside the structure, were richly modeled and painted. The shroud-wrapped body was dressed in a luxurious regal costume, including a jadeite and shell pectoral and belt, both with mosaic masks and jadeite pendants, and a highly polished pair of jadeite earflares. This pair of earflares, however, was placed next to his body as an offering; their heirloom status is indicated by the text, which names an earlier ruler as their owner.

References:
150: Carrasco Vargas 1998a, 381–82; Schmidt et al. 1998; Carrasco Vargas 2000, 17; Laporte 1995, 2000, 14–15; Rodríguez Campero. 2000, 25–26
151: Carrasco Vargas 1998a, 384; García-Moreno and Granados 2000, 29

152

Head of K'inich Ajaw as Jester God

Belize, Altun Ha, Structure B-4, Tomb B-4/7,
AD 550–650
Jadeite
5⅞ in. (14.9 cm)
Institute of Archaeology, Belmopan, Belize

This sculpted head is the largest single piece of jadeite known to have been carved by the Maya, and its imagery interweaves the primary ideological and supernatural foundations of Classic period rulership. The head portrays the Jester God, here shown with the squint eyes of K'inich Ajaw, the Sun God, and the long beak of the Principal Bird Deity. The trilobed maize symbol of rulership sprouts from the prominent *ajaw* icon on the forehead, underscoring the lordliness of the image.

This sculpture was found in a stone sepulcher constructed near the top of Structure B-4's main stairway. In the tomb were the remains of a man more than fifty years of age, who was a ruler of Altun Ha. The cloth-wrapped body was laid upon a woven mat on a wood platform. The right arm cradled this jadeite sculpture, and cloth fragments suggest it had been wrapped, as sacred objects still are among the Maya. He wore a mosaic head-dress and was adorned with more than sixty pounds of jadeite jewelry, including bead necklaces, carved pendants, anklets, bracelets, and earflares. The tomb also contained shells and shell jewelry, ceramics, cloth, nets, a div-ination mirror, and bone and wood objects. Caches that included symbolic eccentric flints, flint chips, and jadeite fragments were found in the corners and under the floor.

The large quantities of jadeite in Tomb B-4/7 not only attest to the ruler's prestige and sacred authority but also imply that Altun Ha was far more important than its small size suggests. Located at the eastern edge of the Maya world, Altun Ha may have had a special association with the rising sun and the world's daily renewal. Artifacts from other Maya sites, as well as from Teotihuacan and Costa Rica, have been found at Altun Ha, and these foreign objects indicate commercial networks that spanned great distances. They may also indicate that Altun Ha was a site for pilgrimages or other ritual events.

References:
Pendergast 1982, 54–75; Taube 1998, 454–60

152

Acknowledgments

Lords of Creation: The Origins of Sacred Maya Kingship as exhibition and catalogue resulted from collaborative efforts on the part of many individuals and institutions in the United States, Mexico and Central America, Canada, and Europe. I would like to express my deep appreciation to my co-curator, Dorie Reents-Budet, who initiated the project planning and organization, and who has provided an enormous amount of energy and expertise to the development of the concepts and their presentation.

Exhibition planning was greatly facilitated by a generous grant from the National Endowment for the Humanities, which supported a meeting of archaeologists, art historians, and epigraphers whose research focuses on Middle and Late Preclassic Mesoamerica. I would like to thank the members of the committee, who not only contributed the pertinent results of their research in the context of early kingship but also provided important insights into communicating these ideas to the public. Many committee members also wrote essays for the catalogue. The committee included Ricardo Agurcia Fasquelle, Jaime Awe, Ramón Carrasco Vargas, Allen Christenson, David Freidel, Richard Hansen, Simon Martin, Kent Reilly, Robert Sharer, and Joel Skidmore; Julia Guernsey, Juan Antonio Valdés, and Carlos Vidal, who were unable to attend the meeting in Los Angeles, also provided advice in the early stages of planning.

I am also grateful to the NEH and to the National Endowment for the Arts for supporting the implementation of the exhibition and catalogue. In addition, the Ethnic Arts Council of Los Angeles and the Arvey Foundation provided grants to support the education programming. I deeply appreciate the ongoing enthusiasm and support for the exhibition and its components expressed by the members of the Ethnic Arts Council and by Margaret and Howard Arvey.

I am grateful for the generous support from Grupo Televisa, and its CEO Emilio Azcárraga Jean, for making the national presentation of the exhibition possible. Univision also provided significant media support for the exhibition in Los Angeles. The efforts of the staff of LACMA's development department made this support possible, and I would especially like to thank Laura Hardy, Stephanie Dyas, Jan Cromartie, and Douglas Rimerman.

On behalf of the Dallas Museum of Art and the Metropolitan Museum of Art, I would like to thank the lenders for generously parting with their works; lenders' names are listed on page 262. Over the course of the past five years, Dorie Reents-Budet and I have benefited from the generosity and support of many individuals at numerous institutions throughout the United States, Mexico and Central America, Europe, and Canada. We are especially grateful to our colleagues Carol Robbins, Dallas Museum of Art, and Julie Jones, Metropolitan Museum of Art, for their ongoing interest and enthusiasm for bringing the exhibition to their institutions. We would also like to thank the following colleagues in the United States for their gracious encouragement and assistance: Kristen Mable, American Museum of Natural History; Nancy Rosoff, Brooklyn Museum; Susan Bergh, Cleveland Museum of Art; Margaret Young-Sanchez, Denver Art Museum; Loa Traxler and Jennifer Younger, Dumbarton Oaks Research Library and Collections; Kathleen Berrin and Jennifer Moore, Fine Arts Museums of San Francisco; Dirk Van Tuerenhout, Houston Museum of Natural Science; Jennifer Casler Price, Kimbell Art Museum; Katie Getchell and Patrick McMahon, Museum of Fine Arts, Boston; Frances Marzio, Museum of Fine Arts, Houston; Natasha Johnson and Erik Satrum, National Museum of the American Indian; Patricia

Capone, Barbara Fash, Viva Fisher, and Gloria Greis, Peabody Museum of Archaeology and Ethnology, Harvard University; Roger Colten, Peabody Museum of Natural History, Yale University; Gillett Griffin, Maureen McCormick, and John M. D. Pohl, Princeton University Art Museum; Juana Dahlan, University of Pennsylvania Museum of Archaeology and Anthropology; and Vicki Cain and Susan Matheson, Yale University Art Gallery.

We are also grateful for the generous assistance and support from the following individuals: Stacy Goodman, Alphonse Jax, Alec and Gail Merriam, Assen and Christine Nicolov, David T. Owsley, John Stokes, and the late Leroy Cleal. We would like to thank Allen Christenson, who not only generously shared his advice and contributed to the catalogue and exhibition film but also lent to the exhibition. For their willingness to share their knowledge on art historical, epigraphic, and related exhibition matters, we would like to express our appreciation to Marilyn Beaudry-Corbett, Michael Carrasco, Elizabeth Graham, Nikolai Grube, Simon Martin, Mary Miller, Sandra Noble, David Pendergast, Kent Reilly, Karl Taube, and Marc Zender, who so generously contributed their time and expertise.

In Canada, we would like to express our appreciation to Mark Engstrom and Mima Kapches, Royal Ontario Museum.

The support and encouragement of various officials in Mexico were critical to the organization of the exhibition and catalogue. We are especially thankful to Sari Bermúdez, president; Jaime Nualart, technical secretary; Alberto Fierro Garza, national coordinator of international projects; and Carlos Enríquez Verdura, director of international cultural exchange, at the Consejo Nacional para la Cultura y las Artes (CONACULTA). We are grateful to Sergio Raúl Arroyo, former general director, and Luciano Cedillo, current director; Moisés Rosas Silva, technical secretary; José Enrique Ortiz Lanz, national coordinator of museums and exhibitions; Elvira Báez García Mariscal, director of international exhibitions; and Ivonne Morales Canales, logistics coordinator, at the Instituto Nacional de Antropología e Historia (INAH). Thanks also to Carlos Vidal, Centro Regional INAH de Campeche; Rubén Morante López, Museo de Antropología de Xalapa; Marco Antonio Carbajal, Museo Histórico Fuerte de San Miguel, Baluarte de San Miguel; Felipe Solís Olguín, Museo Nacional de Antropología; Roberto Ramos Maza, Museo Regional de Chiapas; Blanca González Rodríguez, Museo Regional de Yucatan "Palacio Canton"; Rubén Cabrera Castro, Néstor Paredes C., Leonardo López Lujan, and Saburo Sugiyama, Proyecto Pirámide de la Luna, Teotihuacan; Graciela Bourger, Parque Museo de La Venta. We are especially grateful to Claudio X. González, Mauricio Maillé, and Diana Mogollón González, Fundación Cultural Televisa A.C. We would like to express our appreciation to Sylviane Boucher and Carlos Navarrete, who provided expert guidance, and Enrique Florescano, who contributed to the catalogue. At the United States Embassy in Mexico, we are most grateful to Ambassador Antonio O. Garza, Jr., Jefferson Brown, public affairs officer, Marjorie Coffin, cultural affairs officer, and special thanks to Bertha Cea Echenique, senior cultural affairs specialist, for her tireless and dedicated efforts on our behalf.

In Guatemala, we would like to thank the following individuals for their support and assistance: in the Ministerio de Cultura y Deportes, Otilia Lux de Cotí, the former minister, and Manuel de Jesús Salazar Tetzagüic, the current minister; Virgilio Alvarado Ajanel, the former vice minister of culture, and Enrique Matheu Recinos, the current first vice minister of culture; and Byron Ariel Pac Sac and Nora López Olivares, advisers; in the Dirección General del Patrimonio Cultural y Natural, Guillermo Díaz Romeu, the former director, and Arturo Paz, the current director; and Salvador López, the chief of the Departamento de Monumentos Prehispánicos y Coloniales; José Luis Castillo, coordinator, and Emilio Sequén, legal adviser, Comisión de Exposiciones Internacionales. At the Museo Nacional de Arqueología y Etnología, we are especially grateful to Claudia Monzón de Jiménez, director, and Rodolfo Yaquián, collections manager, for their gracious assistance and support. At the Museo de Arte Precolombino y Vidrio Moderno, we would like to thank Susana Campins, director, and Edgar Castillo Sinibaldi for their enthusiasm and generosity; and at the Museo Popol Vuh, we are grateful for the support of Oswaldo Chinchilla Mazariegos, curator. We would also like to thank José Sánchez, administrator of the Parque Nacional Tikal and the Museo Sylvanus G. Morley. For their invaluable advice and assistance, we would like to thank Patricia del Águila Flores, Bárbara Arroyo, Federico Fahsen, Juan Pedro Laporte, Fernando Moscoso Möller, Miguel Orrego, Mónica Pérez Galindo, Christa Schieber de Lavarreda, and Juan Antonio Valdés. We also appreciate the interest and enthusiasm of Jaime Arimany and Melanie de Arimany, Arturo Batres, Carolina Castellanos, Luis Alberto Castillo Arriola, Luisa Anaité Galeotti Moraga, María Eugenia Gordillo, Rolando Rubio, and Agusto Vela Mena. From the United States Embassy in Guatemala, we would like to thank Jennifer Clark, Ida Eve Heckenbach, and Peter Samson for their assistance and support. We are especially grateful to Sofía Paredes Maury for graciously coordinating the many details of our exhibition activities in Guatemala. In Los Angeles, we would like to thank Fernando Castillo, consul general of Guatemala, and Patricia Meigham, vice consul, for their ongoing enthusiasm and support.

In Honduras, we would like to thank the following individuals at the Secretario de Estado en el Despacho de Cultura, Artes y Deportes: Mireya Batres Mejía , the former minister, Arnoldo Avilez, the current minister, and Alfonso Gallardo Zelaya, the secretary general. In addition, we are most grateful for the support of the Instituto Hondureño de Antropología e Historia, especially Margarita Durón de Gálvez, general manager, Carmen Julia Fajardo, and Karla María Calidonio and Nilda Torres. For their expert guidance we would like to thank Seiichi Nakamura, director of the conservation program at the Parque Arqueológico Copan; Oscar Cruz, regional representative, and Norman Martínez, registrar, Copan Museum. Additional support was received from the Instituto Hondureño de Turismo, and we are grateful to Thierry de Pierrefeu, secretary of tourism, Kenia Lima Zapata, marketing manager, and Hattie Conner for their efforts on our behalf. We would also like to thank Gregory M. Adams, press adviser at the United States Embassy. We greatly appreciate the advice and support of Ricardo Agurcia Fasquelle.

In Belize, we would like to thank the staff of the Institute of Archaeology, especially Jaime Awe, director, John Morris, associate director, and Melissa Badillo, Theresa Batty, Claudia Elena, Sherilyne Jones, George Thompson, Annette Waight, and Brian Woodye. We are also grateful to The Honorable Mark Espat, Ministry of Tourism, Investment and Culture; Yasser Musa, president, National Institute of Culture and History; and Paul Francisco, director, Belize National Museum.

In Costa Rica, we would like to thank Francisco Corrales, director, and Marlin Calvo Mora, chief registrar, at the Museo Nacional de Costa Rica, and Amalia Fontana Coto, director, at the Museo del Jade Fidel Tristan, Instituto Nacional de Seguros.

In Europe, the following colleagues provided invaluable assistance: Colin McEwan and Stewart Watson, British Museum, London; Joanna Ostapkowicz, Liverpool Museum; Maria Gaida, Staatliche Museen zu Berlin, Preussischer Kulturbesitz, Ethnologisches Museum.

We would also like to thank Hajime Inagaki, Miho Museum, Japan, for his prompt and gracious response to our requests.

The exhibition and catalogue greatly benefited from the dedication and support of the administration and staff at LACMA, and I would like to express my appreciation to President and Wallis Annenberg Director Andrea L. Rich. From the exhibitions department, assistant director Irene Martín, financial analyst Beverley Sabo, former coordinators Christine Weider Lazzaretto and Kristin Fredricks, and current coordinator Janelle Aieta, with Ayako Yoshida, oversaw all phases of the project. Registrar Ted Greenberg, associate registrar Sandy Davis, and assistant registrar Jennifer Garpner coordinated the complicated logistics of domestic and international loans. From the conservation department, Batyah Shtrum in objects and Catherine McLean in textiles lent their expertise to the task of assessing numerous works. I am especially grateful to Victoria Lyall, curatorial assistant, who contributed to the success of the project in many different ways, and to former curatorial administrator Sarah Sherman and current administrator Megan Knox for their close attention to the minutiae of exhibition management.

The educational programs accompanying the exhibition were coordinated by Jane Burrell, head of art museum education. We are especially grateful for the inspired efforts of Joel Skidmore, exhibition Web site designer, and David Brent Miller, who guided the production of the exhibition film with the assistance of LACMA's audiovisual department, especially Elvin Whitesides, Megan Mellbye, and Kenneth Olsen.

The exhibition design by Bernard Kester provided an elegant setting for the objects, and I would like to thank him for his sensitive attention to their presentation. Graphic designers Katherine Go and Paul Wehby expertly managed the complexities of the exhibition materials. Juan José Garcia translated the exhibition texts into Spanish with his customary care and efficiency. I am also grateful to Jeff Haskin and the art preparation staff for their dedicated efforts in installing the exhibition. Domenic Morea, formerly of LACMA's communications and marketing department, was also very helpful.

For their insightful contributions, I would like to thank the authors of the catalogue essays, and Dorie Reents-Budet, who cowrote the catalogue entries with me. I would like to thank Stephanie Emerson, LACMA's director of publications, for coordinating the development and production of the catalogue and exhibition texts. I am especially grateful to Nola Butler, editor, who oversaw the complexities of coordinating the many voices of the catalogue with great sensitivity to the material, and to assisting editors Jennifer Boynton and Matt Stevens for their perceptive and painstaking attention to the text. Proofreader Dianne Woo and indexer Diana LeCore contributed excellent work to the catalogue. I am grateful to Rose Vekony for her exceptional translations of the Spanish-language texts. I would also like to thank Katy Homans for her inspired catalogue design. Adrian Kitzinger provided an outstanding map for the catalogue and exhibition. Peter Brenner, supervising photographer, photographic services, and photographer Steve Oliver, managed the quality control of the images, and I would also like to thank Jorge Pérez de Lara, who photographed the exhibition objects in Mexico, Guatemala, Honduras, and Belize with his customary care. Giselle Arteaga-Johnson, rights and reproductions assistant, expertly coordinated the enormous task of securing rights to images, and I am grateful to her.

For their unflagging moral support and good advice, I would like to express my heartfelt thanks to Hollis Goodall, Ilona Katzew, Linda Komaroff, Mary Levkoff, June Li, Maureen Russell, and Kaye Spilker.

Finally, Dorie and I would like to express our warmest appreciation and thanks to Ricardo Budet and David Miller, who have supported the project in more ways than we can count.

Virginia M. Fields
Curator of Pre-Columbian Art
Los Angeles County Museum of Art

Lenders to the Exhibition

American Museum of Natural History, New York

The British Museum, London

The Brooklyn Museum

Centro Regional de Investigaciones Arqueológicas, Copan, Honduras

Allen J. Christenson

Dallas Museum of Art

The Denver Art Museum

Dumbarton Oaks Research Library and Collections, Washington, D.C.

Fine Arts Museums of San Francisco

Fundación Televisa A.C., Mexico City

Houston Museum of Natural Science

Institute of Archaeology, Belmopan, Belize

Instituto de Cultura de Tabasco, Dirección de Patrimonio Cultural, Parque Museo de La Venta, Villahermosa

Instituto Hondureño de Antropología e Historia, Tegucigalpa, Honduras

Kimbell Art Museum, Fort Worth

Los Angeles County Museum of Art

The Metropolitan Museum of Art, New York

Miho Museum, Shigaraki, Japan

Municipal Museum, Copan, Honduras

Museo de Arte Precolombino y Vidrio Moderno, Antigua, Guatemala

Museo de Sitio de Teotihuacan, Mexico

Museo del Jade Lic. Fidel Tristán, Instituto Nacional de Seguros, San José, Costa Rica

Museo Histórico Fuerte de San Miguel, Baluarte de San Miguel, Campeche, Mexico

Museo Nacional de Antropología, Mexico City

Museo Nacional de Arqueología y Etnología, Guatemala City

Museo Popol Vuh, Guatemala City

Museo Regional de Chiapas, Tuxtla Gutiérrez, Mexico

Museo Regional de Yucatan "Palacio Cantón," Merida, Mexico

Museo Sylvanus G. Morley, Tikal, Guatemala

The Museum of Fine Arts, Houston

National Museum of the American Indian, Washington, D.C.

David T. Owsley

Peabody Museum of Archaeology and Ethnology, Harvard University, Cambridge

Peabody Museum of Natural History, Yale University, New Haven

Princeton University Art Museum

Royal Ontario Museum, Toronto

Staatliche Museen zu Berlin, Preussischer Kulturbesitz, Ethnologisches Museum, Berlin

University of Pennsylvania Museum of Archaeology and Anthropology, Philadelphia

Yale University Art Gallery, New Haven

References Cited

Abbreviations

Works and institutions frequently cited have been identified by the following abbreviations:

Dumbarton Studies:
Studies in Pre-Columbian Art and Archaeology (Washington, DC: Dumbarton Oaks)

Maya Reports:
Research Reports on Ancient Maya Writing (Washington, DC: Center for Maya Research)

Pap New World Archaeol Found:
Papers of the New World Archaeological Foundation (Provo, UT: Brigham Young University)

RES:
RES: Anthropology and Aesthetics

UNAM:
Universidad Nacional Autónoma de México

Adams, Richard E. W., ed. 1977. *The Origins of Maya Civilization*. Albuquerque: Univ. of New Mexico Press.

———. 1999. *Río Azul: An Ancient Maya City*. Norman: Univ. of Oklahoma Press.

Agrinier, Pierre. 1960. *The Carved Human Femurs from Tomb 1, Chiapa de Corzo, Chiapas, Mexico*. Pap New World Archaeol Found 6.

Agurcia Fasquelle, Ricardo. 2004. "Rosalila, Temple of the Sun-King." Chap. 6 in Bell et al., *Understanding Early Classic Copan*.

Altman, Patricia B., and Caroline D. West. 1992. *Threads of Identity: Maya Costume of the 1960s in Highland Guatemala*. Los Angeles: UCLA Fowler Museum of Cultural History.

Ambrosino, James N., Traci Ardren, and Travis W. Stanton. 2003. "The History of Warfare at Yaxuná." In Brown and Stanton, *Ancient Mesoamerican Warfare*.

Ardren, Traci. 2002. "Death Became Her." In *Ancient Maya Women*, ed. Traci Ardren, 68–88. Walnut Creek, CA: AltaMira Press.

Asturias de Barrios, Linda. 1997. "Weaving and Daily Life." In Schevill, *The Maya Textile Tradition*, 65–87.

Aveni, Anthony F., Anne S. Dowd, and Benjamin Vining. 2003. "Maya Calendar Reform?" *Lat Am Antiq* 14 (2): 159–78.

Aveni, Anthony F., and Horst Hartung. 1989. "Uaxactun, Guatemala, Group E, and Similar Assemblages." In *World Archaeoastronomy*, ed. Anthony F. Aveni, 441–61. Cambridge: Cambridge Univ. Press.

Awe, Jaime J., and Nikolai Grube. 2001. "La Estela 9 de Cahal Pech." *Los investigadores de la cultura Maya* 9 (1): 55–65. Campeche: Universidad Autónoma de Campeche.

Balandier, Georges. 1980. *Le pouvoir sur scènes*. Paris: Balland.

Ball, Joseph W. 1974. "A Teotihuacan-Style Cache from the Maya Lowlands." *Archaeology* 27 (1): 2–9.

———. 1977. *The Archaeological Ceramics of Becan, Campeche, Mexico*. Middle American Research Institute Publication 43. New Orleans, LA: Tulane Univ.

———. 1983. "Teotihuacan, the Maya, and Ceramic Interchange." In Miller, *Highland-Lowland Interaction in Mesoamerica*, 126–46.

Balser, Carlos. 1974. *El jade de Costa Rica: un album arqueológico*. San Jose, Costa Rica: Lehmann.

Bardawil, Lawrence W. 1976. "The Principal Bird Deity in Maya Art." In *The Art, Iconography, and Dynastic History of Palenque*, pt. 3, ed. Merle Greene Robertson, 195–209. Proceedings of the Segunda Mesa Redonda de Palenque, 1974. Pebble Beach, CA: Robert Louis Stevenson School.

Beetz, Carl, and Linton Satterthwaite. 1981. *The Monuments and Inscriptions of Caracol, Belize.* University Museum Monographs 45. Philadelphia: Univ. of Pennsylvania.

Bell, Ellen E., Marcello A. Canuto, and Robert J. Sharer, eds. 2004a. *Understanding Early Classic Copan.* Philadelphia: University of Pennsylvania Museum of Archaeology and Anthropology.

Bell, Ellen E., Robert J. Sharer, Loa P. Traxler, David W. Sedat, Christine W. Carrelli, and Lynn A. Grant. 2004b. "Tombs and Burials in the Early Classic Acropolis at Copan." Chap. 8 in Bell et al., *Understanding Early Classic Copan.*

Benson, Elizabeth P. 1971. *An Olmec Figure at Dumbarton Oaks.* Dumbarton Studies 8.

———. 1996. Cat. entries 68–71, in Benson and de la Fuente, *Olmec Art.*

Benson, Elizabeth P., and Beatriz de la Fuente, eds. 1996. *Olmec Art of Ancient Mexico.* Washington, DC: National Gallery of Art.

Benson, Elizabeth P., and Gillett G. Griffin. 1988. *Maya Iconography.* Princeton, NJ: Princeton Univ. Press.

Berjonneau, Gerald, et al. 1985. *Rediscovered Masterpieces of Mesoamerica: Mexico-Guatemala-Honduras.* Boulogne: Editions Arts.

Blier, Suzanne Preston. 1998. *The Royal Arts of Africa: The Majesty of Form.* New York: Harry N. Abrams.

Borowicz, James. 2003. "Images of Power and the Power of Images." In Braswell, *The Maya and Teotihuacan,* 217–34.

Boucher, Sylviane, Yoly Palomo, and Luz Evelia Campaña V. 2004. "Dramatis personae de la ofrenda funeraria en la Estructura IX de Becan, Campeche." In Cobos, *Culto funerario,* 369–94.

Bove, Frederick J., and Sonia Medrano Busto. 2003. "Teotihuacan, Militarism, and Pacific Guatemala." In Braswell, *The Maya and Teotihuacan,* 45–79.

Bove, Frederick J., Sonia Medrano Busto, Brenda Lou Pichiyá, and Bárbara Arroyo, eds. 1993. *The Balberta Project: The Terminal Formative-Early Classic Transition on the Pacific Coast of Guatemala.* Memoirs in Latin American Archaeology 6. Pittsburgh: Univ. of Pittsburgh Press.

Braswell, Geoffrey E., ed. 2003a. *The Maya and Teotihuacan: Reinterpreting Early Classic Interaction.* Austin: Univ. of Texas Press.

———. 2003b. Intro. to *The Maya and Teotihuacan.*

Brown, Kenneth L. 1977. "The Valley of Guatemala." In Sanders and Michels, *Teotihuacan and Kaminaljuyu,* 205–395.

Brown, M. Kathryn. 2003. "Emerging Complexity in the Maya Lowlands: A View from Blackman Eddy, Belize." PhD diss., Southern Methodist Univ.

Brown, M. Kathryn, and James F. Garber. 1998. "The Origin and Function of Late Preclassic Mask Facades in the Maya Lowlands." Paper presented at the 63rd annual meeting of the Society for American Archaeology, Seattle, WA.

———. 2003. "Evidence of Conflict during the Middle Preclassic in the Maya Lowlands." In Brown and Stanton, *Ancient Mesoamerican Warfare.*

Brown, M. Kathryn, and Travis W. Stanton, eds. 2003. *Ancient Mesoamerican Warfare.* Walnut Creek, CA: AltaMira Press.

Buikstra, Jane E., T. Douglas Price, Lori E. Wright, and James A. Burton. 2004. "Tombs from the Copan Acropolis." Chap. 10 in Bell et al., *Understanding Early Classic Copan*.

Bunzel, Ruth Leah. 1952. *Chichicastenango*. American Ethnological Society 22. Seattle: Univ. of Washington Press.

Campaña V., Luz Evelia. 1995. "Una tumba en el Templo del Buho Dzibanche." *Arqueol Mex* 3 (14): 28–31.

Campaña V., Luz Evelia, and Sylviane Boucher. 2002. "Nuevas imágines de Becan, Campeche." *Arqueol Mex* 10 (56): 64–69.

Campbell, Lyle R., and Terrence S. Kaufman. 1976. "A Linguistic Look at the Olmecs." *Am Antiq* 41 (1): 80–89.

Carmack, Robert M., and James L. Mondloch, eds. 1983. *El título de Totonicapan*. Mexico City: UNAM.

———. 1989. *Título de Yax, y otros documentos quichés de Totonicapan, Guatemala*. Mexico City: Centro de Estudios Mayas, UNAM.

Carrasco Vargas, Ramón. 1998a. "The Metropolis of Calakmul, Campeche." In Schmidt et al., *Maya*, 373–85.

———. 1998b. Cat. entry 431, in Schmidt et al., *Maya*.

———. 2000. "El *cuchcabal* de la Cabeza de Serpiente." *Arqueol Mex* 7 (42): 12–21.

———. 2004. "Ritos funerarios en Calakmul." In Cobos, *Culto funerario*, 231–44.

Castro-Leal, Marcia. 1996. Cat. entry 51, in Benson and de la Fuente, *Olmec Art*.

Chang, Kwang-Chih. 1984. "Ancient China and Its Anthropological Significance." *Symbols* (spring/fall): 2–4, 20–22.

Cheek, Charles D. 1977. "Teotihuacan Influence at Kaminaljuyu." In Sander and Michels, *Teotihuacan and Kaminaljuyu*, 441–52.

Chinchilla Aguilar, Ernesto. 1963. *La danza del sacrificio y otros estudios*. Guatemala: Ministerio de Educación Pública; Central Editorial José de Pineda Ibarra.

Chinchilla Mazariegos, Oswaldo. 1999. "Desarrollo de la escritura en Mesoamérica durante el Preclásico." In *Epoca Prehispánica*, ed. Marion Popenoe de Hatch, 1: 557–62. Guatemala: Asociación de Amigos del País.

Christenson, Allen J. 1996. "Bare Bones and the Divine Rights of Kings: An Analysis of the Chiapa de Corzo Carved Femurs." Master's thesis, Univ. of Texas at Austin.

———. 2001. *Art and Society in a Highland Maya Community*. Austin: Univ. of Texas Press.

———. 2003. *"Popol Vuh": The Sacred Book of the Maya*. 2 vols. Winchester, England: O Books.

Clancy, Flora. 1985. Cat. entries 19, 33, 48–49, in Gallenkamp and Johnson, *Maya*.

———. 1990. "A Genealogy for Freestanding Maya Monuments." In Clancy and Harrison, *Vision and Revision*, 21–31.

———. 1999. *Sculpture in the Ancient Maya Plaza: The Early Classic Period*. Albuquerque: Univ. of New Mexico Press.

Clancy, Flora S., and Peter D. Harrison, eds. 1990. *Vision and Revision in Maya Studies*. Albuquerque: Univ. of New Mexico Press.

Clark, John E., and Michael Blake. 1994. "The Power of Prestige." In *Factional Competition and Political Development in the New World*, ed. Elizabeth M. Brumfiel and John W. Fox, 17–30. Cambridge: Cambridge Univ. Press.

Clark, John E., and Richard D. Hansen. 2001. "The Architecture of Early Kingship." In Inomata and Houston, *Royal Courts*, 2: 1–45.

Clark, John E., and Mary E. Pye, eds. 2000a. *Olmec Art and Archaeology in Mesoamerica*. Washington, DC: National Gallery of Art.

Clark, John E., and Mary E. Pye. 2000b. "The Pacific Coast and the Olmec Question." In Clark and Pye, *Olmec Art*.

Cobos, Rafael, ed. 2004. *Culto funerario en la sociedad maya*. Memoria de la Cuarta Mesa Redonda de Palenque. Mexico, D.F.: Instituto Nacional de Antropología e Historia.

Coe, Michael D. 1957. "Cycle 7 Monuments in Middle America." *Am Anthropol* 59: 597–611.

———. 1966. *An Early Stone Pectoral from Southeastern Mexico*. Dumbarton Studies 1.

———. 1973. *The Maya Scribe and His World*. New York: Grolier Club.

———. 1977. "Olmec and Maya: A Study in Relationships." In Adams, *Origins of Maya Civilization*, 183–96.

Coe, Michael D., and Justin Kerr. 1997. *The Art of the Maya Scribe*. London: Thames & Hudson.

Coe, Michael D., and Mark Van Stone. 2001. *Reading the Maya Glyphs*. London: Thames & Hudson.

Coe, William R. 1990. *Excavations in the Great Plaza, North Terrace, and North Acropolis of Tikal*. Tikal Report 14. 6 vols. Philadelphia: Univ. of Pennsylvania Museum.

Coe, William R., and John J. McGinn. 1963. "Tikal." *Expedition* 5 (2): 24–32.

Coggins, Clemency C. 1975. "Painting and Drawing Styles at Tikal: An Historical and Iconographic Reconstruction." PhD diss., Harvard Univ.

———. 1979. "A New Order and the Role of the Calendar." In *Maya Archaeology and Ethnohistory*, ed. Norman Hammond and Gordon R. Willey, 38–50. Austin: Univ. of Texas Press.

———. 1985. Cat. entries 13, 15–17, 22, 26, 38, in Gallenkamp and Johnson, *Maya*.

———. 1998. "Portable Objects," in Schmidt et al., *Maya*, 248–69.

Cortez, Constance. 1986. "The Principal Bird Deity in Late Preclassic and Early Classic Maya Art." Master's thesis, Univ. of Texas at Austin.

Cowgill, George. 2003. "Teotihuacan and Early Classic Interaction." In Braswell, *The Maya and Teotihuacan*, 315–35.

Culbert, T. Patrick. 1993. *The Ceramics of Tikal: Vessels from the Burials, Caches, and Problematical Deposits*. University Museum Monographs 81. Philadelphia: Univ. of Pennsylvania.

———. 2004. "Intervención política en las Tierras Bajas Mayas." Paper presented at the Fifth Mesa Redonda de Palenque, Palenque, Mexico, 2–5 June 2004.

Cyphers, Ann. 1999. "From Stone to Symbols." In Grove and Joyce, *Social Patterns*, 155–82.

Demarest, Arthur A., and Antonia E. Foias. 1993. "Mesoamerican Horizons and the Cultural Transformations of Maya Civilization." In *Latin American Horizons*, ed. Don S. Rice, 147–91. Washington, DC: Dumbarton Oaks.

Diehl, Richard A. 1990. "The Olmec at La Venta." In *Mexico: Splendors of Thirty Centuries*, 51–71.

Domínguez Carrasco, María del Rosario. 1994. *Calakmul, Campeche: un analisis de la cerámica.* Colección arqueológica 4. Campeche: Universidad Autónoma de Campeche.

Drucker, Philip, Robert F. Heizer, and Robert J. Squier. 1959. *Excavations at La Venta, Tabasco, 1955.* Bureau of American Ethnology Bulletin 170. Washington, DC: Smithsonian Institution.

Dyckerhoff, Ursula, Federico Fahsen, William L. Fash, Barbara W. Fash, Nikolai Grube, G. Hasemann, J. Henderson, K. Hirth, S. Hirth, and M. López B. 2001. *Maya' Amaq': Mundo Maya.* Guatemala: Cholsamaj.

Easby, Elizabeth Kennedy. 1966. *Ancient Art of Latin America from the Collection of Jay C. Leff.* New York: Brooklyn Museum.

Easby, Elizabeth Kennedy, and John F. Scott. 1970. *Before Cortés: Sculpture of Middle America.* New York: Metropolitan Museum of Art.

Ekholm, Gordon F. 1964. "A Maya Sculpture in Wood." Studies 4. New York: Museum of Primitive Art.

Ekholm, Susanna M. 1969. *Mound 30a and the Early Preclassic Ceramic Sequence of Izapa, Chiapas, Mexico.* Pap New World Archaeol Found 25.

Ellwood, Robert S. 1973. *The Feast of Kingship: Accession Ceremonies in Ancient Japan.* Tokyo: Sophia Univ. Press.

Emmerich, André. 1984. *Masterpieces of Pre-Columbian Art from the Collection of Mr. and Mrs. Peter G. Wray.* New York: André Emmerich and Perls Galleries.

Estrada-Belli, Francisco, Nikolai Grube, Kristen Gardella, Claudio Lozano Guerra-Librero, and Raul Archila. 2003. "News from the Holmul Hinterland." *Mexicon* 25 (2): 59–61.

Estrada Monroy, Agustín. 1979. *El mundo K'ekchi' de la Vera Paz.* Guatemala: Editorial del Ejército.

Fahsen, Federico. 1992. "Dearrollo dinástico de las tierras bajas mayas durante la transición Preclásico Tardío-Clásico Temprano." *Utz'ib* 1 (3): 8–16.

———. 1995. "La transición Preclásico Tardío-Clásico Temprano." In Grube, *The Emergence of Lowland Maya Civilization*, 151–62.

———. 2001a. "From Chiefdoms to Statehood in the Highlands of Guatemala." In Grube, *Maya*, 86–95.

———. 2001b. Cat. entries 40, 44, in Dyckerhoff et al., *Maya' Amaq'.*

Fash, William L. 1991. *Scribes, Warriors, and Kings: The City of Copan and the Ancient Maya.* London: Thames & Hudson.

———. 1998. Cat. entry 284, in Schmidt et al., *Maya.*

Fash, William L., Barbara W. Fash, and Karla L. Davis-Salazar. 2004. "Setting the Stage." Chap. 4 in Bell et al., *Understanding Early Classic Copan*.

Feeley-Harnik, Gillian. 1985. "Issues in Divine Kingship." *Annu Rev Anthropol* 14: 273–313.

Fialko, Vilma. 1988. "Mundo Perdido, Tikal." *Mayab* 4: 13–21.

Fields, Virginia M. 1982. "Political Symbolism among the Olmec." Manuscript on file, Department of Art and Art History, Univ. of Texas at Austin.

———. 1989. "The Origins of Divine Kingship among the Lowland Classic Maya." PhD diss., Univ. of Texas at Austin.

———. 1991. "The Iconographic Heritage of the Maya Jester God." In *Sixth Palenque Round Table*, 1986, ed. Virginia M. Fields, 167–74. Norman: Univ. of Oklahoma Press.

Fields, Virginia M., and Dorie Reents-Budet. 1992. "Historical Implications of the Jade Trade between the Maya Lowlands and Costa Rica during the Early Classic Period." In *The World of Jade*, ed. Stephen Markel, 81–88. Bombay, India: Marg Publications.

Florescano, Enrique. 1995. *El mito de Quetzalcoatl*. Mexico City: Fondo de Cultura Económica. Translated by Lysa Hochroth under the title *The Myth of Quetzalcoatl*. Baltimore, MD: Johns Hopkins Univ. Press, 1999.

Folan, William J., Joyce Marcus, Sophia Pincemin Deliberos, María del Rosario Domínguez Carrasco, Laraine Fletcher, and Abel Morales. 1995. "Calakmul." *Lat Am Antiq* 6 (4): 310–34.

Frankfort, Henri. 1948. *Kingship and the Gods: A Study of Ancient Near Eastern Religion as the Integration of Society and Nature*. Chicago: Univ. of Chicago Press.

Frazer, James. 1905. *Lectures on the Early History of the Kingship*. London: Macmillan and Co.

Freidel, David A. 1979. "Cultural Areas and Interaction Spheres." *Am Antiq* 44 (1): 36–54.

———. 1990. "The Jester God." In Clancy and Harrison, *Vision and Revision*, 67–78.

Freidel, David A., Barbara MacLeod, and Charles K. Suhler. 2003. "Early Classic Maya Conquest in Words and Deeds." In Brown and Stanton, *Ancient Mesoamerican Warfare*, 189–215.

Freidel, David A., Kathryn Reese-Taylor, and David Mora Morín. 2002. "The Origins of Maya Civilization." In Masson and Freidel, *Ancient Maya*, 41–86.

Freidel, David A., and Linda Schele. 1988a. "Kingship in the Late Preclassic Maya Lowlands." *Am Anthropol* 90 (3): 547–67.

———. 1988b. "Symbol and Power." In Benson and Griffin, *Maya Iconography*, 44–93.

Freidel, David A., Linda Schele, and Joy Parker. 1993. *Maya Cosmos: Three Thousand Years on the Shaman's Path*. New York: William Morrow.

Freidel, David A., and Charles K. Suhler. 1995. "Crown of Creation." In Grube, *The Emergence of Lowland Maya Civilization*, 137–50.

Gage, Thomas. 1958 [1648]. *Travels in the New World*. Edited and with an intro. by J. Eric S. Thompson. Norman: Univ. of Oklahoma Press.

Gallenkamp, Charles, and Regina Elise Johnson, eds. 1985. *Maya: Treasures of an Ancient Civilization*. New York: Harry N. Abrams, in assoc. with the Albuquerque Museum.

Garber, James F. 1983. "Patterns of Jade Consumption and Disposal at Cerros, Northern Belize." *Am Antiq* 48 (4): 800–807.

Garber, James F., M. Kathryn Brown, Jaime J. Awe, and Christopher J. Hartman. 2004. "Middle Formative Prehistory of the Central Belize Valley." In *The Ancient Maya of the Belize Valley: Half a Century of Archaeological Research*, ed. James F. Garber. Gainesville: Univ. Press of Florida.

García-Moreno R., Renata, and Josefina Granados G. 2000. "Tumbas reales de Calakmul." *Arqueol Mex* 7 (42): 28–33.

Gendrop, Paul. 1984. "El tablero-talud en la arquitectura mesoamericana." *Cuadernos de arquitectura mesoamericana* 2: 5–27.

González-Lauck, Rebecca. 1996. Cat. entry 10, in Benson and de la Fuente, *Olmec Art*.

Gordon, George B. 1896. *Prehistoric Ruins of Copan, Honduras*. Memoirs of the Peabody Museum of American Archaeology and Ethnology 1 (1). Cambridge, MA: Harvard Univ.

Graham, John A., Robert F. Heizer, and Edwin M. Shook. 1978. "Abaj Takalik 1976." Contributions of the University of California Archaeological Research Facility 36, 85–113. Berkeley.

Graham, Mark Miller. 1998. "Mesoamerican Jade and Costa Rica." In *Jade in Ancient Costa Rica*, ed. Julie Jones, 39–57. New York: Metropolitan Museum of Art.

Grove, David C., ed. 1987. *Ancient Chalcatzingo*. Austin: Univ. of Texas Press.

Grove, David C., and Rosemary A. Joyce, eds. 1999. *Social Patterns in Pre-Classic Mesoamerica*. Washington, DC: Dumbarton Oaks.

Grube, Nikolai. 1990a. "Die Entwicklung der Mayaschrift." Acta Mesoamericana 3. Berlin: Verlag von Flemming.

———. 1990b. *A Reference to Water-Lily Jaguar on Caracol Stela 16*. Copan Notes 68. Austin: Univ. of Texas at Austin.

———, ed. 1995. *The Emergence of Lowland Maya Civilization: The Transition from the Preclassic to the Early Classic*. Acta Mesoamericana 8. Möckmühl: Verlag Anton Saurwein.

———, ed. 2001a. *Maya: Divine Kings of the Rain Forest*. Cologne: Könemann.

———. 2001b. Cat. entries 5, 29, 35, 57, in Dyckerhoff et al., *Maya' Amaq'*.

———. 2004. "Ciudades perdidas mayas." *Arqueol Mex* 12 (67): 32–37.

———. Forthcoming. *Kunstwerke der Klassischen Maya im Ethnologischen Museum, Berlin*. Munich: Prestel.

Grube, Nikolai, and Simon Martin. 2001. "The Coming of Kings: Writing and Dynastic Kingship in the Maya Area between the Late Preclassic and the Early Classic." In *Notebook for the 25th Maya Hieroglyphic Forum at Texas*, pt. 2. Austin: Maya Workshop Foundation.

———. 2004. "Patronage, Betrayal, and Revenge." In *Notebook for the 28th Maya Hieroglyphic Forum at Texas*, pt. 2. Austin: Maya Workshop Foundation.

Guernsey Kappelman, Julia. 1997. "Of Macaws and Men: Late Preclassic Cosmology and Political Ideology in Izapan-style Monuments." PhD diss., Univ. of Texas at Austin.

———. 2002. "Carved in Stone." In Stone, *Heart of Creation*, 66–82.

————. 2004. "Demystifying the Late Preclassic Izapan-style Stela Altar 'Cult'." *RES* 45: 99–122.

Guernsey Kappelman, Julia, and F. Kent Reilly III. 2001. "Paths to Heaven, Ropes to Earth." *Ancient America* 2/3: 33–49. Barnardsville, NC: Center for Ancient American Studies.

Hall, Grant D., Stanley Tarka, W. Jeffrey Hurst, David Stuart, and Richard E. W. Adams. 1990. "Cacao Residues in Ancient Maya Vessels from Río Azul, Guatemala." *Am Antiq* 55 (1): 138–43.

Hansen, Richard D. 1990. *Excavations in the Tigre Complex, El Mirador, Peten, Guatemala.* Pap New World Archaeol Found 62.

————. 1991. "An Early Maya Text from El Mirador, Guatemala." Maya Reports 37.

————. 1992a. "The Archaeology of Ideology: A Study of Maya Preclassic Architectural Sculpture at Nakbe, Peten, Guatemala." PhD diss., Univ. of California at Los Angeles.

————. 1992b. "El Proceso Cultural de Nakbe y el Area del Peten Nor-Central: Las Epocas Tempranas." In *V Simposio de Investigaciones Arqueológicas en Guatemala*, ed. Juan Pedro Laporte, Héctor L. Escobedo, and Sandra Villagrán de Brady, 81–96. Guatemala: Museo Nacional de Arqueología y Ethnología; Ministerio de Cultura y Deportes; Instituto de Antropología e Historia de Guatemala; Asociación Tikal.

————. 1996. "El Clásico Tardío del norte del Peten." *Utz'ib* 2 (1): 1–15.

————. 1998. "Continuity and Disjunction." In Houston, *Function and Meaning*, 49–122.

————. 2001. "The First Cities." In Grube, *Maya*, 50–65.

Hansen, Richard D., Steven Bozarth, John Jacob, David Wahl, and Thomas Schreiner. 2002. "Climatic and Environmental Variability in the Rise of Maya Civilization." *Anc Mesoam* 13 (2002): 273–95. Cambridge: Cambridge Univ. Press.

Harrison, Peter D. 1999. *The Lords of Tikal: Rulers of an Ancient Maya City.* New York: Thames & Hudson.

Hellmuth, Nicholas. 1986. "The Surface of the Underwaterworld: Iconography of Maya Deities of Early Classic Art in Peten, Guatemala." PhD diss., Karl-Franzens-Universität, Graz, Austria.

————. 1987. *Monster und Menschen in der Maya-Kunst.* Graz, Austria: Akademische Druk- u. Verlagsanstalt.

Hocart, Arthur M. 1927. *Kingship.* London: Oxford Univ. Press.

Houston, Stephen D., ed. 1998. *Function and Meaning in Classic Maya Architecture.* Washington, DC: Dumbarton Oaks.

————. 2000. "Into the Minds of Ancients." *J World Prehist* 14 (2): 121–201.

Houston, Stephen D., and Michael D. Coe. 2003. "Has Isthmian Writing Been Deciphered?" *Mexicon* 25 (6): 151–61.

Houston, Stephen D., and David Stuart. 1989. "The *Way* Glyph." Maya Reports 30.

————. 1996. "Of Gods, Glyphs and Kings." *Antiquity* 70 (268): 289–312.

————. 2001. "Peopling the Classic Maya Court." In Inomata and Houston, *Royal Courts*, 1: 54–83.

Inomata, Takeshi, and Stephen D. Houston, eds. 2001. *Royal Courts of the Ancient Maya.* 2 vols. Boulder, CO: Westview Press.

Joralemon, Peter David. 1971. *A Study of Olmec Iconography*. Dumbarton Studies 7.

———. 1974. "Ritual Blood-Sacrifice among the Ancient Maya: Part 1." In *Primera Mesa Redonda de Palenque*, pt. 2, ed. Merle Green Robertson, 59–76. Pebble Beach, CA: Robert Louis Stevenson School.

———. 1976. "The Olmec Dragon." In *Origins of Religious Art and Iconography in Preclassic Mesoamerica*, ed. H. B. Nicholson, 27–71. Los Angeles: UCLA Latin American Center.

———. 1988. "The Olmec." In *The Face of Ancient America: The Wally and Brenda Zollman Collection of Pre-Columbian Art*, ed. Lee A. Parsons, John B. Carlson, and Peter David Joralemon, 9–50. Indianapolis: Indianapolis Museum of Art.

———. 1996a. "In Search of the Olmec Cosmos." In Benson and de la Fuente, *Olmec Art*, 51–59, 212–15.

———. 1996b. Cat. entries 50 and 116, in Benson and de la Fuente, *Olmec Art*.

Justeson, John S. 1986. "The Origin of Writing Systems." *World Archaeol* 7: 437–58.

Justeson, John S., and Peter Mathews. 1991. "Evolutionary Trends in Mesoamerican Hieroglyphic Writing." *Visible Lang* 24 (1): 88–132.

Justeson, John S., William M. Norman, and Norman Hammond. 1988. "The Pomona Flare." In Benson and Griffin, *Maya Iconography*, 94–151.

Kaufman, Carol. 2003. "Maya Masterwork." *Natl Geogr* 204 (6): 72–77.

Kaufman, Terrence S., and John S. Justeson. 2001. "Epi-Olmec Hieroglyphic Writing and Texts." In Wanyerka, *Coming of Kings*, 93–224.

Kerr, Justin, ed. 1997. *The Maya Vase Book*. 6 vols. New York: Kerr Associates.

Kidder, Alfred V., and Gordon F. Ekholm. 1951. "Archaeological Specimens from Pomona, British Honduras." *Notes on Middle American Archaeology and Ethnography* 6 (102). Washington, DC: Carnegie Institution of Washington, Division of Historical Research.

Kidder, Alfred V., Jesse D. Jennings, and Edwin M. Shook. 1946. *Excavations at Kaminaljuyu*. Carnegie Institution of Washington Publication 561. Washington, DC.

Lacadena, Alfonso García-Gallo. 1995. "Evolución formal de las grafías escriturarias mayas: implicaciones históricos y culturales." PhD diss., Universidad Complutense de Madrid.

Laporte, Juan Pedro. 1989. "Alternativas del Clásico Temprano en la relación Tikal-Teotihuacan; Grupo 6C-XVI, Tikal, Peten, Guatemala." PhD diss., UNAM.

———. 1995. "Preclásico a Clásico en Tikal." In Grube, *The Emergence of Lowland Maya Civilization*, 17–34.

———. 2000. "Ofrendas funerarias y cambio social en el Mundo Perdido, Tikal, Guatemala." *Utz'ib* 2 (8): 1–32.

———. 2003. "Architectural Aspects of Interaction between Tikal and Teotihuacan during the Early Classic Period." In Braswell, *The Maya and Teotihuacan*, 199–216.

Laporte, Juan Pedro, and Vilma Fialko. 1987. "La cerámica del Clásico Temprano desde el Mundo Perdido, Tikal." In *Maya Ceramics: Papers from the 1985 Maya Ceramic Conference*, ed. Prudence Rice and Robert J. Sharer, 123–82. British Archaeological Reports International Series 345. Oxford: British Archaeological Reports.

———. 1990. "New Perspectives on Old Problems." In Clancy and Harrison, *Vision and Revision*, 33–66.

Longyear, John M., III. 1952. *Copan Ceramics. A Study of Southeastern Maya Pottery*. Carnegie Institution of Washington Publication 597. Washington, DC.

Looper, Matthew G. 1995. "The Three Stones of Maya Creation Mythology at Quirigua." *Mexicon* 17 (2): 24–30.

———. 2003. *Lightning Warrior: Maya Art and Kingship at Quirigua*. Austin: Univ. of Texas Press.

Lounsbury, Floyd. 1973. "On the Derivation and Reading of the 'Ben-Ich' Prefix." In *Mesoamerican Writing Systems*, ed. Elizabeth P. Benson, 99–143. Washington, DC: Dumbarton Oaks.

Love, Michael. 1991. "Style and Social Complexity in Formative Mesoamerica." In *The Formation of Complex Society in Southeastern Mesoamerica*, ed. William R. Fowler Jr., 47–76. Boca Raton, FL: CRC Press.

———. 1998. "Economía e ideología en El Ujuxte, Retalhuleu." In *XI Simposio de Investigaciones Arqueológicas en Guatemala, 1997*, ed. Juan Pedro Laporte and Héctor L. Escobedo, 309–18. Guatemala: Ministerio de Cultura y Deportes; Instituto de Antropología e Historia; Asociación Tikal.

———. 1999. "Ideology, Material Culture, and Daily Practice in Pre-Classic Mesoamerica." In Grove and Joyce, *Social Patterns*, 127–53.

———. 2002. *Early Complex Society in Pacific Guatemala: Settlements and Chronology of the Río Naranjo, Guatemala*. Pap New World Archaeol Found 66.

———. 2004. "Etnicidad, identidad, y poder en la costa del Pacifico en el Preclásico Tardío." In *XVI Simposio de la Arqueología Guatemalteca*, ed. Juan Pedro Laporte and Héctor L. Escobedo. Guatemala: Museo Nacional de Arqueología y Etnología.

Love, Michael, and Beatriz Balcárcel. 2000. "Ofrendas rituales en la plaza central de Ujuxte." In *Trabajos de análisis del Proyecto Ujuxte: informe preliminar entregado al Instituto de Antropología e Historia de Guatemala*, ed. Michael Love and Donaldo Castillo, 63–74. Guatemala: Instituto de Antropología e Historia.

Love, Michael, Donaldo Castillo, and Beatriz Balcárcel. 1996. *Investigaciones arqueológicas en El Ujuxte, Retalhuleu 1995–96: informe preliminar*. Guatemala: Instituto de Antropología e Historia.

Lowe, Gareth W. 1977. "The Mixe-Zoque as Competing Neighbors of the Early Lowland Maya." In Adams, *Origins of Maya Civilization*, 197–248.

———. 1981. "Olmec Horizons Defined in Mound 20, San Isidro, Chiapas." In *The Olmec and Their Neighbors*, ed. Elizabeth P. Benson, 231–55. Washington, DC: Dumbarton Oaks.

———. 1990. Cat. entries 22–24, in *Mexico: Splendors of Thirty Centuries*.

Lowe, Gareth W., Thomas A. Lee Jr., and Eduardo Martínez Espinosa. 1982. *Izapa: An Introduction to the Ruins and Monuments*. Pap New World Archaeol Found 31.

Mace, Carroll Edward. 1970. *Two Spanish-Quiche Dance Dramas of Rabinal*. New Orleans, LA: Tulane Univ.

MacLeod, Barbara, and Dennis E. Puleston. 1980. "Pathways into Darkness." In *Tercera Mesa Redonda de Palenque*, vol. 4, ed. Merle Greene Robertson and Donnan Call Jeffers, 71–77. Proceedings of the Tercera Mesa Redonda de Palenque, 11–18 June 1978, Palenque. Monterey, CA: Pre-Columbian Art Research Center.

Marcus, Joyce. 1989. "Zapotec Chiefdoms and the Nature of the Formative Religion." In *Regional Perspectives on the Olmec*, ed. David C. Grove and Robert J. Sharer, 148–97. Cambridge: Cambridge Univ. Press.

———. 2003. "The Maya and Teotihuacan." In Braswell, *The Maya and Teotihuacan*, 337–56.

Martin, Simon. 1996. "Calakmul y el enigma del glifo Cabeza de Serpiente." *Arqueol Mex* 3 (18): 42–45.

———. 1997. "The Painted King List." In Kerr, *Maya Vase Book*, 5: 846–67.

———. 2001. "Power in the West." In Grube, *Maya*, 98–113.

———. Forthcoming. "Cacao in Ancient Maya Religion: First Fruit from the Maize Tree and Other Tales from the Underworld." In *The Origins of Chocolate: Cacao in the Americas*, ed. Cameron L. McNeil. Gainesville: Univ. Press of Florida.

Martin, Simon, and Nikolai Grube. 1995. "Maya Superstates." *Archaeology* 6 (48): 41–46.

———. 2000. *Chronicle of the Maya Kings and Queens*. London: Thames & Hudson.

Masson, Marilyn A., and David A. Freidel, eds. 2002. *Ancient Maya Political Economies*. Walnut Creek, CA: AltaMira Press.

Matheny, Ray T. 1986. "Investigations at El Mirador, Peten, Guatemala." *Natl Geogr Res* 2 (3): 332–53.

———. 1987. "Early States in the Maya Lowlands during the Late Preclassic Period: Edzna and El Mirador." In *City States of the Maya*, ed. Elizabeth P. Benson, 1–44. Denver: Rocky Mountain Institute for Pre-Columbian Studies.

Mathews, Jennifer P., and James F. Garber. 2004. "Models of Cosmic Order." *Anc Mesoam* 15 (1): 49–59.

Mathews, Peter, and John S. Justeson. 1984. "Patterns of Sign Substitution in Mayan Hieroglyphic Writing." In *Phoneticism in Mayan Hieroglyphic Writing*, ed. John S. Justeson and Lyle R. Campbell, 185–231. Institute for Mesoamerican Studies Monograph 9. Albany: State Univ. of New York.

Mathews, Peter, and David M. Pendergast. 1979. "The Altun Ha Jade Plaque." Contributions of the University of California Archaeological Research Facility 41. Berkeley.

McAnany, Patricia A., Ben S. Thomas, Steven Morandi, Polly A. Peterson, and Eleanor Harrison. 2002. "Praise the Ajaw and Pass the Kakaw." In Masson and Freidel, *Ancient Maya*, 123–39.

McDonald, Andrew J. 1983. *Tzutzuculi: A Middle Preclassic Site on the Pacific Coast of Chiapas, Mexico*. Pap New World Archaeol Found 47.

McEwan, Colin. 1994. *Ancient Mexico in the British Museum*. London: British Museum Press.

McNeil, Cameron L., W. Jeffrey Hurst, and Robert J. Sharer. Forthcoming. "Cacao at Copan." In *The Origins of Chocolate: Cacao in the Americas*, ed. Cameron L. McNeil. Gainesville: Univ. Press of Florida.

Mendelson, E. Michael. 1957. *Religion and World-View in a Guatemalan Village*. Microfilm Collection of Manuscripts on Middle American Cultural Anthropology 52. Chicago: Univ. of Chicago Library.

———. 1958a. "A Guatemalan Sacred Bundle." *Man* 58: 121–26.

———. 1958b. "The King, the Traitor, and the Cross." *Diogenes* 21: 1–10.

————. 1965. *Las escándolas de Maximon*, pub. 19. Guatemala: Seminario de Integración Social Guatemalteca.

Mendieta, Fray Gerónimo de. 1993. *Historia eclesiástica indiana*. Mexico: Editorial Porrua.

Merwin, Raymond, and George Vaillant. 1932. *The Ruins of Holmul, Guatemala*. Memoirs of the Peabody Museum of American Archaeology and Ethnology 3 (2). Cambridge, MA: Harvard Univ.

Mexico: Splendors of Thirty Centuries. 1990. New York: Metropolitan Museum of Art.

Miller, Arthur G., ed. 1983. *Highland-Lowland Interaction in Mesoamerica: Interdisciplinary Approaches*. Washington, DC: Dumbarton Oaks.

Miller, Mary Ellen, and Simon Martin. 2004. *Courtly Art of the Ancient Maya*. San Francisco: Fine Arts Museums of San Francisco; New York: Thames & Hudson.

Mora Marín, David. 1997. "The Origin of Maya Writing." *U Mut Maya* 6: 133–64.

————. 2001. "The Grammar, Orthography, Content, and Social Context of Late Preclassic Portable Texts." PhD diss., State Univ. of New York at Albany.

————. 2002. "Texto jeroglífico de la cuchara de jadeíta." In *Arte Precolombino Costarricense*, ed. Zulay Soto Méndez, 16. San Jose, Costa Rica: Museo del Jade Marco Fidel Tristán (del Instituto Nacional de Seguros).

Morales, Paulino. 2001. "Rasgos arquitectónicos y prácticas rituales en el Grupo Maler de Yaxha, Peten." In *XIV Simposio de Investigaciones Arqueológicas en Guatemala, 2000*, ed. Juan Pedro Laporte, Ana Claudia de Suasnávar, and Bárbara Arroyo, 157–76. Guatemala: Ministerio de Cultura y Deportes; Instituto de Antropología e Historia; Asociación Tikal.

Munoz Cosma, Gaspar, Cristina Vidal Lorenzo, and Juan Antonio Valdés Gómez, eds. 1999. *Los Mayas: ciudades milenarias de Guatemala*. Zaragoza, Spain: Ayuntamiento de Zaragoza.

Nakamura, Seiichi. 2004. "Culto funerario de Copán en el siglo VI." In Cobos, *Culto funerario*, 245–53.

Neff, Hector. 2000. "Neutron Activation Analysis for Provenance Determination in Archaeology." In *Modern Analytical Methods in Art and Archaeology*, ed. Enrico Ciliberto and Giuseppe Spoto. Chemical Analysis Series 155. New York: John Wiley and Sons.

Newsome, Elizabeth A. 1998. "The Ontology of Being and Spiritual Power in the Stone Monument Cults of the Lowland Maya." *RES* 33: 115–36.

————. 2001. *Trees of Paradise and Pillars of the World: The Serial Stela Cycle of "18-Rabbit-God K," King of Copan*. Austin: Univ. of Texas Press.

Norman, V. Garth. 1976. *Izapa Sculpture*, pt. 2. Pap New World Archaeol Found 30.

O'Connor, David, and David P. Silverman. 1995. *Ancient Egyptian Kingship*. Leiden: E. J. Brill.

Ohi, Kuniaki, ed. 1994. *Kaminaljuyu*. Tokyo: Tobacco and Salt Museum.

The Olmec World: Ritual and Rulership. 1995. Princeton, NJ: Princeton Univ. Art Museum.

Orrego Corzo, Miguel, and Christa Schieber de Lavarreda. 2001. "Compendio de monumentos expuestos en Abaj Takalik." In *XIV Simposio de Investigaciones Arqueológicas en Guatemala, 2000*, ed. Juan Pedro Laporte, Ana Claudia de Suasnávar, and Bárbara Arroyo, 917–38. Guatemala: Ministerio de Cultura y Deportes; Instituto de Antropología e Historia; Asociación Tikal.

Ortiz, Ponciano, and María del Carmen Rodríguez. 2000. "The Sacred Hill of El Manatí." In Clark and Pye, *Olmec Art*.

Pagliaro, Jonathan B., James F. Garber, and Travis W. Stanton. 2003. "Evaluating the Archaeological Signatures of Maya Ritual and Conflict." In Brown and Stanton, *Ancient Mesoamerican Warfare*.

Parsons, Lee A. 1967–69. *Bilbao, Guatemala*. 2 vols. Publications in Anthropology 11 and 12. Milwaukee: Milwaukee Public Museum.

———. 1986. *The Origins of Maya Art: Monumental Stone Sculpture of Kaminaljuyu, Guatemala, and the Southern Pacific Coast*. Dumbarton Studies 28.

Pendergast, David M. 1982. *Excavations at Altun Ha, Belize, 1964–70*, vol. 2. Toronto: Royal Ontario Museum.

———. 2003. "Teotihuacan at Altun Ha." In Braswell, *The Maya and Teotihuacan*, 235–47.

Pincemin Deliberos, Sophia. 1994. *Entierro en el palacio: la tumba de la Estructura III, Calakmul, Campeche*. Colección arqueologíca 5. Campeche: Universidad Autónoma de Campeche.

Poe, William C. 2000. "Site Organization at Ujuxte and Neighboring Sites." Paper presented at the 63rd annual meeting of the Society for American Archaeology, Philadelphia, PA.

Pohl, Mary D. 1983. "Maya Ritual Faunas." In *Civilization in the Ancient Americas: Essays in Honor of Gordon R. Willey*, ed. Richard M. Leventhal and Alan L. Kolata, 55–103. Albuquerque: Univ. of New Mexico Press.

———. 1985. "The Privileges of Maya Elites." In *Prehistoric Lowland Maya Environment and Subsistence Economy*, ed. Mary D. Pohl, 133–45. Peabody Museum Papers 77. Cambridge, MA: Harvard Univ.

Pohl, Mary E. D., Kevin O. Pope, and Christopher von Nagy. 2002. "Olmec Origins of Mesoamerican Writing." *Science* 298: 1984–87.

Pohorilenko, Anatole. 1996. Cat. entry 95, in Benson and de la Fuente, *Olmec Art*.

Porter, James B. 1996. "Celtiform Stelae." In *Beyond Indigenous Voices: LAILA/ALILA 11th International Symposium on Latin American Indian Literatures*, ed. Mary Preuss, 65–72. Lancaster, CA: Labyrinthos.

Prechtel, Martin, and Robert S. Carlsen. 1988. "Weaving and Cosmos amongst the Tzutujil Maya." *RES* 15: 122–32.

Price, Barbara J. 1978. "Secondary State Formation." In *Origins of the State: The Anthropology of Political Evolution*, ed. Ronald Cohen and Elman R. Service, 161–86. Philadelphia: Institute for the Study of Human Issues.

Proskouriakoff, Tatiana. 1993. *Maya History*. Ed. Rosemary A. Joyce. Austin: Univ. of Texas Press.

Quenon, Michel, and Genevieve Le Fort. 1997. "Rebirth and Resurrection in Maize God Iconography." In Kerr, *Maya Vase Book*, 5: 884–99.

Rattray, Evelyn, and Garman Harbottle. 1992. "Neutron Activation Analysis and Numerical Taxonomy of Thin Orange Ceramics from the Manufacturing Sites of Rio Carnero, Puebla, Mexico." In *Chemical Characterization of Ceramic Pastes in Archaeology*, ed. Hector Neff, 221–31. Madison, WI: Prehistory Press.

Reents-Budet, Dorie. 1991. "The 'Holmul Dancer' Theme in Maya Art." In *Sixth Palenque Round Table, 1986*, ed. Virginia M. Fields, 217–22. Norman: Univ. of Oklahoma Press.

Reents-Budet, Dorie, Joseph W. Ball, Ronald L. Bishop, Virginia M. Fields, and Barbara MacLeod. 1994. *Painting the Maya Universe: Royal Ceramics of the Classic Period*. Durham and London: Duke Univ. Press.

Reents-Budet, Dorie, Ellen E. Bell, Loa P. Traxler, and Ronald L. Bishop. 2004a. "Early Classic Ceramic Offerings at Copan." Chap. 9 in Bell et al., *Understanding Early Classic Copan*.

Reents-Budet, Dorie, and Ronald L. Bishop. 1987. "Late Classic Maya Codex Style Pottery." In *Memorias del Primer Colóquio Internacional de Mayistas*, ed. Mercedes de la Garza et al. Mexico City: Centro de Estudios Mayas, UNAM.

Reents-Budet, Dorie, and T. Patrick Culbert. 1999. "Las ofrendas del período Clásico Temprano de Tikal y Kaminaljuyu." Paper presented at the XIII Simposio de Arqueología y Etnología de Guatemala, Museo Nacional de Arqueología y Etnología, Guatemala City.

Reents-Budet, Dorie, and Virginia M. Fields. 1987. "Incised Classic Maya Jades and Slate Disks from Costa Rica." Paper presented at the Denver Jade Conference, 20–22 August.

Reents-Budet, Dorie, Simon Martin, Richard D. Hansen, and Ronald L. Bishop. 1998. "Codex-Style Pottery." Paper presented at the 14th Maya Hieroglyphic Workshop, Univ. of Texas at Austin.

Reents-Budet, Dorie, Juan Antonio Valdés, Ronald L. Bishop, and Jim Blackman. 2004b. "La cerámica de Kaminaljuyu." Paper presented at the XVIII Simposio de Investigaciones Arqueológicas en Guatemala, Museo Nacional de Arqueología y Etnología, Guatemala City.

Reese-Taylor, Kathryn, and Debra S. Walker. 2002. "The Passage of the Late Preclassic into the Early Classic." In Masson and Freidel, *Ancient Maya*, 87–122.

Reilly, F. Kent, III. 1989. "The Shaman in Transformation Pose." *Record of the Art Museum* (Princeton Univ.) 48 (2): 4–21.

———. 1991. "Olmec Iconographic Influences on the Symbols of Maya Rulership." In *Sixth Palenque Round Table, 1986*, ed. Virginia M. Fields, 151–66. Norman: Univ. of Oklahoma Press.

———. 1994a. "Enclosed Ritual Spaces and the Watery Underworld in Formative Period Architecture." In *Seventh Palenque Round Table, 1989*, ed. Virginia M. Fields, 125–35. San Francisco: Pre-Columbian Art Research Institute.

———. 1994b. "Visions to Another World: Art, Shamanism, and Political Power in Middle Formative Mesoamerica." PhD diss., Univ. of Texas at Austin.

———. 1994c. "Cosmología, soberanismo, y espacio ritual en Mesoamérica." In *Los olmecas en Mesoamérica*, ed. John E. Clark, 239–59. Mexico City: El Equilibrista.

———. 1995a. "Middle Formative Origins of the Early Classic Maya Stela Cult." Paper presented at the 94th annual meeting of the American Anthropological Association, Washington, DC, 18 Nov. 1995.

———. 1995b. "Art, Ritual, and Rulership in the Olmec World." In *The Olmec World*, 27–45.

———. 1996. "The Lazy-S." In *Eighth Palenque Round Table, 1993*, ed. Martha Macri and Jan McHargue, 413–24. San Francisco: Pre-Columbian Art Research Institute.

———. 1999. "Mountains of Creation and Underworld Portals." In *Mesoamerican Architecture as a Cultural Symbol*, ed. Jeff K. Kowalski, 14–39. Oxford: Oxford Univ. Press.

———. 2001. "Middle Formative Period Origins of the Mesoamerican Ritual Act of Bundling." Paper presented at the 99th annual meeting of the American Anthropological Association, Washington, DC.

————. 2002. "The Landscape of Creation." In Stone, *Heart of Creation*, 34–65.

Ricketson, Oliver Garrison, Jr. 1928. "Notes on Two Maya Astronomic Observatories." *Am Anthropol* 30 (3): 434–44.

Robertson, Merle Greene. 1974. "The Quadripartite Badge." In *Primera Mesa Redonda de Palenque*, pt. 1, ed. Merle Greene Robertson, 77–93. Pebble Beach, CA: Robert Louis Stevenson School.

Rodríguez, María del Carmen, and Ponciano Ortiz. 2000. "A Massive Offering of Axes at La Merced, Hidalgotitlán, Veracruz, Mexico." In Clark and Pye, *Olmec Art*, 155–68.

Rodríguez Campero, Omar. 2000. "La gran plaza de Calakmul." *Arqueol Mex* 7 (42): 22–27.

Sanders, William T., and Joseph W. Michels, eds. 1977. *Teotihuacan and Kaminaljuyu: A Study in Prehistoric Culture Contact*. University Park: Pennsylvania State Univ. Press.

Santley, Robert S. 1983. "Obsidian Trade and Teotihuacan Influence in Mesoamerica." In Miller, *Highland-Lowland Interaction*, 69–124.

Saturno, William. 2002. "Archaeological Investigation and Conservation at San Bartolo, Guatemala." Foundation for the Advancement of Mesoamerican Studies. http://www.famsi.org/reports/01038/index.html.

Saturno, William, and Mónica Urquizú. 2004. "Programa arqueológico regional San Bartolo." Paper presented at the XVIII Simposio de Investigaciones Arqueológicas en Guatemala, Museo Nacional de Arqueología y Etnología, Guatemala City.

Schele, Linda. 1985. "The Hauberg Stela." *Fifth Palenque Round Table, 1983*, ed. Virginia M. Fields, 135–49. San Francisco: Pre-Columbian Art Research Institute.

————. 1997. Foreword to Schevill, *The Maya Textile Tradition*.

Schele, Linda, and David A. Freidel. 1990. *A Forest of Kings: The Untold Story of the Ancient Maya*. New York: William Morrow.

Schele, Linda, and Peter Mathews. 1998. *Code of Kings: The Language of Seven Sacred Maya Temples and Tombs*. New York: Scribner.

Schele, Linda, and Jeffrey H. Miller. 1983. *The Mirror, the Rabbit, and the Bundle: "Accession" Expressions from the Classic Maya Inscriptions*. Dumbarton Studies 25.

Schele, Linda, and Mary Ellen Miller. 1986. *The Blood of Kings: Dynasty and Ritual in Maya Art*. Fort Worth, TX: Kimbell Art Museum.

Schevill, Margot Blum, ed. 1997. *The Maya Textile Tradition*. New York: Harry N. Abrams.

Schieber de Lavarreda, Christa. 1994. "Abaj Takalik." In *VII Simposio de Investigaciones Arqueológicas en Guatemala, 1993*, 95–111. Guatemala: Ministerio de Cultura y Deportes; Instituto de Antropología e Historia; Asociación Tikal.

Schmidt, Peter. 1998. Cat. entry 164, in Schmidt et al., *Maya*.

Schmidt, Peter, Mercedes de la Garza, and Enrique Nalda, eds. 1998. *Maya*. New York: Rizzoli.

Sedat, David W., and Fernando López. 2004. "Initial Stages in the Formation of the Copan Acropolis." Chap. 5 in Bell et al., *Understanding Early Classic Copan*.

Sharer, Robert J. 1992. "The Preclassic Origin of Lowland Maya States." In *New Theories on the Ancient Maya*, ed. Elin C. Danien and Robert J. Sharer, 131–36. Philadelphia: Univ. of Pennsylvania Museum.

———. 1999. "Archaeology and History in the Royal Acropolis, Copan, Honduras." *Expedition* 41 (2): 8–15.

———. 2003a. "Tikal and the Copan Dynastic Founding." In *Tikal: Dynasties, Foreigners, and Affairs of State*, ed. Jeremy A. Sabloff, 319–53. Santa Fe, NM: School of American Research Press.

———. 2003b. "Founding Events and Teotihuacan Connections at Copan, Honduras." In Braswell, *The Maya and Teotihuacan*, 143–65.

Sharer, Robert J., Loa P. Traxler, David W. Sedat, Ellen E. Bell, Marcello A. Canuto, and C. Powell. 1999. "Early Classic Architecture beneath the Copan Acropolis." *Anc Mesoam* 10 (1): 3–23.

Shook, Edwin M. 1965. "Archaeological Survey of the Pacific Coast of Guatemala." In *Handbook of Middle American Indians*, ed. Robert Wauchope, 2: 180–94. Austin: Univ. of Texas Press.

Shook, Edwin M., and Robert F. Heizer. 1976. "An Olmec Sculpture from the South (Pacific) Coast of Guatemala." *J New World Archaeol* 1 (3): 1–8.

Shook, Edwin M., and Alfred V. Kidder. 1952. *Mound E-III-3, Kaminaljuyu, Guatemala*. Contributions to American Anthropology and History 53. Carnegie Institution of Washington 596. Washington, DC.

Smith, A. Ledyard. 1982. "Major Architecture and Caches." In *Excavations at Seibal, Department of Peten, Guatemala*. Memoirs of the Peabody Museum of Archaeology and Ethnology 15 (1). Cambridge, MA: Harvard Univ.

Smith, A. Ledyard, and Alfred V. Kidder. 1943. *Explorations in the Motagua Valley, Guatemala*. Contributions to American Anthropology and History 41. Carnegie Institution of Washington 546. Washington, DC.

Stephens, John L. 1969 [1841]. *Incidents of Travel in Central America, Chiapas, and Yucatan*. New York: Dover.

Stone, Andrea J. 1989. "Disconnection, Foreign Insignia, and Political Expansion." In *Mesoamerica after the Decline of Teotihuacan, AD 700–900*, ed. Richard A. Diehl and Janet C. Berlo, 153–72. Washington, DC: Dumbarton Oaks.

———, ed. 2002. *Heart of Creation: The Mesoamerican World and the Legacy of Linda Schele*. Tuscaloosa: Univ. of Alabama Press.

Stross, Brian. 1985. "Color Symbolism of a Maya Glyph." *Journal of Mayan Linguistics* 5 (1): 73–112.

Stuart, David S. 1992. "The Iconography of Flowers in Maya Art." Paper presented at the 8th Texas Symposium on Maya Hieroglyphic Writing, Univ. of Texas at Austin.

———. 1996. "A Reconsideration of Stelae in Ancient Maya Ritual." *RES* 29/30: 148–71.

———. 2000. "The Arrival of Strangers." In *Mesoamerica's Classic Heritage: From Teotihuacan to the Aztecs*, ed. David Carrasco, Lindsay Jones, and Scott Sessions, 465–513. Boulder: Univ. Press of Colorado.

———. 2002. "Names in Stucco: Observations on the Earliest Maya Writing." Paper presented at the 100th Annual Meeting of the American Anthropological Association, New Orleans.

———. 2004. "Beginnings of the Copan Dynasty." Chap. 11 in Bell et al., *Understanding Early Classic Copan*.

Sugiyama, Saburo, and Rúben Cabrera C. 2003. "Hallazgos recientes en la Pirámide de la Luna." *Arqueol Mex* 11 (64): 42–49.

Tate, Carolyn. 1995. "Art in Olmec Culture." In *The Olmec World*, 47–67.

Taube, Karl A. 1988. "A Study of Classic Maya Scaffold Sacrifice." In Benson and Griffin, *Maya Iconography*, 331–51.

———. 1995. "The Rainmakers." In *The Olmec World*, 83–104.

———. 1996. "The Olmec Maize God." *RES* 29/30: 39–81.

———. 1998. "The Jade Hearth." In Houston, *Function and Meaning*, 427–78.

———. 2000. "Lightning Celts and Corn Fetishes." In Clark and Pye, *Olmec Art*.

———. 2001. "The Classic Maya Gods." In Grube, *Maya*, 262–77.

———. 2003a. "Tetitla and the Maya Presence at Teotihuacan." In Braswell, *The Maya and Teotihuacan*, 275–314.

———. 2003b. "Ancient and Contemporary Maya Conceptions about Field and Forest." In *The Lowland Maya Area: Three Millennia at the Human-Wildland Interface*, ed. Arturo Gómez-Pompa, Michael F. Allen, Scott L. Fedick, and Juan J. Jiménez-Osornio, 461–92. New York: Food Products Press.

———. 2004a. "Structure 10L-16 and Its Early Classic Antecedents." Chap. 13 in Bell et al., *Understanding Early Classic Copan*.

———. 2004b. "Flower Mountain." *RES* 45: 69–98.

Tedlock, Dennis, ed. and trans. 1985. *"Popol Vuh": The Definitive Edition of the Mayan Book of the Dawn of Life and the Glories of Gods and Kings*. New York: Simon and Schuster.

Thompson, J. Eric S. 1973. "Maya Rulers of the Classic Period and the Divine Right of Kings." In *The Iconography of Middle American Sculpture*, 52–71. New York: Metropolitan Museum of Art.

Urcid Serrano, Javier. 2001. *Zapotec Hieroglyphic Writing*. Dumbarton Studies 34.

Valdés, Juan Antonio. 1992a. "The Beginning of Preclassic Maya Art and Architecture." In *The Ancient Americas: Art from Sacred Landscapes*, ed. Richard Townsend, 147–57. Chicago: Art Institute of Chicago.

———. 1992b. "El crecimiento de la civilización maya en el area central durante el Preclásico Tardío." *Utz'ib* 1 (2): 16–31.

Valdés, Juan Antonio, and Federico Fahsen. 1995. "The Reigning Dynasty of Uaxactun during the Early Classic." *Anc Mesoam* 6: 197–219.

Valdés, Juan Antonio, Federico Fahsen, and Héctor L. Escobedo. 1999. *Reyes, tumbas, y palacios: la historia dinástica de Uaxactun*. Mexico City: UNAM; Guatemala: Instituto de Antropología e Historia.

Valdés, Juan Antonio, and Lori E. Wright. 2004. "The Early Classic and Its Antecedents at Kaminaljuyu." Chap. 16 in Bell et al., *Understanding Early Classic Copan*.

Valeri, Valerio. 1985. *Kingship and Sacrifice: Ritual and Society in Ancient Hawaii*. Trans. Paula Wissing. Chicago: Univ. of Chicago Press.

Varela Torrecilla, Carmen, and Geoffrey E. Braswell. 2003. "Teotihuacan and Oxkintok." In Braswell, *The Maya and Teotihuacan*, 249–71.

Vinicio García, Edgar. 1997. "Excavaciónes en el acceso a la Terraza 3, Abaj Takalik." In *X Simposio de Investigaciones Arqueológicas en Guatemala, 1996*, ed. Juan Pedro Laporte and Héctor L. Escobedo, 167–91. Guatemala: Ministerio de Cultura y Deportes; Instituto de Antropología e Historia; Asociación Tikal.

Wanyerka, Phil, 2001. *The Coming of Kings*. Proceedings of the 25th Maya Hieroglyphic Workshop. Austin: Univ. of Texas at Austin.

———. ed. 2004. *Patronage, Betrayal, and Revenge: Diplomacy and Politics in the Eastern Maya Lowlands*. Proceedings of the 28th Maya Hieroglyphic Workshop. Austin: Univ. of Texas at Austin.

Webster, David L., and Ann Corinne Freter. 1990. "Demography of Late Classic Copan." In *Pre-Columbian Population History in the Maya Lowlands*, ed. T. Patrick Culbert and Don S. Rice, 37–61. Albuquerque: Univ. of New Mexico Press.

Willey, Gordon R. 1978. "Artifacts." In *Excavations at Seibal, Department of Peten, Guatemala*. Memoirs of the Peabody Museum of Archaeology and Ethnology 14 (1). Cambridge, MA: Harvard Univ.

Winfield Capitaine, Fernando. 1988. "La Estela 1 de La Mojarra, Veracruz, Mexico." Maya Reports 16.

Wright, Lori E. 1998. "Los niños de Kaminaljuyu." In *XII Simposio de Investigaciones Arqueológicas en Guatemala*. 2 vols. Guatemala: Instituto de Antropología e Historia.

Ximénez, Fr. Francisco. 1967. *Escolios a las historias de origin de los indios*. Sociedad de Geografía e Historia de Guatemala. Special Publication no. 13. Guatemala: Sociedad de Geografía e Historia de Guatemala.

Zender, Marc. 2004. Cat. entry 34, in *Ancient Civilizations of the Americas*, 86–88, 193–94. Shigaraki, Japan: Miho Museum.

Illustration Credits

Most photographs are reproduced courtesy of the lenders of the material depicted. For certain artwork and documentary photographs we have been unable to trace copyright holders. The publishers would appreciate notification of additional credits for acknowledgement in future editions.

Pages 2 (left), 12, 25, 102, 106 (top left), 124–25, 126 (bottom), 132 (right), 133, 144, 169, 178, 206, 210: © Michel Zabé; pages 2 (right), 3, 8, 23, 59 (bottom), 87, 104, 105, 109, 110, 114 (bottom), 116, 117, 120 (top right), 120 (bottom), 122, 126 (top), 142, 145, 152, 153, 156 (bottom), 162–63, 164, 168, 170, 175, 176, 181 (bottom), 182, 183, 186, 198, 201, 204–5, 208, 211, 212, 213, 216, 218–19, 220, 222, 223, 224, 226, 227 (top), 228, 230, 231, 232, 233, 234, 236–37, 238, 246, 247, 248, 249, 250, 251, 252, 253, 254: © Jorge Pérez de Lara; pages 6, 101, 106 (top right), 106 (bottom), 108, 127, 139 (top), 174, 180 (left), 221, 225, 229: © 2005 Museum Associates/LACMA; page 14: Adrian Kitzinger; pages 16, 35 (left), 53, 77 (bottom), 114 (top), 194 (bottom), 196 (right): Linda Schele. © David Schele, courtesy FAMSI, www.famsi.org; page 18: Merle Greene, 1975; pages 20, 56–57, 83: David Brent Miller; page 22: Felipe Dávalos; pages 27, 118, 132 (left), 134, 158, 159, 165, 172–73, 177, 195, 214, 217, 240, 243: © Justin Kerr; page 28: Jeremy R. Bauer; page 31: David C. Grove; page 32 (top): Frank Kent Reilly III after Peter David Joralemon, *A Study of Olmec Iconography*, Dumbarton Studies 7, 1971, p. 50, fig. 145; page 32 (bottom): The Merrin Gallery, New York; page 35 (right): © Sotheby's, Inc.; page 38 (left): James Porter, courtesy of John Graham and the University of California, Berkeley, Abaj Takalik Project; pages 38 (right), 42: Michael Love; page 39: John Graham; pages 40, 43: Ayax Moreno, courtesy of John Clark and the New World Archaeological Foundation; page 44: Constance Cortez after V. Garth Norman, *Izapa Sculpture*, pt. 1, Papers of the New World Archaeological Foundation, 30, Provo, UT, Brigham Young University, 1973, pls. 3, 4; page 45: Constance Cortez after Lee A. Parsons, "Altars 9 and 10, Kaminaljuyu, and the Evolution of the Serpent-Winged Deity," in *Civilization in the Ancient Americas: Essays in Honor of Gorden R. Willey*, ed. Richard M. Levanthal and Alan L. Kolata, University of New Mexico Press, Albuquerque, and Peabody Museum, Harvard University, Cambridge, MA, 1983, figs. 5.2b and 5.2c; pages 46, 48, 50: James F. Garber; page 51: Jason Weirsema; pages 52, 120 (top left): David Freidel; pages 54, 60: Dorie Reents-Budet; page 61: Jody L. Hansen and Richard D. Hansen; page 62: Centro INAH Campeche; page 63: © Rocío Ruiz-Rodarte; page 65 (top): Ricardo Alvarado Tapia; pages 65 (bottom), 255: Simon Martin; pages 68–69, 70: Virginia Fields; page 71: Nikolai Grube and Simon Martin after Christopher Jones and Linton Satterthwaite, *The Monuments and Inscriptions of Tikal: The Carved Monuments*. Tikal Report 33, pt. A, University of Pennsylvania Museum, Philadelphia, 1982; page 72: Christopher Klein/National Geographic Image Collection; page 73: Enrico Ferorelli; pages 74, 77 (top), 79, 200: Nikolai Grube; page 80: Enrique Franco Torrijos; page 85: Juan Antonio Valdés Gómez; page 90: Alfred P. Maudslay, courtesy Royal Geographic Society; page 92: © 1994 The Art Institute of Chicago. All rights reserved.; pages 94, 95: Allen Christenson; page 96: Eduard Seler, *Gesammelte Abhandlungen zur Amerikanischen Sprach- und Altertumskunde*, vol. 5, Ascher–Behrend, Berlin, 1902–23, fig. 192; pages 98–99, 107: © 1980 The Metropolitan Museum of Art; page 100: Hawkinson Photography; page 103: © 1996 John Bigelow Taylor; pages 111 (left), 157, 187 (top), 227 (bottom): © 2004 Trustees of Princeton University, Bruce White; page 111 (right): © 1996 The Metropolitan Museum of Art, New York; pages 112, 119, 154–55, 161 (right), 244, 245: courtesy Peabody Museum of Archaeology and Ethnography, Harvard University; pages 113 (left), 161 (left), 194 (top), 196 (left), 207: courtesy Dumbarton Oaks Research Library and Collections, Washington, D.C.; pages 115, 123, 139 (bottom), 156 (top), 192, 235: © The British Museum; page 121: © Hughes Dubois, Brussels, Paris; pages 128, 147: © Denver Art Museum. All rights reserved.; page 129 (top): courtesy The Brooklyn Museum; page 129 (bottom): courtesy Yale University Art Gallery; pages 130, 131: courtesy National Gallery of Art, Washington, D.C.; pages 135, 187 (bottom): © Royal Ontario Museum; pages 136–37, 143 (top): David Heald; page 138: Heather Hurst/National Geographic Image Collection; pages 140, 184, 185: courtesy Fine Arts Museums of San Francisco; page 141: © 2005 Museum of Fine Arts, Boston; pages 146, 181 (top), 190, 242: © 1991 Dallas Museum of Art. All rights reserved.; page 149: Bildarchiv Preussischer Kulturbesitz/Art Resource, NY. Photos by Martin Franken; pages 150, 166, 167: © 2004 The Metropolitan Museum of Art, New York; pages 151, 180 (right): © 2005 Kimbell Art Museum, Michael Bodycomb; pages 160, 209: courtesy Dallas Museum of Art; page 171: courtesy The Museum of Fine Arts, Houston; page 179: University of Pennsylvania Museum (neg. #T4-2965c); pages 188–89, 199, 202: © 2000 The Metropolitan Museum of Art, New York; page 191 (top): Justin Kerr, courtesy The Brooklyn Museum; page 193 (left): © 2005 Peabody Museum of Natural History, Yale University, William Sacco; page 193 (right): Diane G. Peck; page 203: Thomas R. DuBrock; page 215: Benjamin Blackwell; page 241 (top): courtesy Miho Museum, Japan; page 241 (bottom): Linda Schele after Lin Crocker. © David Schele, courtesy FAMSI, www.famsi.org; page 256: courtesy Institute of Archaeology, Belmopan, Belize

Index

Page numbers in *italic* type indicate catalogue illustrations; those in **boldface** indicate figures.